Ashok Gurung
March 15th, 2010

GROWING CITIES IN A SHRINKING WORLD
The Challenges of Urbanism in India and China

Antonio Scarponi, www.conceptualdevices.com Human World 2001. The map distorts the geography of the world flag map originally by artist Alighiero Boetti by reducing or enlarging the size of each country's boundaries according to the national population. For example, Russia and Canada shrink to a size much smaller than its territorial boundaries, while India and China dominate the world map due to their enormous populations. Scale 1 Pixel = 1000 People.

Source: United Nation, 2000.

The maps of the various countries, including India and China as shown on the cover are an artistic representation and do not in any way reflect the actual territorial boundries of the various countries as approved by their Governments.

Cover Design: Kaushal Shrestha

GROWING CITIES IN A SHRINKING WORLD
THE CHALLENGES OF URBANISM IN INDIA AND CHINA

Editors
Ashok Gurung • Brian McGrath • Jianying Zha

Foreword by
Arjun Appadurai

INDIA CHINA INSTITUTE
THE NEW SCHOOL

in association with

MACMILLAN

INDIA CHINA INSTITUTE
THE NEW SCHOOL

© *India China Institute, 2010*

All rights reserved. No part of this publication may be reproduced or transmitted, in any form or by any means, without permission. Any person who does any unauthorised act in relation to this publication may be liable to criminal prosecution and civil claims for damages.

First published, 2010

MACMILLAN PUBLISHERS INDIA LTD
Delhi Bangalore Chennai Kolkata Mumbai
Ahmedabad Bhopal Chandigarh Coimbatore Cuttack
Guwahati Hubli Hyderabad Jaipur Lucknow Madurai
Nagpur Patna Pune Thiruvananthapuram Visakhapatnam

Companies and representatives throughout the world

ISBN 10: 0230-32928-4
ISBN 13: 978-0230-32928-7

Published by Rajiv Beri for Macmillan Publishers India Ltd
2/10, Ansari Road, Daryaganj, New Delhi 110 002

Printed at Sanat Printers
312 EPIP, Kundli, Sonipat 131 028

US Contract Address
India China Institute
66 Fifth Avenue, 9th Floor
New York, NY 10011 USA
Tel.: +1 212 229 6812
Fax: +1 212 627 0369
E-mail: indiachina@newschool.edu

This volume is the first in a series of endeavors by the India China Institute at The New School, New York, to create a space for trilateral conversations on the emerging issues of globalization, urbanization, political economy, development and governance that can enrich and expand intellectual collaboration across diverse disciplines in India, China and the US. It presents shifting perspectives on urbanization and globalization in India and China over the past few decades, at the dawn of this new era when both countries are actively removing barriers to reach out to each other and the rest of the world.

It is hoped that this volume will prove to be the front runner in stimulating productive dialogue that is bereft of preconceived notions and misconceptions and focused on asking the right questions and finding the more elusive answers. Academics, policy-makers, practitioners, professionals, bureaucrats, and journalists from India, China and the US have contributed to this compendium to provide an immensely enriching and insightful read for their brethren all over the world.

Contents

About Starr Foundation and ICI	x
Acknowledgements	xi
Foreword	xiii
Preface	xv
List of Abbreviations	xvii
List of Tables, Figures, and Boxes	xix

Introduction — 1
– *Ashok Gurung, Brian McGrath, and Jianying Zha*

Part One
COMPARING THE INCOMPARABLE: ENGAGEMENT, INNOVATION, AND LEGITIMACY

1. Two Countries, Diverse Systems, A Shared Future?: An Essay on the Global Significance of India and China's Increasing Engagement — 9
   – *Aromar Revi*

2. Comparative Analysis of National Innovation Systems of China and India — 24
   – *Xiaobo Wu*

3. Perspectives on China's Integration with the World Economy — 42
   – *Hiren Doshi*

4. A Comparative Study of State Response to the Educational Needs of Informal Settlers in Indian and Chinese Cities — 58
   – *Amita Bhide and Yang Yao*

Part Two
GOVERNING URBAN SPACES: ECONOMY, DESIGN, AND GOVERNANCE

5. Urban Development and Governmental Approach: Experiences in China and India — 85
   – *Zongyong Wen*

6. Land Acquisition and the Protection of Farmers' Interests: The Practice in Hangzhou, China — 91
   – *Zuojun Yang*

7. Silicon Valley in Paradise: Wiring the Urban Water Body of Hangzhou, China — 106
   – *Brian McGrath*

8. Beginning a Conversation on Chinese Urbanization — 118
   — *Partha Mukhopadhyay*

Part Three
DISPATCHES FROM THE FIELD: INTELLECTUALS, FAT CATS, AND DEMOCRACY

9. Social Transition in India and China — 143
   — *Chakrapani Ghanta*

10. How Intellectuals Misinterpret Each Other: Globalization, Market Economy and Chinese Peasants — 174
    — *Yukuan Guo*

11. A Future for Disinterested Governance? — 183
    — *Yang Yao*

Subject Index — 191
Editors and Contributors — 199

The Starr Foundation

Special thanks go to the Starr Foundation for their generous grant of USD10 million in 2004 to The New School, NY towards the establishment of the India China Institute. The foundation was both visionary and bold in establishing a unique entity that looks at India, China and the United States together. Without this initial trust in the tradition of critical inquiry at The New School, a new community of scholars would not have been possible.

For more information visit www.starrfoundation.org

The India China Institute at The New School

The India China Institute (ICI) is based at The New School. Founded in 1919, The New School is a legendary, progressive university based in New York City. The university's eight schools are bound by a common, unusual intent: to prepare and inspire its 9,400 undergraduate and graduate students to bring actual, positive change to the world through innovation in the arts, design, humanities, public policy, and the social sciences.

ICI advances this tradition by fostering study, research, and connections between India, China, and the United States-countries that increasingly share interests and challenges, but have not yet been fully engaged in three-way conversations. The institute is the hub of an international network of institutions and activities that nurtures these conversations and deepens our understanding of global processes.

ICI is committed to analyzing major issues and trends in India, China, and the United States, and to helping leaders, managers, public opinion-leaders, intellectuals, and academics in all three countries address key challenges through collaborative solutions. ICI will provide a vibrant platform for the circulation of people and ideas within The New School's overall mission to develop the knowledge and skills necessary to promote social change.

For more information visit: www.newschool.edu/ici, www.indiachinainteractions.org

Acknowledgements

The editors have numerous people to thank. Many individuals and institutions have contributed in countless ways to creating a new community of scholars, students, and experts which is committed to a trilateral conversation between India, China, and the United States. They continue to help the India China Institute (ICI) become the hub of an international network of institutions and activities that nurtures and facilitates transdisciplinary research, teaching, and policy analysis, which is deepening our understanding of the re-emergence of India and China in the world.

First, we would like to sincerely thank the Starr Foundation for its generous grant, which established ICI in 2004, without which this edited volume and the many discussions and ideas which it supported would not be possible. We are grateful for its continued support as well.

Second, we are grateful for the bold vision and continued active support and commitment to ICI from the leadership of The New School. We convey our heartfelt gratitude to Bob Kerrey, President of The New School for not only securing the support of the Starr Foundation but also for making important resources of the university available to ICI. In addition, thanks go to Professors Arjun Appadurai and Benjamin Lee, two noted scholars, who have a long history of friendship and collaboration, for providing the critical intellectual focus and guidance in the establishment of ICI, including its signature India China Fellowship Program. Here, we would like to thank Arjun Appadurai for most enthusiastically writing a Foreword that succinctly captures both the larger vision and the importance of the work in this edited volume and for help with the title of this volume. In addition, we are grateful to Tim Marshall, Ronald Kassimir, and Elizabeth Ross in the Provost's office for providing crucial support and guidance in making this edited volume a possibility.

Third, we would like to thank the First Cohort of ten Fellows from India and China, who were later joined by five faculty members from The New School, for not only contributing to the volume, but also for being enthusiastic pioneers in building a new community of scholars and experts. While this volume represents just part of their initial work, we are confident that additional serious and important scholarship and policymaking will soon follow.

Fourth, several people worked directly on bringing this volume to fruition. Here, special thanks go to Philip K. Oldenburg, who worked closely with many of the authors, providing valuable advice and helping to conceptualize the preliminary framework for the volume. Lucid Solutions, ICI's editorial consultant in Delhi, deserves deep appreciation for developing the manuscript into a book form—particularly in terms of careful attention to detail, and substantive editorial and design work. For that, we are indebted to Shreemoyee Patra, Director, Lucid Solutions for envisioning the structure of the book and steering it through the publishing process. Thanks and appreciation go to Kaushal Shrestha for designing the cover of the edited volume. We are also grateful and highly appreciative of Antonio Scarponi for allowing us to use his brilliant map for the cover of this volume. The map deliberately distorts the geography of the world flag map by artist Alighiero Boetti by reducing or enlarging the size of each country's boundaries according to the national population, hence, it captures both the spirit and the essence of the work of ICI Fellows in this volume.

As is the case with most complex collaborative projects of this nature, several research assistants, associates, and consultants at ICI played an important role, often beyond the limelight, in producing this volume in a timely manner. Most notably Brenna Foster, who together with Jonathan Cogliano, Chris Eberhardt, Shoshana Goldstein, He XiaoXue, Irene Leung, Michelle Raffanti, Scott Rosefield, Tina Shrestha, Jonathan Stiles, Josephine Vu, and Yiwen Wu worked hard and diligently in fact-checking, initial editing, and coordinating multiple tasks and follow-ups with individuals and institutions in three countries to ensure the timely publication of this volume. Special kudos to the ever-smiling and ever-ready Grace Hou, ICI Office Manager for ensuring that office and university resources were mobilized in a timely manner to make this volume happen.

'A trans-disciplinary and trans-national project like this edited volume would not be possible without the generous intellectual insights, advice, and networks of many. Here, we would like to extend special thanks to the growing group of the Friends of ICI, including Ackbar Abbas, Jonathan Bach, Sherry Brabham, Tan Chung, Michael Cohen, Frank Fu, Gang Gong, He Jin, Kavita Iyengar, Justin Yifu Lin, L.H.M. Ling, Pratap Bhanu Mehta, Colleen Macklin, Pan Gongkai, S. Parasuraman, Natalie Polvere, Paul Ross, Vyjayanthi Rao, Tansen Sen, Anwar Shaikh, K.C. Sivaramakrishnan, Francisco Tezen, Joel Towers, Patricia Uberoi, I-Hsien Wu, Vinod Khanna, Nandan Maluste, C.V. Ranganathan, and Nirupama Rao for their direct and indirect help in making this volume a reality.

In addition, we would like to thank Anita Patil-Deshmukh, Executive Director of PUKAR, who is an advisor to ICI and was the first Representative of ICI in India. We would also like to thank Arthur Tai of the Commission on Scholarly Communications with China (CSCC), our initial partner in China. We are grateful to Victor Yue Yuan, Xi Feng, and Zeng Jing (Emma), Horizon Research Consulting Group, ICI partners in China for all the help they have given ICI. We especially thank Shubhagato Dasgupta, ICI Representative in India, whose thoughtful attention to detail and follow-up was crucial in working closely with the authors, coordinating with Lucid Solutions and of course the Macmillan Publishers India Ltd.

Last but not least, we are pleased and thankful to Macmillan Publishers India Ltd for being highly flexible and enthusiastic about partnering with us in producing this edited volume. In particular, special thanks to Suresh Gopal, Senior Editorial Consultant and his team of editors at Macmillan Publishers India Ltd for their final copy-editing and design of the volume.

Ashok Gurung
Brian McGrath
Jianying Zha

Foreword

This important volume represents several milestones. It is the first major published result of collaborative research projects initiated by the India China Institute (ICI) at The New School. The Institute was the result of a major gift to The New School from the Starr Foundation in 2004, and supported the formation of a unique transnational collaboration. The Institute was the home of a Fellowship program geared to selecting a group of mid-career leaders in academia, industry, policy and public life in both countries, who were then encouraged to develop collaborative research projects that would require them to spend time in each other's countries as well as in New York.

When the first group of Fellows was selected and had their first meeting in New York in 2006, it was during the first flush of global recognition that India and China were major global economic giants, that their mutual relationships were likely to be major factors in the history of the 21st century and that the United States needed to learn from each of them and to contribute to open-minded cultural dialogue with them, outside of the constraints of politics, security and trade. The meetings and discussions that took place between these American, Chinese and Indian academics in the years since that date, in the context of mentoring and shaping the research of the ICI Fellows, marked a new phase in intellectual collaborations between the three countries. These relations had so far been overwhelmingly bilateral and had generally emphasized the primacy of US institutions and scholars in shaping these bilateral scholarly agendas. In the case of the ICI Fellows, what emerged was the first sustained trilateral dialogue between scholars and public intellectuals in the United States, India and China, supported and enriched by American academic institutions and scholarly concerns. This volume is therefore a document of a unique moment in the relationship between American public intellectuals and their counterparts in India and China.

It is within this context that the India China Institute decided that the theme for the first cohort of ICI Fellows would be that of urbanization as a global process with significant implications for India and China. The New School already had a large cohort of scholars spread across many schools of the University, with special interests in urban planning, design and cultural studies. India and China had already begun to make urban policy and urban studies major priorities in both countries. The ICI Fellows whose work is showcased in this volume were all engaged in research and public debate on the major challenges of urbanization in their respective countries. What emerged in the course of their collaborative work was a series of insights, initially sparked by their national perspectives and priorities and increasingly reshaped by their comparative and mutual dialogues and experiences in all three countries. The papers in this volume reflect this set of overlapping and mutually provocative set of conversations, whose results have taken the form of academic studies, cultural insights and public media contributions on both sides of the Himalayas.

There is no doubt that these essays break new scholarly ground and will be the subject of critical appraisal in the academic and policy worlds for some years to come. It is equally important that they be seen as the record of a unique trilateral conversation, which opened the doors to new topics, new methodologies and new friendships across national borders. In the end, it may prove that the deepest resource created by this collaborative project was that it sowed the seeds of transnational friendships that will endure. These friendships have shaped the research that is reported in this volume and it might well be that this volume also marks a new mode of international collaboration which emerges from sustained social solidarity between partners across borders. The research results may well be debated and modified over time, and indeed they should be, but the friendships and solidarities behind these pages will endure and multiply.

February 2010

Arjun Appadurai
Former Provost of The New School
Founding Member of India China Institute
Professor, New York University

Preface

Since its inception in 2004, the India China Institute (ICI) has dedicated significant energy and resources to creating a new community of scholars and experts from multi-disciplinary backgrounds, committed to building friendships based on issues of mutual interest and concern. ICI has been engaging in a sustained conversation focused on the critical and interrelated issues that India, China, and the United States encounter in the daily business of living and growing together in a globalizing world. As the institute has matured and grown, it has surpassed all my expectations, and this publication is proof that the ICI community is both strongly connected and actively engaged in the critical inquiry and collaborative scholarship that it was founded to promote. As my esteemed former colleague and endowed professor at ICI, Professor Arjun Appadurai, has said, 'if we can get thinkers in India, China, and the United States not only to agree about the biggest questions, but to decide the shape and scope of them, then the answers will have a certain range and durability that answers in the past have not had.' This volume is evidence of our journey towards creating a community focused on producing enduring answers.

The first cohort of India China Institute Fellows focused their collaborative research on the theme of Urbanization and Globalization, a topic of lasting importance, that this volume is also dedicated to addressing. These fellows provided the initial groundwork for imagining a community of scholars dedicated to trans-disciplinary, multilateral, and critical inquiry through four residencies and independent research in India, China, and the United States. The diversity of professional backgrounds and academic disciplines represented by the fellows in all three countries helped immensely in advancing innovative ideas and inquiry, as well as in supporting a strong international community committed to working on the same issues and questions. The ICI community, an interconnected, although geographically separated, group of scholars and experts, may never have had the opportunity to communicate without the ICI Fellowship Program. The advent of these new friendships has fostered greater trust and willingness to learn and converse across national and disciplinary borders.

For many years, scholars have studied India and China separately, subscribing to the area studies model. While this is now changing, most current literature on India and China is still framed in terms of (economic and political) competition that continues to ignore the more complicated and subtle relationship between the two countries. Our Fellows have expanded the dialogue on India-China issues beyond the normative arguments, conventional frameworks of service industry versus manufacturing, or competition for resources, to further deepening our knowledge about such topics as efficacy of government and the significance of social and cultural exchange. In this volume, we build on our earlier work and move to a different level of analysis that broadens and brings into conversation seemingly unconnected viewpoints, opinions, and perspectives valuable to understanding contemporary India-China interactions.

Given the complexity and historically specific context of issues pertaining to India and China and the challenges they present, the subject matter covered in this volume should neither be taken as the entire scope of what could be done nor be regarded as the ultimate source of knowledge in the area. The conversations and collaborative work initiated by the authors of this volume will be further developed by the two subsequent cohorts of India China Institute Fellows, who are working on the two interrelated themes of 'Prosperity and Inequality' and 'Social Innovation for Sustainable Environments.'

This volume is not meant to be an exhaustive catalogue of all the issues facing India and China in the future, but rather a sample of some of the unique perspectives and collaborative research that the ICI Fellows have contributed to the ongoing conversation on these issues. I hope that you, as a reader, will gain further understanding of the complex and interrelated nature of these issues, as well as the nature of the dialogue our Fellows have been creating. We encourage you to visit us and participate in various web-based resources of India China Institute at www.newschool.edu/ici.

Ashok Gurung
Senior Director
India China Institute, The New School
New York

List of Abbreviations

ASEAN	Association of Southeast Asian Nations
BOA	Board of Approval
BOE	Bureau of Education
BTA	Bilateral Trade Agreement
CAS	Chinese Academy of Sciences
CBE	Commune and Brigade Enterprise
CCP	Chinese Communist Party
DDR	Doha Development Round
DFI/FDI	Foreign Direct Investment
DTA	Domestic Tariff Area
EEC	European Economic Community
EIUS	Environmental Improvement of Urban Slums
EOU	Export Oriented Unit
EPZ	Export Processing Zone
ESC	Educational Subsidy Certificate
EU	European Union
FAI	Fixed Asset Investment
FII	Foreign Institutional Investor
FTA	Foreign Trade Agreement
GATT	General Agreement on Tariffs and Trade
ICI	India China Institute
IIT	Indian Institute of Technology
IP	Intellectual Property
IPR	Intellectual Property Rights
IT	Information Technology
JDFHBC	Jianggan District Farmer House Building Center
JV	Joint Venture
KIP	Knowledge Innovation Program

MNC	Multinational Corporation
NAFTA	North American Free Trade Agreement
NGO	Non-governmental Organization
NIS	National Innovation Systems
OCP	Organochlorine Pesticide
OECD	Organization for Economic Cooperation and Development
PAH	Polycyclic Aromatic Hydrocarbon
PBOC	People's Bank of China
PC	Personal Computer
PLA	People's Liberation Army
PPP	Purchasing Power Parity
PRC	People's Republic of China
R&D	Research and Development
RMB	Renminbi
S&T	Science and Technology
SAPI	Strategic Action Plan for Science and Technology
SEPA	State Environmental Protection Administration
SEZ	Special Economic Zone
SNP	Slum Networking Programme
SOE	State Owned Enterprises
TPA	Trade Pact Agreement
TVE	Township and Village Enterprise
WTO	World Trade Organization

List of Tables, Figures, and Boxes

CHAPTER 2

Table 1	NIS Evaluation Index	29
Figure 1	NIS Summary Chart	29
Table 2	Infrastructure Comparison	32
Table 3	Education System Comparison	35
Table 4	Comparison of Innovation Input and Output in China and India	36
Table 5	Economic Performance Comparisons	37

CHAPTER 4

Table 1	Elimination of Jiedufei for Migrant Children in Selected Provinces/Municpalities	67
Figure 1	Growth of Migrant Students in Seven Rui'an Schools, Fall 2002 to Fall 2006	72
Table 2	Effect of ESCs on Students	73
Figure 2	Growth of Migrant Students in Seven Yueqing Schools, Fall 2002 to Fall 2006	73

CHAPTER 6

Figure 1	Strategic Location of Xintang	97
Figure 2	Aerial Photograph of Xintang Village	97
Figure 3	Typical Urban Village Residential Buildings in Hangzhon	98
Figure 4	Land-use Plan of Xintang Community	99
Figure 5	Detailed Land Use Plan: Site Allocation	100
Figure 6	Land-use of Xintang Village before Planning	101
Figure 7	Land Use for Xintang Village after Planning	102
Figure 8	Master Plan of Xintang Community	103
Figure 9	Bird's-eye View of the Xintang Community	103
Figure 10	Apartments Completed	104
Figure 11	Apartments Under Construction	104
Figure 12	Completed Apartment in Xintang	104

CHAPTER 8

Figure 1	India's Exports and Imports as a Share of GDP	119
Figure 2	Growing Savings and Investment in India	121
	(a) Composition of Savings	
	(b) Gross Investment as a share of GDP	
Figure 3	Projections of Urban Population Shares in China and India	122

Box 1	Gujarat's Industrial Pollution Corridor	124
Figure 4	Construction Growth Rates in India 1997-8 to 2008-9	126
Figure 5	Growth in China's Real Estate Sector	128
Figure 6	Nail House in Chongqing	135

CHAPTER 9

Figure 1	New Driving Force	145
Figure 2	Pulling Its Weight	145
Figure 3	Growth in GDP, Merchandise Trade and FDI Inflows 2000–05	148
Table 1	SEZs in China and India	163

Introduction

ASHOK GURUNG, BRIAN MCGRATH, AND JIANYING ZHA

When India joined China in removing barriers to globalization and trade in 1991, a new era in India-China relations began. But unlike the chaste remove of the two ancient civilizations separated by the Himalayas and the Tibetan Plateau, or the contentious cold-war era border disputes of the two new Republics, India and China are entering into an era of competition and engagement. This volume presents shifting perspectives on the challenges of urbanism in India and China over the past few decades, at the dawn of this new era of growing cities in a shrinking world.

The people of China and India have traded, philosophized, debated and deliberated for thousands of years through numerous upheavals and transformations in the world around them. References to ancient China have been recorded in the Mahabharata, while Chinese silk is mentioned in the Arthashastra, India's earliest economic policy document written in the 3rd century BC. The spread of Buddhism from India to China dates back to the 1st century AD, and it has flourished over centuries of extraordinary journeys and translations between the two languages and cultures.

Yet, in a more recent context, the two most populous states in the world have been described as follows: 'China and India are very prickly, both hypersensitive, emotional countries. Their power has grown faster than their political maturity.'[1] In the second half of the 20th century, during the difficult stage of modern nation-state building, relations between the People's Republic of China and the Republic of India turned belligerent, creating barriers to mutual understanding and the exchange of ideas. Forums that are free from preconceived notions and guarded opinions where such discussions could take place were conspicuously absent. Leaders, academics and professionals from each country have, in the recent past, found it difficult to talk to each other, share common issues, ideas, problems and questions that vex them.

This volume documents the first in a series of endeavors by the India China Institute at The New School, New York, to create space for trilateral conversations on the emerging issues of globalization, urbanization, political economy, development and governance that can enrich and expand intellectual collaboration across diverse disciplines in India, China, and the US. The India China Fellowship Program was founded on the conviction that Chinese, Indian and American scholars and professionals would need to construct the key questions about the future of their countries first, before they could devise innovative and creative solutions to the

---

[1] Jehangir Pocha, who worked in Beijing for three years and is now editor in chief of the Indian NewsX TV channel in India, quoted in http://www.washingtonpost.com/wp-dyn/content/article/2009/12/13/AR2009121302527_2.html

problems and puzzles of so vast a landscape. The theme for the first India China Fellowship was Urbanization and Globalization. The New York experience was extremely memorable with intense debates and discussions, work on collaborative projects, and the forging of great cross border friendships.

The essays in this compendium are divided into three sections. The first section, entitled *Comparing the Incomparable: Engagement, Innovation, and Legitimacy*, includes related studies on economic development and possible areas of dialogue between China and India. It pairs Aromar Revi's essay 'Two Countries, Diverse Systems, a Shared Future?' with Xiaobo Wu's, 'Comparative Analysis on National Innovation Systems of China and India'. Included in this section, Hiren Doshi's 'Perspectives on China's Integration with the World Economy' compiles select articles previously penned by him for The Financial Express, to analyze China's economy for Indian readers from his perspective as an employee of an Indian multinational living in Beijing. Also within this section is a contribution from Amita Bhide and Yang Yao entitled 'A Comparative Study of State Response to Informal Settlers in Indian and Chinese Cities'. This joint chapter grew from a collaborative project that took a close look at state action in the field of educational provisioning to informal settlers in Mumbai, India and to migrants in Rui'an, China.

Aromar Revi's essay moves from looking at India and China as countries distanced by their images of each other, to examining how their separate economic and political endowments have pulled them together in the global political economy, and finally to analyzing the prospects for closer economic ties between them. The 1962 China–India Border War led to a freeze in relations between the two countries. China witnessed rapid economic growth in the 1980s because of significant economic reforms. India started its process of reforms in the early 1990s. Thus China had a head start in the growth process and India has not been able to close the gap. Important factors for China's persistent growth have been a strong human capital base, state provided services, the development of infrastructure, and the availability of foreign capital and technology, and access to foreign markets. However, from the mid-1990s India has also seen a steady increase in economic growth and looks well positioned to surpass China for the longer run.

The western media usually frames the 'India–China Question' in terms of a contest between two emerging economic powerhouses. This chapter, however, follows a different approach by discussing how the long enduring stereotypes of the 'other' do not allow a more meaningful dialogue between the two countries. The movement from a political association towards one defined by economic and cultural interests may prove to be the beginning of a more stable relationship between the two large cultures where the historical barriers of language and distance will no longer be constraints.

Xiaobo Wu presents a comparative study of economic growth in China and India. He discusses the value of the conceptual tools that come under the heading of 'National Innovation Systems' and compares the differing capacities and performances of the two countries. Rather than compare economic outcomes, this approach looks at what helps determine those outcomes, such as the investment in Research and Development. The chapter reveals that the two countries have followed diverse modes of development. Recent studies have investigated key indices of the National Innovation Systems (NIS) of both countries, to gain insights into their economic development process. An NIS 'is a historically rooted subsystem of the national economy in which various institutions impact one another in carrying out innovation activity'. The chapter takes a comprehensive look at the innovative capacities of China and India to get a sense of their development potential, comparing their innovation environments, innovation operations and economic performances.

Each environment for innovation is compared from various perspectives, including scientific research institutions, policy, infrastructure, and human resources. Through a thorough analysis of the innovation operation systems, the chapter concludes that China has an apparent advantage in innovation investments; however, India seems to have an edge in efficiency of Research and Development input and output.

Hiren Doshi's position is special in this cohort of ICI Fellows, in that he is an Indian who worked in China for an extended period of time. He brings significant professional experience with both countries to his examination of China's global economic integration. In the articles introduced and reprinted here, written for a major Indian business newspaper, The Financial Express, Doshi draws on his personal experiences and his job-related expertise with an Indian software company doing business in China. He also brings his analytical skills to bear on a wide range of topics on various facets of contemporary China: the background to the India–China economic collaboration, structural challenges faced by China due to its single-minded focus on economic growth, the political–economic relationship between China and the US, the balance of powers in international trade, turmoil in financial markets, and the increasing importance of the Chinese economy in the world.

In India, the source of legitimacy for the government is the set of procedures regarding elections, laws, and other regulations. This is called procedure-based legitimacy. In China, the legitimacy of the government comes from its ability to continuously deliver performance to the population. This is performance-based legitimacy. The chapter by Amita Bhide and Yang Yao discusses the accountability of the government under these types of legitimacy by studying how the government provides education to informal settlers in cities in China and India. Migrants to cities severely test the existing urban system, and the responses of the state to their needs help to explain how the state really works. The chapter is based on intensive fieldwork which studied the governmental arrangements for informal settlers in Mumbai, India and for migrants in Rui'an, China.

Both case studies show that in terms of ensuring universal access to elementary education, neither system is automatically responsive. The 'procedure-based' system in India is handicapped by the conflicting interests of institutional players and various civil society groups. On the other hand, the performance-based system in China grants immense power to the local government; this often leads to a selective provision of public goods to suit the aims and targets of the government. Bhide and Yao conclude that the there is a need for greater power for social groups to counterbalance government powers in China, and a more competent government that can resolve conflicting interests and work towards common goals in India.

The next section *Governing Urban Spaces: Economy, Design, and Governance* dwells on the recent development experience in urban China in comparison to approaches and practices in India. It contains four essays that look at Chinese and Indian governance challenges in urbanization which resulted from collaborative research between two urban planners from China, an economist from India and an architect from the US. Zongyong Wen, Zuojun Yang, Brian McGrath, and Partha Mukhopadhyay formed a team to look at the land, water, and culture of various cities in China and India. The first essay, by Zongyong Wen, is entitled and *Urban Development and Governmental Approach: Experiences in China and India.* The next two chapters consider urban space and government action in China without making explicit comparisons with India. Both chapters deal with the urbanization experience of Hangzhou, China. Zuojun Yang deals with land acquisition challenges and the practice 'Che Cun Jian Ju (撤村建居)' to protect the interests of affected farmers. Brian McGrath, on the other hand, examines the ecological impact of the rapid urbanization of Hangzhou on its lakes and pristine mountains. He offers the basis for a new urban design model for ecological development in China, which is not necessarily at odds with its development imperatives. Partha Mukhopadhyay presents an intensely comparative piece in which the urbanization issues faced in India and China are analyzed in terms of coping strategies, performance, response and preemptive action prevalent in these countries. He anchors his discourse at various points with the issues highlighted by Zongyong Wen, Zuojun Yang, and Brian McGrath in the volume to develop his thesis.

Zongyong Wen's essay is part analysis of urban growth in China, and the contrast to India, and part personal thoughts on urban development, and questions he has distilled from this research experience. In his chapter, Chinese and Indian experiences are compared in the context of the priorities of the respective governments. Rapid urbanization leads to increasing divergence between development and traditional culture. Chinese economic and social life is undergoing tremendous changes and is witnessing a conflict between the old and the new. However, in India, traditional lifestyles are still observed in various parts of the country.

In China, the rate of urbanization is higher than that of economic development. This is resulting in social and economic conflicts; but at the same time there is greater awareness among the population about protecting their rights and the need to participate in day-to-day governance issues.

The chapter concludes that the priorities of a strong government in a country should be macro-control of the economy, the provision of social services as well as employment security, removal of poverty, etc. If some type of an accountability and performance assessment system is in place, it can help to reduce malpractices by government officials. Past experience proves that single-mode growth and high energy-consuming operations do not allow sustainable development to take place. To maintain a balance across population growth, resources and the environment, a rational outlook on development is required. This should be accompanied by a move towards a comprehensive mode of development that encompasses political, economic, social and human factors. He notes that 'ancient Chinese philosophers had discussed the concept that "man is an integral part of nature" but it is only now that the Chinese are beginning to understand this'.

Like many other cities in China, Hangzhou has witnessed fast urban growth. To meet the needs of urbanization, the administrative region of Hangzhou has continuously been enlarged in the past two decades. Zuojun Yang in his chapter provides a detailed and luxuriously illustrated evaluation of how Hangzhou has succeeded in implementing plans for transforming agricultural land into urban spaces, while protecting the interests of the farmers whose land was used. He discusses the Che Cun Jian Ju (撤村建居) process started in 1999 in which farmers from about 70 per cent of the villages within the Hangzhou Ring Road were relocated to multistoried apartment blocks from individual dwelling units to unlock land. This policy has played an important role in the efficient use of land resources in Hangzhou. It is interesting to note that this transformation has been achieved with the full support of farmers affected by the project.

The chapter discusses the specific experience of Xintang village which is now no longer categorized as rural. All erstwhile villagers are now Hangzhou urban residents with access to benefits that ordinary Hangzhou urban residents receive. The interests of the farmers of Xintang community have been fully protected. The farmers are getting land for relocation of their houses and land for the future development of the community. They will also receive compensation for the acquired land, including the cost of the land and compensation for the demolition of their former residential buildings.

In conclusion, the chapter argues that the incremental demand for land, invariably leads farming households to give up both their land and livelihood. Generally speaking, the majority of such households do not have the skills to survive without land and nor are there enough job opportunities to absorb unskilled labour. Hence, the transition to an industrial or service economy from an agrarian economy is not easy. If the urban growth process is to be sustained, agrarian communities need to be supported through the process of transition in a manner that protects food, livelihood security and quality of life.

Hangzhou is among the most scenic cities in China due to its location between the Qiantang River, the Grand Canal and West Lake, and its beautiful mountain views. In the recent past, economic planners have encouraged the creation of an information technology hub in Hangzhou while at the same time promoting its physical charms. Brian McGrath's chapter, 'Silicon Valley in Paradise', provides the foundation for a new model for ecological urban development in China, using an ancient sensibility to create a new urban metabolism around an intricate ecosystem of water, land and cultural relationships.

The chapter focuses on the environmental, social and experiential possibilities of combining 'Silicon Valley' with 'Paradise on Earth'. A scientific literature search reveals a number of environmental problems and ongoing ecological monitoring in West Lake, the Grand Canal, the Qiantang River as well as in the headwater mountain area which nourishes the rapidly developing agricultural delta. The question that the chapter asks relates to Hangzhou's challenge in maintaining its intimate connection with its water bodies in the face of such enormous changes at the regional scale and with the commoditization of its landscape and scenery.

This study is part of a larger research quest concerning sustainable urbanization and development in India and China in a networked world. Can these two ancient cultures with rich traditions of skillful environmental design bypass the most severe environmental problems of western industrialization and create a socially and environmentally resilient urban future? In asking this question, this chapter echoes Wen's hopes for China.

The chapter by Partha Mukhopadhyay is structured as a series of responses provoked by his three partners in inquiry—Zongyong Wen, Zuojun Yang, and Brian McGrath. Following an introductory section that examines the broad features of economic transformation in India and China, it addresses specific issues related to various aspects of urbanization, responding largely to issues raised by Wen. It then situates the specific model of urban transformation described by Yang in an Indian comparative context before concluding with an agenda for future conversations, drawing on McGrath, who emphasizes the importance of the specificity of the Indian and Chinese urban experience.

The last section *Dispatches from the Field: Intellectuals, Fat Cats and Democracy* includes articles by the widely published Indian academic and journalist, Chakrapani Ghanta and Chinese journalist turned academic Yukuan Guo. It also contains the concluding essay on China's incredible journey to economic development by Yang Yao. Ghanta and Guo exchanged turns as guides to the most marginalized members of the Indian and the Chinese society, the dalit weaving and coal mining villagers in India, and minority groups deep in rural China. Ghanta has been studying economic reforms and the ongoing debate about the impact of the market economy and globalization, particularly on the lower income groups for over a decade. The section captures snapshot reflections on social and political economic discourses in China and India around the developmental impact of a globalizing regime in terms of social stratification, migration, displacement and dislocation in the form of a series of essays by Ghanta. Some of these articles appeared in the Telegu newspaper Andhrajyothy and feminist magazine Bhumika and Ghanta has translated them himself for reproduction in this volume. This section also carries a chapter by Yukuan Guo which is essentially a critique of the long-held concept of a leftist in China and situates its ramifications in the context of what is globally considered a true 'leftist' approach. Guo expresses amused puzzlement at how Indian intellectuals of leftist persuasion seem to misinterpret China's new policies that opened the country to global influences with significant impact on Chinese peasants.

Ghanta has made a series of contributions on the impact of reform processes in India and China, foreign investments, Special Economic Zones and lessons that India can learn from the Chinese experience. In his last article, the author discusses the status of women in China who like Indian women experienced thousands of years of suppression by patriarchal and traditionally oppressive customs before being granted equal political, economic, social and cultural rights and also equal wages for equal work under the Communist government led by Mao Zedong (毛泽东).

Yukuan Guo in his chapter demonstrates how intellectuals the world over misinterpret one another when they discuss issues of globalization and the market economy. The majority of left-wing intellectuals in the West criticize globalization and the market economy and ostensibly espouse the same causes as the 'Chinese New Left' who showcase the miseries faced by Chinese peasants in their discourses against globalization, magnifying capitalist hegemony and oppression. However, it is hard for these thinkers to even imagine the oppression faced by Chinese peasants during Mao's era. Of all the cases of contemporary capitalism in the world, it is hard to pick out one that subjugates peasants to the same degree of deprivation as Mao's regime did. Guo presents an extended meditation on how Chinese peasants have in fact benefited from globalization and China's open door policies, and the paradox that 'leftists' from India and elsewhere seem to think that the damage apparently done by globalization in places like India must have happened in China also, while in Guo's opinion, what is needed is more of the same.

Guo interweaves his reflections on how Indian and Chinese intellectuals talk past each other on these issues. The author firmly believes that intellectuals should adopt the truth-seeking 'mentality of logical coherence'. Equipped with their insights, they should question the fundamental adversities of human beings. Alliances formed on ambiguous political platforms, such as 'anti-globalization' cannot work in the long run. A true intellectual must always retain objectivity and breadth of vision to not be restricted by specific ideology that creates barriers to the pursuit of true knowledge.

Yang Yao concludes this section with an essay which seeks to explain the remarkable success of China's economic development. He argues that China achieved this success, not by creating a new economic model such as proposed by the so-called 'Beijing Consensus', but by following the economic policies close to those proposed by standard neoclassical economics, summarized by the 'Washington Consensus'. However, the success of those policies is not universal in the developing world. Yao believes that China's successful adoption has a lot to do with the existence of a 'disinterested government', meaning one that is unbiased and does not favor any single interest group in decision making, but only looks to a policy which assures steady economic growth. The foundation for a disinterested government is social equality, especially the absence of strong dominant social groups. However, there are signs that strong interest groups are emerging in China. Yao believes that greater democratization allowing ordinary citizens to participate in the political process is the key to help China maintain a disinterested government.

The challenges in globalization and urbanization in India and China form the broad theme that runs through the three sections of the book, and these powerful drivers of change in India and China touch every aspect of social life and the physical environment. The perspectives of the authors shift between India and China, the macro and the micro, the elite and the marginalized, the conceptual and the real. It is rare that a single volume captures such a broad range of territories, views, and disciplinary lenses.

PART ONE

Comparing the Incomparable: Engagement, Innovation, and Legitimacy

1

Two Countries, Diverse Systems, A Shared Future?

An Essay on the Global Significance of India and China's Increasing Engagement

AROMAR REVI

LONG CONTACT AND THE SHOCK OF SUDDEN ENGAGEMENT

In a long and expansive view, India and China are two adjacent civilizations, separated by the largely impassable Himalaya and the forbidding Tibetan plateau, the Indian Ocean and five millennia of autonomous development of state systems, culture, faith and identity. Over the last two millennia, largely land and limited maritime contact between them has been almost continuous. This has involved an exchange of goods, ideas, culture and religion mediated by the elite and the courageous individuals who made the arduous and often dangerous journey in their pursuit of new frontiers of knowledge (Frank 1998; Hsu 1995). Yet, at a popular level, each was constructed as a distant 'other'— close enough to be alluring, but far enough not to stir up serious conflict.

The late 1940s saw the liberation of both countries. India achieved its Independence in 1947 from 150-year old British colonial regime, through a majorly non-violent struggle led by Mahatma Gandhi and the Congress party. In 1949, after years of fighting to defeat the Japanese, the Chinese Communist Party (CCP) trounced the Guomintang in a vicious post-World War II civil war. The Mao-led consolidation of the revolution led to the integration of an autonomous Tibet into China in 1956.

This led to a sharp discontinuity in the historical low-level interstate engagement between China and India. They were suddenly thrown together as neighbors along an 1800 km border between Tibet, an arc of five north Indian states, and the former kingdom of Nepal sandwiched in the center. The shock of this relatively recent contact persists in the longest unsettled terrestrial border in spite of decades of tortuous negotiations (Maxwell 2006).

A conflict along two zones of this border in 1962, led to a near freeze in bilateral relations between these Asian giants that began to thaw mildly a quarter of a century later. As a result, soon after the establishment of a long common border, trade as well as economic, cultural and people-to-people contact dwindled to less than a trickle (Ranganathan and Khanna 2004). This heightened the historical gap in knowledge and shared experience between the Indian and Chinese elite, further widening the huge gulf between ordinary people in both countries. As a new wave of post-Soviet globalization rolled out across the world in the mid- and late-1980s, changes in domestic politics and economic strategy led both countries down divergent political and economic paths (Deshpande and Acharya 2001).

China was striving hard to regain its position as a 'Great Power' and the 'primary driver' of the global economy, after having made the transition from a poor to a middle income country with a globally competitive manufacturing sector, broad self-sufficiency in agriculture and a modern military system. India started on the path of reforms later, and with greater disabilities, but rapidly caught up in terms of growth, modernization of its economy and creation of a globally competitive information technology (IT) services sector within the framework of a mixed economy and plural democracy (Amin 2005; Bloom et al., 2006).

POST 1980 DIVERGENCE

Differing domestic initial conditions and priorities; a fundamental divergence in the nature of founding political settlements and hence political systems; and a strategic divergence for over a decade in economic- and trade-based engagement with the rest of the world have taken China and India to very different places in the global economy, geopolitics and the space for future development and transformation.

Mao's China went through a roller-coaster of attempts to enforce structural change and consolidate communist power via multiple traumatic passages of the Great Leap Forward and the resulting famine that killed over 30 million people and the decade-long (1966–76) Cultural Revolution that probably destroyed more human and cultural capital than many twentieth century interstate conflicts. In spite of these terrible dislocations, by the late 1970s China had made considerable progress in education, health, agrarian reform, basic industrialization and national security, even though in economic terms, it wasn't dramatically better off in per capita output than its Indian neighbor.

Post-Mao China rapidly opened up to globalization via Organization for Economic Cooperation and Development (OECD) investments, firms and technology; export and investment-led growth, largely on its own terms. The CCP simultaneously pushed pragmatic domestic economic and political reform focused on growth, industrial modernization and price competitive exports, and strengthened the nationalist state system to maintain stability and order and maintained its own centrality to the Chinese state (Barnett et al., 2004). With the exception of hiccups, as in Tiananmen Square in the late 1980s, China has been largely successful in recapturing its historical place at the center of the world economy through sheer growth, though at the significant cost of loss of political, socio-cultural and ecological resilience. Only history will be able to judge the long-term consequences of this trade-off.

After leading a successful and largely non-violent struggle against British colonialism in India, Gandhi, Nehru, Patel and their successors built the foundations of a stable, plural Parliamentary democracy in a highly diverse ethnic, regional, linguistic and religious terrain. This was despite the traumatic partition of India and Pakistan in 1947.

Post-independence economic performance of India was better than that under the British colonial yoke in the first half of the twentieth century, but it was still slow. The creation of a modern industrial sector, technological capability and market-based systems, did not succeed in addressing the well-entrenched asymmetries of caste, gender, ethnicity and unequal agrarian relations. A committed, development-oriented state was constructed from an imperial steel-framed bureaucracy; however, it was rapidly captured by special interests and rampant corruption to become the entrenched 'Licence–Permit Raj', that held the Indian economy and polity in a vice-like grip until the mid-1990s (Jalan 2002; Kapur and Mehta 2005).

Yet India, with a robust and well-crafted Constitution and slowly deepening democracy managed to deal with multiple economic and political challenges. This included three wars with Pakistan—the 1971 war eventually leading to the creation of Bangladesh; the rapid righting of the ship of state after the imposition of the draconian National Emergency (1975–7); and the slow move towards a 'social revolution' led by resurgent intermediate and lower castes and excluded populations that led to a series of radical responses from both the Left and nationalist Hindu extremes of the political spectrum, starting in the late 1980s (Frankel 2005).

A significant divergence between India and China began in the early 1980s, with the beginning of rapid Chinese economic growth led by a burst of productivity in rural China as collectivist constraints were released; an opening up to the world economy; and a series of significant reform measures introduced by Deng and his successors. India also embarked on a path of halting economic reforms from the mid-1980 onwards. Progress was patchy till the early 1990s. This provided China an early and significant lead that has been difficult for India to close. A strong human capital base; the ability of the state to deliver services, infrastructure and access to foreign capital and technology and eventually export markets; and the creation of a strong framework for 'command capitalism' are cited as important factors in a 30-year run of strong economic growth in China (Friedman and Gilley 2005; Dollar 2007).

AN INDIAN CATCH UP?

Starting in the mid-1990s, there was a steady increase in India's economic growth and efficiency, and savings and investment. Around 2008, development indicators for India were beginning to slowly close in on the long-range Chinese averages (Bussolo et al., 2006). India has: steadily resolved problems related to poverty and deprivation; improved public services delivery in areas such as drinking water, elementary education and rail transport; built a better-regulated national market and strong domestic financial sector; and enabled innovation and market-forces to expand the delivery of telecom, IT, air transport and financial services to domestic and international markets (Dahlman & Utz, 2005, Bound, 2007).

International remittances, foreign institutional investor (FII) portfolios and, more recently, foreign direct investment (FDI) growth, have transformed the flow of financial resources, in what was once a capital-starved economy (Das 2006).

A few commentators speak of India catching up or even being ahead of China in some areas (Khanna and Huang 2003). On many economic counts, however, India is currently at the point where China was a decade or more ago. With a reduction in the growth differential between the two countries, exponentially increasing opportunities of India–China trade and economic engagement, and the rapid consolidation of both domestic markets, a key question is whether some form of convergence around a pan-Asian market structure is possible (and desirable?) If it is, then what are the changes in perception and particular strategic choices that could help to achieve this potential?

Rather than examining the India–China question in relative terms or as the western media construct of a 'neck-and-neck' race between two emerging Asian economies, a more useful approach would be to examine how the wide (late twentieth century) gaps in mutual understanding and knowledge of each others' cultures and persistent stereotypes of the 'other', constrain a deeper engagement between the two countries.

GOING BEYOND CONSTRUCTED NATIONAL STEREOTYPES

The most common Indian stereotype of China, centers around the 'betrayal' of the promise of a collective Asian future enshrined in the 1950s political slogan *Hindi–Chini bhai bhai* (Indo-China brotherhood) following the 1962 border conflict, in which China is perceived by Indians as the unprovoked aggressor (Ranganathan and Khanna 2004). On the Chinese side, this series of historical events is ascribed to a mix of Indian political naiveté; an inability and refusal to read multiple Chinese warning signals; and internalization of a British colonial perception of hard borders versus soft perceptions of zones of influence. This translates into continuing surprise at the Indian sensitivity to what is seen as a non-event of which most Chinese have little or no recollection.

Similarly, the portrayal of India in many Chinese school textbooks, and hence in the popular perception, as China's 'failed' Asian neighbor is a difficult stereotype to undo. This strongly governs contemporary Chinese perceptions of India that are ironically almost Orientalist in their construction.

A more recent stereotype in the making is the idea of *Chindia*—the largest market opportunity in the twenty-first century (Ramesh 2005). This is projected to provide space for greater prosperity, equity and hence, peace for the people of both countries. A number of transnational companies are beginning to address this joint business opportunity (Khanna 2008). This approach could also become a fulcrum around which the deconstruction of the post-World War II—conception of development becomes possible. This could be posited as a search for an 'advanced' western-style economy and liberal democracy to an exploration of the nation state with a distinct Asian flavor and strong Chinese (or Indian) characteristics.

This paper attempts to engage the three stereotypes mentioned above as metaphors to examine the dramatically different global context of the twenty-first century and the multiple transitions that contemporary India and China are making to find their niches. These processes are transforming the economic, political and social relations within and outside their boundaries. They are also creating immense opportunities for mutual engagement. Appropriately directing the sheer size and momentum of these two economies, could potentially alter the nature and trajectory of the world system to a more sustainable, harmonious and humane direction (Krueger 2005; Arrow et al., 2006).

This provides a compelling reason to study the internal dynamics, interaction and engagement of these two ancient Asian cultures and the chrysalis of the two modern nation states in the making that currently encapsulates them.

INDIA AS CHINA'S 'FAILED' ASIAN NEIGHBOR?

An uninformed observer may well agree with the stereotype of India as China's 'failed' Asian neighbor that appears in some school textbooks and has colored the perception of at least two generations of the Chinese population.

Part of the critique is partially justified. India made a late start in addressing its post colonial challenges of human development. It began to effectively universalize primary education only in the 1990s and, reform its failing public health care systems after 2005. It has, in the recent past, embarked on a serious reform of its massive higher education system. Deep rural and urban poverty and deprivation, poor transportation and power infrastructure and public service delivery, widespread corruption, and severe regional development imbalances make early twenty-first century India, similar to China in an earlier period (Baru 2006).

India's development has been strategically constrained like that of late twentieth century China by the per capita availability of arable land and water, a lack of domestic oil and gas resource, hence a strong dependence on coal, and a severe shortage of domestic capital. China's early investment in education and health care, better physical and economic infrastructure, a strong focus of the economy on export and secondary sectors since the early 1980 and an emphasis on economic performance catapulted it into center stage of the global economy in the 1990s, placing it way ahead of India in terms of most development indicators.

China addressed the challenge of capital availability in the medium run, by encouraging massive external investments in manufacturing and markets both from the OECD and partial round tripping from Taiwan and Hong Kong. It pursued a conservative foreign exchange and fiscal policy and encouraged high savings and investment rates that in turn led to the economic growth. China now has the largest foreign exchange reserves in any country, ever, and this effectively (along with Japan and Arab oil states) not only props the US budget deficit, but also underwrites the immense trade and macroeconomic deficit that powers US and to a some extent European consumption.

Yet, India's fundamental achievement and divergence from China has been in building the largest stable and plural democracy in recent human history. This is probably why India's polity is of greater interest to Chinese scholars than its economy. The counterfactual is Pakistan's parallel 60-year rocky trajectory that provides a subtle counterpoint to India's stable Constitutional history that the US and even China are starting to acknowledge (Guha 2007; Austin 1999).

India has maintained steady economic growth, typically over 6 per cent since the mid-1990s, along with a process of economic reform supported across the political spectrum. This has survived the post-1990 era of coalition politics in New Delhi. A recent spurt in growth, savings and investment appears set to spur a relatively steady period of medium-term economic growth (Jadhav et al., 2006). Strong domestic demand, the rapid growth of some of the lowest cost infrastructure services in the world (for example, India has overtaken China as the largest national market for cellular phones), an aggressive process of financial market deepening, the new found confidence of Indian corporations, consumers and a post-liberalization generation poised to enter the workforce in millions is dramatically changing India's economic landscape (Khanna 2008; Bijapurkar 2007).

THE RESILIENCE OF CHINA'S CURRENT DEVELOPMENT TRAJECTORY

China has managed to sustain a long 30-year period of relatively steady economic growth. This is poised to overtake the late nineteenth century and post-World War II economic boom in the US as the longest sequence of growth in recorded economic history, in spite of the hiccups caused by the 2008–9 recession. However, the development has not been without costs. Rapid growth and prosperity in some regions has led to a sharp increase in inequality and regional disparities, leading to a clear expression and apparent tolerance of dissent across China (Virmani 2005).

There have been some political hiccups in China as well, especially the use of force in Tiananmen in 1989. However, the continual chatter of local and ethnic disaffection has never been regime-threatening. Within China, it appears that Deng's gamble of catalyzing a transition from an extreme form of Maoism at the end of the Cultural Revolution to a Chinese form of Party-led 'command capitalism' seems to have paid off, at least in the short run.

The tolerance of Chinese society of command capitalism, in the face of hyper-modernization may, however, be shorter than anticipated. The decline of the family with entry of 'Young

Emperors' (a direct outcome of the one-child policy) into the workforce, the burning aspiration to emulate and outdo the West in mass consumption, the linked resurgence of faith traditions to fill the deepening psychological and social void and the insidious impact of new media and global connectedness which is creating new networks of relationships and institutions in China, could challenge the smooth social and political transition into a postmodern future, even one with strong Chinese characteristics.

China is facing at least two fundamental challenges. The first is political transition to a more widely-held form of governance within the frame of 'One China' that returns it to its eighteenth century place as the largest global economic power (Thornton 2008). This will almost certainly require an incipient social transition with interlinked modern and postmodern elements, as older forms of social organization and hegemony—clan, community and Confucian hierarchy—change or breakdown. The second is to enable the first transition within the constraints imposed by an increasingly interdependent global capitalist economy; an economy driven by trade and expanding influence of transnational corporations; underpinned by the availability of cheap fossil fuels; a near-real time global financial system that is open to considerable volatility and yet subject to little global governance; threatened by a fractured global landscape of power dominated by a single superpower sometimes in retreat and often in denial; over three billion people across the world living in poverty, many in failing nation states and cultures that are seeking hard to reconcile multiple regional identities with the increasingly alien (post September 11) standard of western liberal democracy (Deng and Moore 2004). This shifting and increasingly fractal and postmodern *glocal* geopolitical landscape seems to imply the opening up of multiple spaces for the exploration of plural regional institutions and interest groups in a rather different narrative to that of the centralized modern nation state promoted by contemporary Beijing propaganda.

Therefore, a key conceptual challenge for Beijing, Chinese provinces and semi-autonomous metropolitan regions (for example, Shanghai) is to weave an acceptable frame and culture of governance; adapting central command and control systems by providing considerable autonomy at the peripheries; enabling decentralized self-organization from the bottom up—using a mix of community organization, market forces and active political participation. Simultaneously, it is also essential to protect against a backslide to a more rigidly structured incarnation of the current centralized bureaucracy or the endless revolutionary nightmare of a new Cultural Revolution.

When faced with these apparent choices, Guided Democracy seems the safest way forward to a new generation of Chinese reformers (Yang 2007). This is underpinned by a number of critical caveats: as long as the center holds; the peripheries are kept in check with a mix of economic incentives and military force; an extension of a Chinese zone of economic power and soft influence via aid, trade, investment and the Chinese diaspora in search of resources, markets and security in Asia, Africa and Latin America; western economies remaining addicted to consumption at low Chinese export determined prices and other regional powers like Japan, Russia and India being content, do not challenge this trend of events.

Given this context, a number of strategic questions emerges on India-China relationship:

1. Will the Chinese domestic market-centered push to accelerate growth of its service sector allow it to become the 'workshop, office and market' of the world by the 2020s (PRC 2006)? What will this mean for the stability of the global economy and the future of western capitalism and transnational corporations (Wilson and Purushothaman 2003)?

2. Will China be willing to cede its dominant position in manufacturing to India and other emerging economies in the 2030s onwards as its economy becomes larger than that of the US, matures, and as a consequence slows in terms of growth (Srinivasan 2006)? What will that mean for the stability of the Chinese state and the global balance of power?
3. Will India be able to maintain its current lead in services-export, deepen and widen its manufacturing base to cater to the exploding domestic demand and potential exports and simultaneously enable a transition of over 500 million people from agriculture-based livelihoods and rural areas into secondary or tertiary sector urban occupations (de Vries and Revi 2007)?
4. Will this process be relatively smooth, with little inter-state competition but intense firm competition across Chindia as both countries jostle for dominance (Singh 2005)? Will this be the largest market opportunity in history, or will it be constrained by the US and European edge in soft, economic and military power (Wallerstein 2006)?

Both China and India are cognizant of these opportunities and the attendant domestic challenges. Some are common to both emerging nations: burgeoning inequality across income cohorts and regions; universal access to quality education and health care services and other public goods; natural resource 'hunger' and crises, especially around water, agriculture and forests; managing the global commons, especially the atmosphere and the impact of climate change and accelerating access to, and deepening of, domestic markets (Winter and Yusuf 2006).

The central questions for India are: whether it will be able to address its ongoing challenges of poverty and deprivation and enable social transformation in the face of growing inequality, sectarian polarization and globalization. Issues for China include its resilience to internal shocks, potential slowdowns in economic growth, and the inevitable separation of power between the Party and the Chinese state aka a soft political landing, in an environment of slow economic growth (World Economic Forum 2007).

THE INTEREST OF THE ELITE IN INDIA AND CHINA IN GLOBALIZATION AND DEVELOPMENT

The political and business elite both in India and China express a high-level of confidence in the future (McKinsey 2007). This is largely ascribed to expectations of steady economic growth and transfer of much of the incremental gains of globalization towards these economies. Upsetting the current globalization applecart is posited being against national interest (as established by the elite) in both countries, even though it causes economic dislocation, negative environmental impacts and politically articulated angst among a fair section of the population.

The elite in both countries claim that the current version of globalization is essential to fuel the growth of their economies and thereby their incomes, wealth, well-being and dominance. Being pragmatic, however, they hope that they can facilitate a number of difficult transitions before global or regional instability; economic slowdown and volatility; declining regime legitimacy and climate change (independently or in conjunction) can slam the narrow global window of opportunity on their faces. The primary vehicle of elite aspiration is a mix of the nation state (domestic) and the transnational corporation in the space between nations. This may well prove to be an unstable mix in addressing the increasing global and regional challenges of security, governance and development.

The tolerance of the current unipolar world order by the elite in both countries, in spite of their strong nationalistic tendencies, is due to the pragmatic approach that great risk and responsibility are associated with the aspiration to achieve Great Power status, even if it is thrust upon them by economic and political circumstances. China and India both recognize that the 1943 Yalta global political settlement and the global institutions that uphold the United Nations and Bretton Woods institutions are dated and unequal to many emerging regional and global challenges.

The importance of manufacturing exports to China and services to India; the dependence of both on a global supply chain of oil and gas, strategic minerals and the limited ability of either to project conventional strong power beyond their immediate regions, implies that the development of a new global security architecture is of crucial interest to both as US dominance has declined with time (Tellis 2007). Yet, Asian caution may stay the course of political and economic adventurism, given the eighteenth to mid-twentieth century colonial experiences of India, China and much of Asia, and bitter memories of Japan's failed twentieth century imperial experiments in China (Cohen 2002; Lal 2006; Wadhva 2006).

The same cannot be said of hyper-nationalism, the transnational battle for religious and cultural identity; and the slow shift of the global balance of power in favor of transnational corporations, mobile finance capital and high-net-worth individuals, who have overtaken nation states as the largest and most powerful economic entities in the world. This is the space that the elite from both nations are learning to work in.

China as a strong state has developed an entire ecosystem of domestic institutional relationships binding the new elite into the older structures of power and patronage. This ranges from state and enterprises owned by the People's Liberation Army to Party-member run business empires that are dependant on guanxi (guanxi expresses the relationship of one person to another, or one party to another) and other forms of patronage. India's political and bureaucratic elite, however, has long emigrated to the US and to a lesser extent to Europe, to make their children experience the security of 'good life' that knows no borders.

Both the Chinese and Indian elite diaspora are crucial to a new range of global relationships, enterprises and prosperity, starting to flow into up-market localities in Beijing, New Delhi, Shanghai, Mumbai and Bangalore. They have helped to facilitate the flow of both FDI and FII, the high technology revolution that is starting to sweep many sectors of the economy and have increasing clout in political processes in their home countries, as well as in the US and parts of Europe.

In a quirk of contemporary history, the second generation diaspora elite of both India and China are closely allied in economic, cultural and value terms to those in the US. This makes for interesting contradictions, especially in the articulation of regional identity. The longer range question is the emerging vector between current economic and political power and interests of particular elite and those of subaltern political and regional economic voices, who are less invested in globalist values.

Inter-state relations between China and India, since the 1950s, have been the monopoly of the political and bureaucratic elite (Frankel and Harding 2004). This is changing rather quickly with the rapid expansion of trade, tourism and, more recently, educational and cultural exchange between the two countries. As the penetration of markets deepens into rural and peripheral urban Chindia; the local resistance to globalization crystallizes in the peripheral areas of both countries; new forms of engagement may become possible between mass and subaltern groups in these billion-plus populations that may fundamentally change the relationships between the two cultures and their mediation by various elite groups. These processes are embedded in a range of global and regional transitions that provide structural constraints and opportunities.

CHINDIA: EMBEDDED IN SIX SIMULTANEOUS GLOBAL TRANSITIONS

The economic and geopolitical resurgence of China and India and the opportunity for the creation of the largest market of the twenty-first century are captured in Chindia (Ramesh 2005). Chindia, however, masks the considerable divergence in the socio-cultural and political systems of the two Asian giants, starting with their almost simultaneous post-colonial journey in the late 1940s.

There are, however, a number of structural similarities that are often missed in a comparative analysis of both countries, whose elite stand to be among the most significant beneficiaries of the current wave of globalization. Among these, six global and regional transitions stand out.

A **demographic transition** from a rapid population growth to stabilization combined with significant aging. China will experience aging first and more strongly than India, ironically because of the 'success' of its population policies including its draconian 'one-child policy' (Cheng 2003). This could change not only future demography and consumer behavior in China but also its engagement with modernity, individualism and consumption, similar to the age of the baby boomers in the US.

China's aging population will not only present a challenge of becoming ' grey before becoming rich' but force it to construct a twenty-first century Chinese version of the western European social safety net. Unlike the European experience that was part of the social compact forged in western democracies during the post-World War II economic boom, the Chinese initiative may well be another test of performance-based legitimacy demanded of the State.

India, on the other hand, can make the best of its projected demographic dividend by rapidly scaling-up the provision of public services in health and education and improving both quality and innovation in these sectors to enable a rapid build-up of human capital and its productive engagement across the economy (Dyson, Cassen & Visaria, 2004). The development of a social safety net for India will demand significant innovations both in terms of per capita incomes and public expenditure, which may be much lower than those possible in China for a while.

China is close to achieving an **education transition** from the universalization of elementary education, to the near universal provision of secondary education. India, however, continues to lag behind China by almost a decade and a half, with universal elementary education expected to be achieved on the ground post-2015. Even though the transition into a tertiary-education dominated knowledge economy is unclear in either country, it may well become a reality for small parts of both populations, if their globally connected elite can wield their influence in diverting resources and setting up special institutions.

The scale of this education transition in China and India dwarfs the creation of human capital (in both size and quality) in any other period of human history (Hughes and Hillibrand 2006). It is greater in scale than the dramatic schooling and adult education revolutions that swept Europe and North America in the late nineteenth century and the former Soviet Union in the early and mid-twentieth century, providing the basis for the 'modernization' of these societies. The momentum of this early twenty-first century transition in India and China is set to transform both global economic history and the nature of social systems and politics. Yet, the battle for the hearts, minds, identities and pocketbooks of close to three billion people remains among the least researched areas of contemporary social science.

An **urban transition** from rural to 'urban' areas will only be complete (in spite of the official UN projections) when both China and India have become predominantly urban. China is undergoing the most dramatic urban transformation in human history, with over 15 million people being added to cities and urban areas every year. It is only in contemporary China that the construction of more than a dozen million-plus cities a year can be contemplated.

This scale of urbanization—while providing new opportunities for dramatically higher productivity, income and wealth generation; engagement with new occupations and lifestyles that were unimaginable even in the early 1990s—has a number of inherent contradictions.

There has been a history of discrimination in China between the peasantry in the countryside and urban elite, led by intellectuals and officials. Historical periods of chaos and disaffection have often been linked to the dissonance between these two classes as surplus extraction became unsustainable or a mix of inadequate governance and insufficient coercion led to peasant revolts and uprisings against regional or imperial authorities. Mao's hukou edict of 1956 crystallized this into a rigid system that provided significant entitlements to urban residents while severely constraining and effectively disentitling those in rural areas. This has led to the creation of a huge underclass of urban migrants, who are important participants in China's global manufacturing competitiveness.

The transition into a primarily urban culture implies that China will have to rapidly re-engineer its hukou system, apart from developing a more participative form of urban governance for over 800 million people. This is a class of problems that no state in history, even with a strong central control has encountered or responded to effectively. It is also closely linked to China's future political transition. Hence, multiple experiments in urban governance and democratic innovation are the need of the hour.

A linked challenge to the rapid urbanization of China is its long-term food security as agrarian populations diminish; water and fossil fuels become increasingly scarce and expensive; and the mirage of competing with unsustainable capital and energy intensive North American and European agriculture recedes. It is possible that in time Chinese public policy will reverse its current urbanization drive to address the essential question of food security in a world where trade and fluctuating prices may well become a constraint. A linked question is the labor intensity and sustainability of the agricultural systems that are strengthened as an outcome of it.

An alternate trajectory for China could be to build upon the remaining agrarian populations and decentralized settlement structures to create a sustainable hierarchy of settlements. The ability to make this switch-over in the future will be strongly compromised by the aspiration to outperform and out-compete the US—based on its more ephemeral and unsustainable exports: the energy guzzling city driven strongly by the automobile sector.

India, like much of other South Asian countries, lags behind the rest of the world in its rate of urbanization, given its current lower middle income country status. Over two-thirds of its population still resides in villages. The deceleration of India's urban growth over the period 1981–2001 is an indicator of the current inelasticity and structural constraints to urban growth. This is partially endogenous and linked to the mixed up frame of urban Indian governance; illiquid and vitiated land and housing market functioning and poor infrastructure development.

The strong roots of India's agrarian population to the land and the slow growth of urban economic and social opportunities have constrained greater rural–urban mobility. The developing agrarian crisis in rural India coupled with the potential impact of climate change, the pull of urban economic growth and livelihood and educational opportunities could possibly accelerate urbanization in the direction of China's growth in the next two decades. Unfortunately, unlike China, India still seems unprepared to address this deluge in terms of institutional capacity, human resources, governance and even building an urban culture.

The **energy transition** is among the most diverse contemporary global transformations, encompassing the shift from traditional bio-fuels to conventional fossil fuels such as coal and oil to transition fuels like gas and nuclear energy and renewable source of energy like wind and solar energy. In both India and China, these shifts are taking place simultaneously depending upon location, economic sector, level of modernization and engagement with the global economy. It often reflects the state of the real economy, that is, the mix of traditional, modern and post-industrial sectors and within these, those that are most impacted by globalization.

The most important energy sources for both India and China are coal and oil. Coal underpins much of the industrial production and a large fraction of power generation. Oil and petrochemicals provide critical chemical feed stock and support the bulk of the rapidly growing transport sectors that these economies have developed with the growth of both domestic and export markets, more pertinently in China. In India, a traditional biomass-based subsistence energy economy still persists in many rural areas areas as only half the households have access to electricity.

Hence, a dual challenge needs to be addressed. The first is to provide universal access to basic energy to address domestic and livelihood needs. The other is to simultaneously implement widespread energy-efficiency measures and a transformation of its economy that is oriented towards large scale use of renewable energy (de Vries and Revi 2007).

A key constraint in both countries is that the bulk of their oil and gas is imported. The dramatic rise in fossil fuel prices and the location of new resources in difficult or conflict-ridden locations implies that the strategic imperative to hasten the development of domestically abundant coal-based power and renewable energy is high. The national environmental and social costs of coal extraction and the global impact of carbon emissions could be very significant. Hence, there is considerable strategic and commercial interest in both countries to develop, incentivize and deploy energy efficient, low carbon and renewable energy technology as quickly as possible (Leadbeater and Wilsdon 2007). This is a clear area of convergence of interest between the US, the European Union, China and India as well as transnational firms and enterprises that can mobilize Research and Development technology and supply chains on a scale that these economies will demand.

The **development transition** is the transition from primary sector-led economies in the mid-twentieth century to a mix of secondary and tertiary-sector led economies in the early twenty-first century. Here, there is a considerable difference between the two countries, with China having taken a more conventional secondary-sector led development path; while in India it is the service sector that became the largest in terms of output share by the mid-1990s (Hu and Khan 1997). The transition to a secondary- and tertiary-sector led economy has happened in both the countries considerably faster than predicted by their per capita gross domestic product (GDP) levels.

The fundamental strategic challenge is to match a rapidly changing economic output and capital structure with the livelihood structure that is often lagging by a few decades, leading to severe economic, regional and social dislocation as human capital and institutions are unable to keep pace with technological and economic change.

The **environmental transition** is the often forgotten transition that has a huge impact on the lives of the poor and vulnerable. Their livelihoods and places of residence are often directly impacted due to their higher risk exposure and vulnerability to a wide range of externalities created by a rapidly expanding economy with weak regulation. All three phases of this environmental transition—the brown (for example, wastewater, sanitation and sewage); the grey (for example, indoor and outdoor air pollution) and the green (for example, efficiency, recycling, reuse and climate change resilience)—are taking place in India as well as China. Both countries have a large share of the more polluted locations on the planet. These are becoming important reasons for local, social and political mobilization as the living and working conditions of large numbers of people become increasingly untenable.

These six transitions help define the structural confines of the challenges and opportunities that India and China are confronted with. Rarely have such a large number of transitions been confronted simultaneously by such large populations in history.

INDIA AND CHINA'S ENGAGEMENT AND WHAT IT COULD MEAN FOR THE WORLD

Pre-2000, the India and China bilateral trade was less than USD 3 billion. It has grown by close to twenty times and is expected to cross USD 60 billion by 2010. China first displaced the European Union (EU), Japan and then the US as India's largest trading partner. As domestic markets continue to integrate and deepen the potential for bilateral trade, commercial services could expand at double-digit rates enabled by the discretionary expenditure of the middle classes growing faster than GDP growth; banking and financial systems could penetrate deeper to reach previously un-served rural and urban residents thereby deepening markets; and open up large numbers of new classes of investors and consumers (Bijapurkar 2007; Khanna 2008).

Trade between China and India, can be expected to have a multiplier impact on South Asian trade, which is very weak because of the historical animosity between potential trading partners. The expansion of bilateral and multilateral trading arrangements between India and other South Asian countries, other trading groups and associations in South-East Asia and West Asia, along with the holy grail of the free trade arrangement between India and China, could alter the landscape of trade in products and services globally. This could also engender a fresh global perspective on contentious issues such as intellectual property rights and mobility of services and service sector workers on which China and India currently share a number of common areas of concern. This could, in turn, be expected to influence global trade negotiations, first for products and later for services in the medium to long term.

This will provide a unique opportunity for domestic firms in both national markets to reach out to the other, using their best strategic advantages. The low cost base and internationally competitive quality of an increasing number of Chinese and Indian firms could make it difficult for Japanese, EU and US multinationals to compete, unless they relocate their manufacturing and service provision centers to either of the two countries. Highly successful transnationals such as GE, have been doing this for more than a decade—leveraging on Chinese manufacturing and Indian IT and marketing skills (Khanna 2008).

In practice, the first true Indian and Chinese transnationals will build their fortunes around a mix of OECD and Chindian markets. It is only a matter of time before entrepreneurs from both sides develop and successfully scale firms that are targeted primarily at these two national markets, with their high heterogeneity, regional and cultural sensitivity, high segmentation across a wide band of price points, and strong oral and increasingly new media tradition. This would be difficult for even well-established OECD transnationals to beat, especially, if access to capital is no longer a constraint.

If moderate to strong growth persists in China and India over the medium run, global growth will become increasingly dependent on the functioning and development of these economies. This can be expected to change the relationship between Asian and OECD countries. The massive growth in savings and investment potential of both these economies (close to 40 per cent) is also a significant factor. This implies that along with Japan, Greater China and India will play an increasingly important role in helping to redefine the new global financial architecture and institutional design.

China currently holds over USD 1 trillion in foreign exchange reserves. When considered along with holdings in Hong Kong, Taiwan and with the Chinese diaspora, China has considerable leverage over the major currencies. In comparison, India's foreign exchange reserves are only approximately USD 350 million. However, it is today in a relatively strong and stable position to service and protect the independence of its monetary and macroeconomic policies, and is unlikely to face a situation like the near bankruptcy of 1991.

The rapid growth of these national economies has led to a dramatic growth in their demand for oil and gas, strategic mineral resources and electricity, often at rates higher than that of their GDP. The establishment of an Asian power, oil and gas grid as proposed by a number of specialists, if executed and maintained effectively, could alter both regional and geopolitical relationships between the two countries, and west and central Asia. The development of clean coal technology is a strategic imperative for both countries and could be the basis for a massive joint R&D program that brings together domestic and international firms.

Both countries are seriously constrained by environmental and resource challenges, especially related to water access, recycling, reuse and conservation. Apart from potential trans-boundary issues on the sharing of waters from Himalayan rivers; a better understanding of the monsoons and defining a suite of mitigation and adaptation interventions to address climate change are other areas of common interest. Similarly, environmental conservation, sustainability and the harmonious development of ecosystem services and natural resources are important experiences to share and possibly address jointly.

Apart from the continuing efforts towards finding a solution to the border question, China and India are working to address common regional and global security concerns, especially the growth of Islamic fundamentalism and terrorist activity on the periphery of both states. The pragmatic way forward that both governments are working on is to allow economic exchanges to lead cultural exchange and the settlement of sensitive political matters like the Himalayan border issue.

The strongest and most sustainable link between India and China has historically been religion and culture. Film, music and the internet will play an important part in deepening this relationship once the technical challenges of transliteration between multiple languages are addressed adequately. The growth of tourism is also expected to be a large money-spinner apart from being one of the most effective ways of closing the knowledge gap between India and China.

The most important actors in these emerging sets of relationships include the private sector, the media, faith traditions, civil society organizations, ordinary citizens and governments. Both national governments have recognized that economic relations should take precedence over the border settlement issue. There has also been some discussion about removing cultural barriers and constructed hostility through an expansion of tourism, film, television, cultural exchanges and deeper academic relations.

The transition from a political and bureaucratic elite-led relationship to one that is increasingly defined by economic and cultural interests is the beginning of a deeper and more stable relationship between the two large cultures. If this works its way through, the historical barriers of language, distance and lack of knowledge will become less relevant in the twenty-first century and a stable, productive and more harmonious relationship between India and China will be possible. This could help redefine the contemporary basis for inter-state relations that were constructed in another continent in another age, when the world was neither 'full' of people and their artifacts', nor networked or challenged by global change.

REFERENCES

Amin, S. (2005) 'India, a Great Power?', *Monthly Review*, Vol. 56, No. 9.

Arrow, K J., P. Dasgupta, L.H. Gouldar, K. Mumford, and K. Oleson (2006) *China, the U.S., and Sustainability: Perspectives Based on Comprehensive Wealth*, Stanford Working Paper, Stanford University and University of Cambridge.

Austin, G. (1999) *Working a Democratic Constitution: A History of the Indian Experience*, Oxford University Press, New Delhi.

Baru, S. (2006) *Strategic Consequences of India's Economic Performance*, Academic Foundation, New Delhi.

Bijapurkar, R. (2007) *We Are Like That Only – Understanding the Logic of Consumer India*, Penguin, New Delhi.

Bloom, D.E., D. Canning, L. Hu, Y. Liu, A. Mahal, and W. Yip (2006) *Why Has China's Economy Taken Off Faster than India's?*, Tsinghua University, China.

Bound, K. (2007) *India: The Uneven Innovator*, Demos, London.

Bussolo, M., R.E. De Hoyos, D. Medvedev, and van der Mensbrughhe (2006) *Global Growth and Distribution: Are China and India Reshaping the World's Development Prospects Group*, The World Bank, Washington DC.

Cheng, K.C. (2003) 'Economic Implications of China's Demographics in the 21st Century', International Monetary Fund, Working Paper, WP/03/29, Asia and Pacific Department.

Cohen, S.P. (2002) *India Emerging Power*, Oxford Univeristy Press, New Delhi.

Dahlman, C. and A. Utz (2005) *India and the Knowledge Economy: Leveraging Strengths and Opportunities*, WBI Development Studies. The World Bank, Washington DC.

Das, G. (2006) 'The India Model', *Foreign Affairs*, July/August, Vol. 85, No. 4, pp. 2–16.

Dollar, D. (2007) 'Asian Century or Multi-polar Century?', World Bank Policy Research Working Paper 4174, March.

Dunaway, S. and E. Prasad (2006) *Rebalancing Economic Growth in China – A Commentary*, International Monetary Fund, Washington DC.

Deng, Y. and T.G. Moore (2004) 'China Views Globalization: Toward a New Great-Power Politics?' *The Washington Quarterly*, Vol. 27, No.3, pp. 117–136.

De Vries, B and A. Revi (2007) *India 2050*, The Netherlands Environmental Assessment Agency, Bilthoven.

Deshpande, G.P. and A. Acharya (eds) (2001) *Crossing a Bridge of Dreams: 50 years of India China*, Tulika, New Delhi.

Dyson, T., R. Cassen, and L. Visaria (eds) (2004) *Twenty-first Century India: Population, Economy, Human Development and the Environment*, Oxford University Press, New Delhi.

Eswar Prasad (ed.) (2004) *China's Growth and Integration into the World Economy: Prospects and Challenges*, International Monetary Fund, Washington DC.

Frank, A. G. (1998) *ReOrient: Global Economy in an Asian Age*, University of California Press, Berkeley.

Frankel, F. R. (2005) *India's Political Economy (1947–2004) The Gradual Revolution*, Oxford University Press, New Delhi.

Frankel, F. R and H. Harding (eds) (2004) *The India-China Relationship Rivalry and Engagement*, Oxford University Press, New Delhi.

Friedman, E and B. Gilley (2005) *Asia's Giants Comparing India and China*, Palgrave, New York.

Guha, R. (2007) *India after Gandhi: The History of the World's Largest Democracy*, Picador, New Delhi.

Hsu, C.Y.I. (1995) *The Rise of Modern China*, Oxford University Press, New York.

Hu, Z. and M. Khan (1997) 'Why Is China Growing So Fast?' International Monetary Fund, Working paper no. 96/75, Washington DC.

Hughes, B.B. and E.E. Hillbrand (2006) *Exploring and Shaping International Futures*, Paradigm, Boulder.

Jadhav, N.R. Ranjan, and H. Sujan (2006) *Re-emerging India a Global Perspective*, ICFAI, Hyderabad.

Jalan, B. (2002) *The Future of India: Politics, Economics and Governance*, Penguin, New Delhi.

Kapur, D. and P.B. Mehta (2005) *Public Institutions in India: Performance and Design*, Oxford University Press, New Delhi.

Khanna, T. and Y. Huang (2003) 'Can India Overtake China?', *Foreign Policy*, pp. 74–81.

Khanna, T. (2008) *Billions of Entrepreneurs: How China and India Are Reshaping Their Futures and Yours*, Harvard Business School Press, USA.

Krueger, A.O. (2004) *Letting the Future In: India's Continuing Reform Agenda*, Keynote Speech to Stanford India Conference, International Monetary Fund, Washington DC.

—— (2005) *Still Achieving, Still Pursuing: The Global Consequences of Asian Growth*, Asia Society, Hong Kong, International Monetary Fund, Washington DC.

Lal. R. (2006) *Understanding India and China Security Implications for the United States and the World*, Praeger, Newport Connecticut.

Leadbeater, C. and J. Wisldon (2007) *The Atlas of Ideas: How Asian Innovation Can Benefit Us All*, Demos, London.

Maxwell, N. (2006) 'Settlements and Disputes – China's Approach to Territorial Issues', *Economic and Political Weekly*, Vol. 41, No. 36, pp. 3873–81.

McKinsey (2007), *Global Survey of Business Executives*, www.mckinseyquarterly.com/Economic_Studies/Productivity_Performance/The_Mckinsey_Global_Survey_of_Business

People's Republic of China (2006) *Guidelines of the Eleventh Five-Year Plan for National Economic and Social Development (2006–2010)*.

Ramesh, J. (2005) *Making Sense of Chindia Reflections on China and India*, India Research Press, New Delhi.

Ranganathan, C.V. and V.C. Khanna (2004) *India and China: The Way Ahead*, Har Anand Publications, New Delhi.

Singh, S. (2005) *China-India Economic Engagement Building Mutual Confidence*, CSH, New Delhi.

Srinivasan, T.N. (2006) *China, India and the World Economy*, Stanford Center for International Development, Stanford University.

Tellis, A. (2007) 'American and Indian Interests in India's Extended Neighborhood' in *India and Transition*, Center for the Advanced Study of India, University of Pennsylvania.

Thornton, J.L. (2008) 'Long Time Coming Prospects of Democracy in China', *Foreign Affairs*, Vol. 87, No. 1.

Virmani, A. (2005) *China's Socialist Market Economy: Lessons of Success*, Occasional Policy Paper, Indian Council for Research on International Economic Relations, New Delhi.

Wadhva, C.D. (2006) *Management of Rising Power by China and India in the Twentyfirst Century and scope for their Strategic Partnership*, Centre for Policy Research, New Delhi.

Wallerstein, I. (2006) *Whose Century Is It Aanyhow? The 20th was America's, But that's History*, Yale University, New Haven.

Wilson, D. and R. Purushothaman (2003) *Dreaming With BRICs: The Path to 2050*, Global Economics Paper No. 99, Goldman Sachs.

Winter, L.A. and S. Yusuf (2006) *Dancing with Giants – China, India, and the Global Economy*, The World Bank and the Institute of Policy Studies.

World Economic Forum (2007) *China and the World: Scenarios to 2025 – Executive Summary*, Switzerland.

Yang, Y. (2007) *Thoughts on My Indian Visit* (personal communication).

2

Comparative Analysis of National Innovation Systems of China and India

XIAOBO WU

INTRODUCTION

In recent times, China and India have been developing constantly in terms of economic and comprehensive strength; the comparative study of the two countries has attracted worldwide attention not only among the media, but also in academic and policy arenas.

On the one hand, there is similarity in the recent histories of China and India. Both were subject to colonial rule during the nineteenth century. Both gained independence in the mid-twentieth century, only after bitter struggles—China in 1949 after the civil war; India in 1947 with a partition which created the west and east Pakistan. Since then, both have been politically independent, and devoted to developing their economies.

On the other hand, China and India are different in terms of development modes and characteristics. Kenneth Rogoff, Professor, Harvard University, once compared the competition between China and India (of developing their economies) to the race between the rabbit and the tortoise; wherein India may exceed China sooner or later.

People with varying academic backgrounds provide different explanations on the comparative growth of China and India. 'The Dragon and Elephant Competition' between China and India first discussed by Huang Yasheng, an MIT scholar who pointed out that China has introduced a great amount of FDI, while India has not. The huge influx of FDI into China, in fact, reflects some defects of the economy rather than strengths, since it implies a greater reliance on foreign investment. In spite of low FDI, India has surpassed China from a microcosmic perspective and has become its major competitor.

Studies that compare software and hardware fundamental facilities in the two countries find that India has an advantage in software facilities and some key areas of promoting economic development. Kapil Sibal, the Union Minister of Science and Technology, visited China in 2006. He observed that China's socialist market oriented economy is driven by the government, led by industry, and accompanied by high domestic savings, large scale investment in fundamental facilities, FDI, and expansion of foreign trade. Whereas. in contrast, India's development mode is unique, valuing consumption rather than investment, internal needs rather than exports, services rather than industry, and high technology industry rather than labor-intensive, low technology industry (Sibal 2006). This provides the Indian economy stronger resistance when the global economy becomes unstable , and gives it a long-term stable growth. The economic growth of

India reflects the contribution of the knowledge oriented economy, the software industry and business process outsourcing (BPO), and a strong development of bio-medicine industry. The Indian economy may in fact be termed the 'world office'.

There are increasing discussions in China's academic circles comparing the two countries' economies. Recent research tends to focus on certain perspectives, such as: the comparison of the ability and method of attracting foreign investment; the comparison of the development of the service industry in the two countries; the environment of industry development or a competitive power comparison or the comparison of a certain industries like software; etc.

There are two ways to approach China and India's development strategies and trajectories. The first is an in-depth investigation of each case on the presumption that the two countries are so huge that comparisons with smaller countries may not be helpful or be superfluous. Several thorough case studies have been published in recent years (Krueger 2002, Lardy 2003). There have also been comparative studies that situate the two countries' experience in a broader perspective (for example, Ahya and Xie 2004). Here, the strategy is to compare and contrast the economic growth of China and India against the background and environmental elements that constitute their technological power. The studies also investigate some key indices of the two countries' National Innovation Systems (NIS), thus gaining insights into their economic development. While innovation elements and their distribution are different across countries, the combination of technological and economic activities determines the performance of its innovations.

The NIS approach was first introduced in the late 1980s (see Freeman 1987; Dosi et al., 1988) and further elaborated in the years thereafter (see Lundvall 1992; Nelson 1993; Edquist and Johnson 1997). An NIS can be perceived as a historically rooted subsystem of the national economy in which various organizations and institutions interact and influence, one another in carrying out the innovative activity. Using the NIS approach implies that the innovative activity is usually analyzed in a broader sense: instead of focusing solely on the number of products introduced and process innovated in a country, it also encompasses the research and development efforts by business firms and public actors, as well as determinants of innovations such as, learning processes, incentive mechanisms and the availability of skilled labor. Hence, the systemic approach to innovation is based on the notion of non-linear and multidisciplinary innovation processes. Interactions at the organizational level as well as the interplay between organizations and institutions are accorded central priority.

Although the growing economic stature of China and India is widely acknowledged, the factors underlying their success are still not well understood. The advantage of a large, low-wage workforce is apparent to everyone, but that alone cannot provide the foundation for them to grow into economic superpowers. True economic leadership comes only with the ability to produce high-quality, high technology goods and services and to create innovative new products and technologies. To appreciate the long-term potential of China and India, we need to take a comprehensive look at their innovative capacities.

The creation of knowledge and the ability to innovate new products and processes has become one of the main driving forces in making national economies and enterprises competitive. It is difficult to directly compare the technology competitive power of the two countries. According to the *2006–7 Global Competitive Power Report* from the 2006 World Economy Forum, China at number 54 is ranked behind India which is at number 43, however, according to the *2006 World Competitive Power Yellow Book* issued by the Lausanne International Management School in Switzerland, mainland China ranks higher than India (the countries scored 71.554 and 64.416 points, ranking 19 and 29 respectively).

THEORETICAL BACKGROUND AND METHODOLOGY

The concept of NIS as an analytical tool was first used by Freeman (1987), Lundvall (1988) and Nelson (1988). Freeman used the concept to analyze the success of Japan over the post-war period. He attributed Japan's success to certain key and distinctive elements in its national system of innovation. He defined the concept as 'the network of institutions in the public and private sectors whose activities and interactions initiate, import, modify and diffuse new technologies'. Lundvall (1992: 22) defined the concept at two levels, wherein the narrow definition of NIS included the organizations and institutions involved in searching and exploring, such as R&D(research and development) departments and technological institutes and universities. The broader definition encompassed 'all parts and aspects of the economic structure and the institutional set-up affecting learning as well as searching and exploring –the production system, the marketing system and the system of finance which present them as subsystems in which learning takes place' (Gu and Lundvall 2006).

Since the late 1990s, several attempts have been made to evaluate and to compare innovation systems in terms of their performance—defined and measured in different ways. In some cases, comparative studies at the system-level have been utilized as a preliminary step to generate NIS rankings (see for example, Porter and Stern 2002). These have been classified in policy-oriented studies and in research-driven advancements of the NIS approach.

The growing number of policy-oriented studies of innovation systems signals that the creation of an innovation-enhancing framework has become an essential objective of policymakers around the globe, particularly in highly industrialized countries. Due to the pragmatic assumptions underlying the NIS concept, as well as the insightful outcomes acquired so far in studies of national innovation patterns, the systemic approach to innovation enjoys growing popularity among technology policymakers as a means to derive technology policy implications. At the same time, learning processes from one's own experience and from those of other countries in the organization of NIS are recognized as important inputs into innovation policy design. This requires broad international comparisons of innovative strength and institutional frameworks, especially of incentive mechanisms for innovative action.

Indeed, political interest and agreements prompted the carrying out of national benchmarking studies while employing the innovation systems terminology. Most importantly, the EU urged its commission to work together with the EU-15 countries in order to 'develop indicators and a methodology for the benchmarking of national research policies' (Ken Guy 2003). The fulfillment of these targets requires a conjunction of benchmarking techniques and a systemic approach to innovation. So scholars currently observe an intended convergence of two conflicting methodological streams, namely, a systemic perception of innovation processes with strong country-specific features, on the one hand and objectives to obtain clear-cut policy recommendations through benchmarking exercises, on the other. Typically, the intended 'benchmarking studies' follow, at least implicitly, a two-step procedure. First, by considering various indicators of innovative efforts/ outcomes, the analyses aim to identify the 'best practice' policies and/or 'best practice' behavior' among the countries under study. In the second step, based on the results of the search for 'best practice', policy recommendations are derived.

The following studies are good examples of this procedure.

1. The analysis carried out by Eichhorst et al. (2001), 'benchmarks' Germany with 17 OECD member countries. Although the study actually concentrates on the German labor market, 'all' the factors affecting its performance are sought to be investigated. These include indicators that

reveal the relative size and strength of the German educational system; those that capture the innovative performance and founding nature of Germany's business sector; and various proxy variables for the degree of product market regulation in Germany.
2. The international comparison of the relations between the private business sector and scientific research bodies by Polt et al. (2001).
3. Work by OECD on the employment situation in several member countries. One fragment of the so-called 'OECD Jobs Study' (OECD 1998) was the discovery of best practiced policies related to technology and innovation.

Apart from this political background, research objectives in the economics of innovation literature can be observed as the second main driver of comparative NIS studies. In order to explain this argument, it may be helpful to review some of the limitations of earlier NIS studies and of the research course pursued: first, these early studies are typically based on qualitative investigation of national innovation patterns, and the number of utilized indicators of innovative activity is rather small; second, early NIS studies usually concentrated on one country in order to thoroughly describe the functioning of the innovation system under consideration, third, the set-up of NIS studies have varied considerably because of a lack of formalized methodology to carry out such studies. These limitations may have stimulated research efforts to carry out system-level comparisons as well as to formalize the NIS concept. The efforts have led to the introduction of descriptive frameworks and the development of analytical models.

A good example of a descriptive model of NIS that is meant to capture the structure and performance is the conceptual framework introduced by Liu and White (2001). This framework is built on five different activities of the innovation process. These activities are research, production, 'end-use (customers of the product or process outputs)', 'linkage' and 'education' (Liu and White 2001). In this respect, the descriptive model differs from the widely-used actor-specific analysis of innovation systems which Liu and White criticize sharply. They apply their descriptive concept to the analysis of the innovation system in China through an inter-temporal comparison between different development stages (or regimes). Differences in the set-up, organization, and the performance between China's former (socially planned) NIS and China's current (democratically organized) NIS are highlighted in detail.

Another model employed to study the composition and strength of a country's innovation system has been introduced by Chang and Shih (forthcoming). Based on previous work by OECD (1999), the model comprises six elements—R&D expenditure, R&D performance, technology policy, human capital development, technology transfer and the climate for entrepreneurial behavior. With these basic criteria, it intends to allow the analysis of structural specifics of an NIS. To capture the performance of a system, four fundamental groups of indicators are employed: formal as well as informal co-operation in R&D, measures of the dissemination of innovations and finally the mobility of the national workforce.

In contrast to these descriptive NIS models, Furman et al. (2002) present a formalized method of cross-country comparisons of innovative performance using the concept of 'national innovative capacity' (NIC). This is based on the combination of three different—though closely related—theoretical concepts: endogenous growth theory (for example, Romer 1990), the theory of international competitiveness (Porter 1986), and the national systems of innovation approach (described above). National innovative capacity is defined as 'the ability of a country to produce and commercialize a flow of innovative technology over a long-term [depending] on the strength of a nation's common innovation infrastructure...the environment for innovation in a nation's industrial clusters, and the strength of linkages between these two'(Furman et al. 2002: 921).

Each of these components, that is, infrastructure, cluster conditions and linkages, is measured by a number of variables. Next, these three components enter the main regression model in the form of complementary independent variable blocks. Patent data, that is, 'the number of patents granted to investors from a particular country other than the US by the USPTO[1] in a given year', are used as the dependent variable. The knowledge-driven endogenous growth model serves as the basis to establish a link between the independent input factors and the dependent output measure of innovations. But again, deviating from standard endogenous growth theory, in which the variation of a country's real economic activity is taken as a dependent variable (the growth rate of GDP, for instance), patent growth (that is, the growth of patent applications per country in the US) is employed as a growth variable in this framework. The sample includes 17 highly industrialized countries in all.

The NIC model can be considered as an ingenious contribution to the NIS approach, because it builds a bridge between elements of economic growth theory and a modern, systemic approach to innovation, which is extended by a (non-descriptive) technique to carry out international comparisons of innovative strength. However, given that various actors contribute to the system's performance in an NIS, a major drawback of the model is that it takes only one output measure of innovation into account. Porter and Stern (2002) recently applied the NIC model to a large number of countries (75) than Furman et al. (2002). Apart from the different sample sizes and differences in the data employed Porter and Stern (2002) used the empirical results in order to generate a ranking of the nations analyzed.

An alternate means for formalized system-level comparisons is discussed by Nasierowski and Arcelus (1999; 2000), where coherent country groups in terms of technological capabilities are identified on the basis of a system of structural equations that consist of inputs, outputs and moderators. Cluster analysis techniques lead to a classification consisting of two country groups, one including technological leaders, the other comprising of the emerging countries that base their technological progress mainly on innovations developed abroad. Through actor analysis methods, the analyzed countries are then ranked according to their technological strength. In addition to these empirical tests, Nasierowski and Arcelus (2003) have developed a data envelopment analysis-based model consisting of two inputs, two moderators, and three output variables, with the aim of studying the efficiency of NIS. The efficiency evaluations are divided into two parts: one concerned with the measurement of efficiency in the generation of innovations, called 'R&D efficiency', while the second is related to 'R&D productivity', which is defined as a country's efficiency in the translation of technological success into national productivity growth. The basic idea underlying the efficiency measurement by Nasierowski and Arcelus (2003) is to perceive the NIS as an isolated sector of the economy. However, such a definition can be misleading because it contradicts the widely held stance that innovation systems are open systems.

Chinese scholars have also been involved in fundamental research on the theory of national innovation. When it comes to an NIS evaluating index, some scholars analyze it from different perspectives, including: the main effect of the NIS, its fundamental nature and the operational rule. They believe that an NIS is a multi-layered system, multivariable, multi-subsystem under a dynamic external environment, including four elements: innovation impetus, innovation resources, innovation operation and innovation values. The promotion of an NIS is accomplished by three systemic processes: innovation-driven system (innovation operation transferred by innovation impetus); innovation marketing process (innovation value transferred by innovation operation); and innovation feedback system (new innovation impetus introduced innovation values [or innovation

---

[1] United States Patent and Trademark Office.

values introduced by new innovation impetus]). The three systems constitute the basic mode of national innovation, under which the effects and combinations of different elements in the NIS result in various innovation results. The general principle of an innovation driven system contains two key stages. The first is the 'innovation actors integration' period, in which various innovation policies lead to diverse combinations of national innovation actors, the second is 'innovation resource optimization deployment', that is, the combination of innovation principle and other innovation resources. Essentially, national innovation always results in an upgradation of national resources, as well as a higher level innovation process. This is the basic mode of national innovation, or the so-called NIS mode—the 4-3-2-1 model.

Based on the understanding of NIS from this research, and using the evaluation framework of NIS proposed by domestic scholars, this study simplifies China's and India's NIS into three parts: the innovation environment subsystem, the innovation operation system, and the innovation economy performance (see Figure 1).

FIGURE 1: NIS SUMMARY CHART

Innovation Environment → Innovation Operation ← Economic Performance

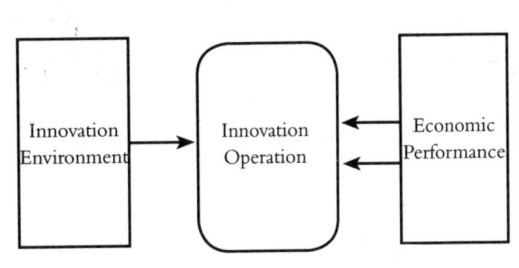

TABLE 1: NIS EVALUATION INDEX

Main index	Sub-index	Third index
Innovation environment	Scientific research institution and innovation policy	
	Infrastructure	Information infrastructure Physical infrastructure
	Education	Financial education investment Percentage of financial education investment in GDP Literacy (among those above 15 years of age) Percentage of people with high education diploma
Innovation operation	R&D input	R&D researchers R&D researchers per million population Spending on R&D Percentage of R&D expenditure in GDP R&D expenditure distribution
	R&D output	Scientific and technical articles Scientific and technical articles per million population Patents granted by US Patent Office Patent applications granted by US Patent Office per million population
	R&D efficiency	USD 1000s of R&D spending per scientific and technical article Million USD of R&D spending per patent granted
Economic performance	Economic growth	GDP GDP growth rate
	Industry structure	Share of the three industries in the increase in GDP Proportion of high-tech in GDP

Source: China Technology Development Strategy Research Group (2008)

According to the above research framework, and considering the availability of data in China and India, we construct the NIS evaluation system in three parts. The evaluation indices include absolute indicators, relative indicators and growth indicators (see Table 1).

THE COMPARISON OF NIS IN CHINA AND INDIA

Innovation Environment Subsystem

Innovation environment subsystem is a key to the capability of the NIS. The technology innovation system involves many elements. This chapter compares the innovation environment in the two countries from various perspectives, including scientific research institutions and innovation policy, the development extent of innovation infrastructure, and innovation for human resources.

Scientific Research Institutions and Innovation Policy

China and India have similar features in terms of their scientific research organizational structure. China has established large-scale comprehensive scientific research institutions such as the Chinese Academy of Sciences (CAS) and China Social Science Institution. Various ministries including technology, agriculture, water resources and others have established professional institutions. Besides, there are key research universities which constitute the principal element of national technology scientific innovation. In India, the central government is responsible for science and technology development policy and plan and supports R&D activities, technology transfer and work in other relevant areas. State government institutions and university research institutions incorporate local resources and coordinate technology activities to solve local problems. The scientific institutions belonging to the government are subordinate to different social and economic departments, thus, the government monitors its subordinate research institutions directly.

In China, the first initiative by CAS was the Knowledge Innovation Program (KIP). The KIP has resulted in serious restructuring of the R&D community—that is, the transformation of state-controlled research institutes into private enterprises, effectively mandating that their activities and operations be pragmatic and profitable. Ten innovation bases have come into being, combining the research forces of relevant CAS institutes in selected areas and thereby becoming special 'thrust areas'.

The Strategic Action Plan for Science and Technology (S&T) Innovation (SAPI), launched in 2001, is seen as a key measure for CAS 'to scale the heights of S&T development and to make fundamental, strategic and forward-looking contributions to China's economic growth, national security and social development. It is also a necessary step for upgrading the national capacity for S&T innovation'. The SAPI comprises an overall plan, four thematic plans (basic research, life sciences and biotechnology, environmental technology, and high-tech R&D) and several 'special programs' (major research projects in key areas, infrastructure and support facilities, new research units, science communication, industrialization of innovations and headquarter reforms). The plan indicates a modification from the earlier very pragmatic approach in China: attracting FDI for cheap mass production, gradually establishing indigenous R&D capabilities, launching pilot operations and scaling up operations if successful. The new development is to simply 'buy' technology by taking over companies in the developed world.

China's current 11th Five-Year Plan for science and technology foresees 'improving the sustainable innovation capacity of science and technology, under which the industrial enterprises shall be made the mainstream for technical innovations focusing on the key technologies for industrial development so as to promote the development of high-tech industries and transform the traditional industries with high technologies, promoting the industrial technical upgrading and restructuring'. The future draft plan for National Economic and Social Development similarly outlines the importance of innovations in select high-tech industrial areas.

In order to compel R&D organizations to work in a demand-driven way, the government initiated major changes in funding and managing of research organizations. For example, the government decreased grants to public research and thereby ensured that research institutes actively and successfully looked for different funding sources. Today, many academic institutions are launching commercial ventures on their own or in collaboration with the corporate sector.

Small and medium enterprises (SMEs) in China act as 'profit units' that have spun-off from state-owned enterprises. These units are in a position to act flexibly, based on the country's competitive advantages. The promotion of innovative high-tech SMEs is largely seen as a key remedy against the existing overcapacity in traditional industries. Thus, a series of far-reaching measures has been launched to promote medium-sized and small scientific and technological enterprises. The Chinese government has identified eight cities as experimental for technical innovation and has established regional and professional service centers there. At present, in China, there are 40 technological innovation service centers, more than 500 productivity promotion centers, over 100 hi-tech enterprise incubators, more than 30 universities, scientific and technological parks and 20 business foundation parks for students returning from different countries after completing their studies overseas. Today, Chinese companies (including SMEs) are interested not only in setting up extremely competitive cost structures but also in developing their innovation capabilities.

In comparison, India has a long tradition in R&D and innovation policy, but has not been very successful until recently. India's Tenth Five-Year Plan (2002–7) recognizes that 'the comparative advantage in the globally integrated knowledge-based world economy today is shifting to those with brain power to absorb, assimilate and adopt the spectacular developments in S&T and harness them for national growth' (Bajwa 2003). The plan is to provide a special thrust to S&T by leveraging the strong institutional S&T framework built in post-independence India.

The Ministry of Science and Technology is the main body governing science, technology and innovation in India. Through its Department of Scientific & Industrial Research (DSIR) and Department of S&T (DST), the ministry is in charge of more than 70 research institutions and laboratories. Its objective is to promote new areas of S&T and to play the role of a nodal department for organizing, coordinating and promoting S&T activities in the country, as well as working towards international cooperation. However, the ministry does not seem to be performing according to expectations. India's ranking in terms of innovation linkages and clustering is low compared to international standards. To create and sustain an effective knowledge based economy with competitive advantages, India needs to undertake systemic integration of reforms in all four domains of the knowledge economy, involving all the relevant ministries.

Small and medium enterprises in India, which constitute more than 80 per cent of total number of industrial enterprises and form the backbone of industrial development (Das et al. 2007), suffer from the problems of sub-optimal scale of operation and technological obsolescence. Although Indian SMEs realize the importance of technological innovation, most still believe in importing technology, rather than developing it in-house or in association with national R&D centers.

Over the years, Indian SMEs have largely ignored R&D and rarely embarked on new product development or technological upgradation. Their biggest source of know-how comprises the suppliers of plant and machinery. Therefore, it seems that any technology upgradation initiative is meaningful only if it involves the manufacturers of plants and machines. Further, any intervention

TABLE 2: INFRASTRUCTURE COMPARISON

Indicator			China	India
Information infrastructure		Telephone lines/1000 inhabitants (2005)	565.3	126.7
		Mobile subscribers /1000 inhabitants (2005)	210.20	24.17
		Personal computers/1000 inhabitants (2005)	27.6	7.2
		Internet users/1000 inhabitants (2005)	104	17
		International Internet bandwidth bits per capita (2004)	57	11
		Information and communications technology as expenditure of GDP (%)(2004)	4.4	3.8
Physical infrastructure	Roadways	Length of roadways (km) (2007)	1,930,544	3,383,344
		Road network, paved (% of total roads) (2007)	81.6	47.4
		National expressways (km) (2007)	41,005	5957
		Freight ton km (100 million ton miles) (2007)	15,080	336
	Railways	Length of transport routes (miles) (2007)	75,438	63,221
		Freight ton km (100 million ton miles)	17,247	3332

Sources: *China Statistical Yearbook 2008*; Indian government budget and economic research website http://indiabudget.nic.in/; World Development Indicators 2006; International Telecommunications Union 2006.

should cover the complete supply chain of the products/ sectors. The National Census of Small Scale Industries shows that 85 per cent of units have no specific source of know-how; 6 per cent received know-how from R&D institutions; 7 per cent have domestic collaborations; and less than 1 per cent have a foreign collaboration (Narayana 2004).

Support policy and service structures for SMEs are now being put into place. The Ministry of Small Scale Industries has established the following policy priorities: developing national modernization plans for selected sectors having high export potential; developing a national plan for technology exchanges; establishing a committee to recommend linkages among R&D institutions, training institutions, technology banks and user groups; and introducing utility patent protection for small innovations. Though there is a wide network of technical support institutions specially meant for small enterprises under the Ministry of Small Scale Industries, many of them suffer from technological obsolescence and their service record is anything but encouraging.

The Ministry has established a Technology Management Division to bring all its initiatives related to technology upgrading and modernization of the small scale sector under one umbrella. Two of these deserve special mention: first, the Small Industries Development Bank of India (SIDBI) which has launched a National Program on Innovation and Incubation for small scale industries. This program assists projects with high R&D content in the small scale sector to grow into viable and strong commercial businesses. Second, the National Science & Technology Entrepreneurship Development Board (www.nstedb.com) promotes high-end entrepreneurship through business incubators, technology entrepreneur parks and other initiatives. However, the government is not in a position to help business development organizations in reaching out to many more entrepreneurs. One way to do this would be through the use of IT. The management and structure of supporting organizations need to be changed in a major way—they should become larger, more sector-specific and more businesslike.

In moving forward, India requires assistance in further energizing its innovation system by increasing linkages with academia and industry; strengthening intellectual property rights and the patent regime; enhancing venture capital; promoting R&D by companies; encouraging new R&D niches, increasing innovation in agriculture; conducting R&D to promote welfare and encourage grass roots innovations and tapping the Indian diaspora.

Innovation in Infrastructure

Infrastructure is considered an important indicator of innovation in a country or a region. The importance of the infrastructure sector also follows from the fact that foreign investors look at infrastructural development as a yardstick before investing in a country. In fact, infrastructural development had taken precedence over wage levels in assessing the investment potential in developing countries. We consider the number of mobile telephones and internet connections, computers, as well as highways, railways and so on as evaluation indicators.

India has only 126.7 telephone subscribers per 1000 inhabitants against China's 565.3 (ITU 2006). The gap is also visible in the case of mobile phones: India has 24.17 cellular mobile subscribers per 1000 inhabitants against China's 210.20 (ITU 2006). In terms of coverage, 41 per cent of the population in India is covered by mobile telephony against China's 73 per cent (2006 World Bank, WDI report). Telephone services are available in 97 per cent of rural areas in China against 87 per cent in India. In order to increase the coverage area, operators can opt for combinations of low cost technologies.

As far as information technology is concerned, access to and availability of personal computers (PCs) is critical, as they enable access to the internet. China has the lead in terms of number of PCs. With respect to international connectivity, that is, international internet bandwidth for transmitting internet traffic between countries, China is at levels five times that of India. All this contributes to China having superior access and services as compared to India. China is not only well-positioned in terms of telecommunication infrastructure, but it also has a huge availability of hardware (PCs, phones and so on) because of a strong local manufacturing base.

If we consider the physical infrastructure which indirectly contributes to the growth of the country, China has much better physical infrastructure as compared to India: in 2007, India had 5,957 miles of national highways against China's 41,005. Road networks in India are in disarray, and India's power production and consumption woes continue. Therefore, it is not surprising that international companies choose China over India when setting up manufacturing plants. According to new estimates, India needs to invest about USD 500 billion on infrastructure in the next five years—in power plants, roads, ports, and airports.[2]

India can certainly learn from China in terms of infrastructure investment. China has invested its huge reservoir of domestic saving—about 40 per cent of GDP—into some of the best infrastructure that can be seen anywhere in the world. It has been brilliant in attracting massive inflows of FDI as the means to acquire technology, managerial expertise, and factories on a large scale. China is, in fact, the largest recipient of FDI in the world—approximately USD 53 billion per year (in 2002–3). India suffers in comparison. India has a 29.1 per cent national saving rate, only a little more than half of that of China. As a result, it has far less by way of internally-generated funds available to put back into infrastructure. It doesn't take much traveling around in India to experience first-hand the seriousness of its infrastructure constraint. The *India Infrastructure Report 2004*, brought out by India's best and brightest minds engaged in this field, reports, '…even relative to our income, our

---

[2] Prime Minister Manmohan Singh's speech: http://www.siliconindia.com/shownews/India_needs_500_Billion_for_core_sector_in_next_five_years_PM-nid-48545.html]

failure in water, roads, sanitation, schooling, and electricity is woeful' (3iNetwork 2004). Nor can India hold a candle to China on FDI. China's inflows in 2003 were more than ten times the USD 4 billion FDI received by India.

Innovative Human Resource

The quality and quantity of innovative human resources directly influence the cost and efficiency of innovative human production, which in turn affect the innovation behavior itself. We evaluate the levels of innovative human resource by comparing the investment into, and performance of, the two countries' education systems.

China has endeavored to build 'first-class universities' in recent years. With heavy investment from central and local governments, the rank of Chinese universities in the world is rising. A study conducted by Shanghai Jiaotong University in 2003 reports that there were 18 Chinese universities among the top 500 universities of the world—the number is about half that of Japan (Yasmeen 2004). Even the undervalued universities in China have gleaming campuses and good facilities which are not too far behind those in developed countries.

In contrast, higher education in India has witnessed a downward spiral with the 'bottom-class universities in the world' (Yasmeen 2004). Although Indian universities have expanded rapidly in recent years, the main proportion of government's allocated resources is focused on primary education. Newly established colleges have tight budgets, often not enough to even maintenance costs. Professors' salaries are low. Sometimes payroll disbursements are delayed by two or three months. The most talented students seldom choose a career as faculty in universities. Even in top schools, lectures are cancelled or suspended from time to time, for the lecturers needs to take a second job to meet their cost of living. Unsurprisingly, India has seen a sharp decline in the status of elite universities. Only three universities in India ranked in the top 500 universities in the world (Yasmeen 2004).

India is built on a meritocracy where performance in exams results in admission to the top-ranked schools and hence access to the best jobs. India's top institutes are considered as good as any in the world, and the Indian Institute of Technology (IIT) rivals MIT as a producer of world-class scientists.

Further, the Indian Institute of Management recently had 200,000 applications for only 250 seats at its top Ahmedabad campus, a ratio that puts the Ivy League's selectivity to shame. Although India does have an 'affirmative action' program for those belonging to the backward castes, the private sector is not subject to these quotas and is, therefore, free to hire 'the best and the brightest'.

There is no doubt that China is also developing top schools, in science as well as business. The latter are particularly important since the Communist system is filled with managers of SOEs whose performance will be woefully inadequate in a private-sector economy. In this area, India is ahead of China.

Also, China has been sending more tertiary level students abroad for education and training, even though it has a much larger tertiary education system than India (in absolute and relative terms). In 2004, more than 15 per cent of the total 2.7 million students studying outside their home country were from China (not counting Hong Kong), and 5 per cent were from India. Foreign education and training are an extremely important means to tap global knowledge. The students not only learn from the syllabi, but a large number of them remain involved in research at higher education institutions around the world. Many also go on to work in the high technology firms in the US and Europe. Until a few years ago, many of them stayed on in their host countries.

TABLE 3: EDUCATION SYSTEM COMPARISON

Indicators	China	India
Financial expenses on education (billion) (2005)	385.06	268.95
Financial expenses on education as percentage of GDP (%)(2005)	3.3	5.0
Public expenditure on education (% of total government expenditure) (2005)	15.0	10.7
Literacy rate (above 15 years old) (%)(2005)	88.4	61.3
The percentage of people with high education diplomas (%)(2005)	5.2	16.2
Percentage of native students on total students studying outside their home country (%)(2005)	15	5

Sources: *China Statistical Yearbook 2006*, Indian government budget and economic research website (http://indiabudget.nic.in/).

However, the past five years have seen a return of many expatriates to China and India. This may be partly attributed to the increasing opportunities in the home countries and the attractive incentive programs designed by the home countries to stem 'brain drain'. The United States has encouraged this trend by making it more difficult for foreigners to obtain student visas post-9/11 period.

Table 3 shows that though the money spent on education in China is more than that in India, in absolute terms expenditure on education in China as a percentage of GDP is 3.32 per cent, which is lower than that in India. In relative terms, India is placed at the same level as developed countries. Basic education in China may be considered to be better than that in India, since the number of people who cannot read in China is much lower than that in India. However, the state of higher education in India is better than that in China. India places great emphasis on technical education, and has invested in the expansion of higher education in engineering, and intensified scientific research programs. India has also achieved economic success in the IT industry, where higher education plays a key role.

In the long run, the quality of education is the crucial factor in technological development and economic growth. It is noteworthy that the Chinese government has reviewed its educational needs (in schools and universities). It has figured out that since it is not possible to build the traditional teaching infrastructure fast enough, it is best to concentrate resources towards setting up the largest online education capability in the world. India has a first class education system for a select section of gifted children, but it doesn't scale up for the universe of school-going kids in the country. China could leapfrog every single country and scale a world class on-line education facility in a few years for those who haven't received formal education in any university.

Innovation Operation Subsystem

In recent years, both China and India have been focusing on R&D. Along with increasing investment, the efficiency of expenditure on R&D has also improved, which is observed in the fields of nuclear technology, space technology and biological technology. By comparing data on investment and production in the two countries, we try to investigate the advantages and disadvantages of innovation.

For R&D input, the most common measures are engineers involved in R&D and expenditure on R&D. Table 4 shows that the number of engineers in China is about eight times as that in India (in 2004) (although there may be some definitional problems).

The expenditure on R&D in China has increased greatly since 2002. In 2004, China spent 1.44 per cent of its GDP on R&D. Although the percentage is still lower than that in developed countries—usually 2–3 per cent—the gap is narrowing gradually. Basic research expenditure was 13.12 billion RMB; applied research expenditure was 43.35 billion RMB and experimental development expenditure was 188.53 billion RMB (the respective proportions are 5.4, 17.7 and 76.9 per cent (respectively) of GDP). The Chinese government announced a 15-year Science and Technology Plan in 2006, which aims to increase R&D spending to 2 per cent of GDP by 2010 and to 2.5 per cent by 2020.[3]

In the last twenty years, the share of R&D expenditure in GDP in India has oscillated between 0.8 and 0.9 per cent, and more than 70 per cent of funding was from the government. According to data published by the Ministry of Science and Technology, the basic research expenditure was 17.6 per cent, applied research expenditure was 39.9 per cent and experimental development expenditure was 33.3 per cent of national R&D investment. However, in the past two years there has been an increased spending by the private sector, particularly in information and communications technology, automobile industry and pharmaceuticals. The bulk of the increase has come from multinational companies that have discovered India as a cost-effective location for R&D.

In terms of R&D output, the number of Chinese science and technology publications has increased rapidly. Although the same has occurred in India as well, the number in China is twice that in India (in 2003). In addition, citation analysis reveals that China's science and technology papers are of higher quality than those of India.[4] A very crude measure of relative efficiency can be constructed by looking at technical publications and patents and per dollar spending on R&D in the two countries (Table 4). This is a rough estimate because it does not control for the quality of output or for the different cost structures in the two countries. The results are suggestive, nonetheless. India appears to be more efficient than China. This probably reflects the lower cost structure, particularly the low salaries of researchers. Chinese researchers' salaries are mentioned as being 20–50 per cent

TABLE 4: COMPARISON OF INNOVATION INPUT AND OUTPUT IN CHINA AND INDIA

Indicators		China	India
Researchers in R&D (2004)		926,252	117,528
R&D researchers per million population (2004)		708	119
Spending on R&D (USD billion) (2004)		27.8	5.9
The percentage of R&D expenditure in GDP (2004)		1.44	0.85
R&D expenditure distribution (%) (2004)	Basic research	5.4	17.6
	Applied research	17.7	39.9
	Experimental research	76.9	33.3
Scientific and technical articles (2003)		29,186	12,774
USD 1000s of R&D spending per scientific and technical article		953	462
Scientific and technical articles per million population		22.7	12.0
Patents granted by US Patient Office (2004)		597	376
USD millions of R&D spending per patent granted		46.6	15.7
Patent applications granted by US Patent Office per million population (2004)		0.46	0.34

Sources: China National Statistic Bureau, Indian Science and Industry Research Department, The World Bank (www.worldbank.org).

[3] http://www.stats.gov.cn/tjsj/

[4] The industry structures of the two countries dating to 2007 in Table 5 provide basis for these comments. Data has been sourced from the World Bank website.

higher than those in India (Qin, Chang 2006). If we consider R&D cost per patent, it probably reflects that in both countries greater emphasis is still placed on science and technology per se rather than on commercializing it. It is also clear from a detailed analysis of the R&D systems in both countries that efficiency is still very low. However, both countries are focusing on improving the allocation, management and monitoring of R&D, as they know that it is increasingly important to improve their competitiveness in this field.

Economic Performance Subsystem

The value of an innovation system in a country ultimately rests on its contribution to economic growth. We can evaluate the economic performance promoted by NIS of the two countries by looking at their GDP, industry structure and production and per capita international competitive strength.

We can see from Table 5 that the two countries have developed very rapidly in recent years. China has shown better performance in terms of economic development because of its earlier market reforms and undertaking of world industry transfer. At present, GDP in China is more than twice that in India, and the development speed is quite rapid. However, an in-depth analysis reveals that the year 2000 is like a dividing line during the period 1990–2007; comparing the economic growth data in the two stages—pre- and post-2000, we see that India's growth rate is even more exciting. This can probably be explained by India's efforts to develop IT and other high-tech industries in the knowledge economy. India has performed better than China in the proportion of output value of high-tech industry in GDP.

The three sector ratio in the two countries could confer the titles of 'world factory' and 'world office' on China and India, respectively. The Chinese economy has undergone significant industrial restructuring over the past 25 years. The share of agriculture in GDP has fallen to 11.3 per cent, while that of industry share has risen to 48.6 per cent—among the highest in the world. The Indian economy has not undergone such drastic structural change. The share of agriculture in GDP is still 17.6 per cent, and that of industry is just 29.4 per cent. In fact, the share of the manufacturing sector has not changed over the past 20 years. However, significant growth has been witnessed in the service sector. Part of this has been due to the (forced) growth of self-employment in low-value service activities due to the inability of the modern sector of the economy to absorb the rapidly growing labor force. However, there has also been a rapid increase in high-value business services. These include not just offshore services, but also the establishment

Table 5: Economic Performance Comparisons

Indicators		China	India
GDP (current USD billion) (2007)		3251	1099
GDP growth rate	1990–2000	10.6	6.0
	2000–5	9.5	6.8
	2005–7	9.9	8.5
GDP per capita (PPP) (2007)		5,300	2,700
Industry Structure (2007)	The proportion of three industries (industrial structure)	11.3 : 48.6 : 40.1	17.6 : 29.4 : 52.9
	Proportion of high-tech in GDP	4.0	4.75
High-tech exports as % of manufactured exports (2007)		30	8

Sources: Indian Science and Industry Research Department, The World Bank (www.worldbank.org), The Central Intelligence Agency (https://www.cia.gov).

of many banking and consulting service operations in India, including those managed by major MNCs such as General Electric, IBM, other technology firms, and investment banks (Dahlman 2007).

CONCLUSION

To conclude, innovation has played a modest role in explaining growth in both China and India in recent years. Since both countries are latecomers in competition and innovation, the two must cope with far more intense rivalries and will probably favor disruptive innovation. By reformulating the rules of competition, they can move faster to higher added values. Judging by the statistical data provided in this chapter, both countries are developing their own NIS and are becoming important nodes in the global networks of research and innovation.

However, as scientific and technological development in the two countries proceeds, the institutions affecting higher education, R&D management and the governance of science and technology will be increasingly challenged. Therefore, developing capacity for ongoing institutional reforms and innovation is likely to help in their emergence as technological powers as much as standard input measures like R&D spending and the education and employment of scientists and engineers.

Despite two decades of institutional reform, the challenges of institutional innovation in China have become more urgent precisely at a time when financial and human resources for S&T have become more abundant and the expectations for R&D have increased. The challenges range from university reforms needed to stimulate greater research creativity in young scientists and engineers to mechanisms for more effective national research coordination. They also include the need to develop quality control and evaluation procedures to promote genuine innovative work and guard against fraud and misconduct. There is also a felt need for mechanisms that create greater transparency and accountability in the use of public money. Perhaps the biggest challenge concerns the infusion of Chinese industrial enterprises with a zest for innovation and an understanding of how R&D and knowledge management can more generally serve their long-term interests. Similar challenges exist in India.

Many of the challenges that both countries face arise from the complexities of determining the government's role in promoting research and innovation. Both countries have experienced the positive effects of government action in human resource development and the initiation of new fields of research. Indeed, without active government policies, we would not be discussing their emergence as technological powers.

At the same time, the actions of the state have also led to resources being wasted on derivative research, and distortions of market signals needed for strategically sound innovation decisions by industrial producers. Thus, the evolution of science-state relations in the two countries warrants continuing attention.

The primary analysis of the environment, operation and performance of the innovation systems in China and India reveals the following:

1. The research organization structures in the two countries are both government-led. China has an apparent advantage in terms of innovation infrastructure. It should increase its investment in higher education to cultivate more R&D professionals and reduce its lag in human resources. It is necessary for India to improve its infrastructure system. India's huge pool of low-cost, english-speaking professionals is attracting BPO services. However, high illiteracy rates and a dearth of qualified engineers could hinder India's growth in the long run.

2. Through an analysis of innovative operation systems, we see that China has an apparent advantage in innovation investments. But its competitive strength is not greater than India's. There seem to be problems in the structure of its national resources. What is more important is that India has a higher efficiency of R&D input and output than China.
3. The R&D expenditure in GDP in the two countries is still low. Although R&D expenditure has increased rapidly in China, most of it is concentrated on experimental development and applied research; basic research investment is extremely scarce. India, in turn, has a more reasonable ratio for R&D expenditure. In the long term, it could have a positive effect on Indian technology development.
4. The innovation performance subsystem reflects that India's economic development has greater potential given the background of the knowledge economy. Although the economic quantity indicator in China is higher than that in India, the third industry-led economic development model of India will be a cause for concern.
5. Interestingly, while China is currently faster and ahead of India, the latter may turn out to be the slower but surer long-run bet. India appears to be developing more solid microeconomic foundations and more staying power. Its capital markets are more efficient, effective and transparent than those in China, its legal system is well developed, and it provides a better environment for entrepreneurs. While China has an advantage at the macroeconomic level (through exports and FDI), India is firmly convinced of its' outstanding performance at the microeconomic level. Also, if the macro economy is shaped by the micro economy, then India may be better poised for sustained future growth (Yasheng and Tarun 2003).

To sum up, the innovation system models in both the countries are in the initial stages. A deeper analysis of the similarities and differences of the innovation systems in the two countries could help in the development of NIS in the knowledge economy according to the laws of economic and technological development, which will further result in sustained economic development.

REFERENCES

3iNetwork (2004), *India Infrastructure Report 2004*, Oxford University Press, New Delhi.

Ahya, C., A. Xie, A. Agarwal, D. Yam, S. Lam, and M. Sheth (2004) *India and China: A Special Economic Analysis*, Morgan Stanley, Shanghai, p.65–9.

Brenner, T. (2001) 'Simulating the Evolution of Localized Industrial Clusters—An Identification of the Basic Mechanisms', *Journal of Artificial Societies and Social Simulation*, Vol. 4, No. 3, p. 4.

Bajwa, G. S. (2003) 'ICT Policy in India in the Era of liberalization: Its Impact and Consequences', *Global Built Environment Review*, Vol. 3, pp. 49–61.

Chenggang, Z. (2000) 'National Innovation System Comparison between Japan and USA', *Japan Academy Forum*, Vol. 1, p.24–27.

China Statistical Yearbook 2001-2006, Chinese Statistic Publishing Company.

China's State Council (2002) *The 16th Central Committee Congress Report*, pp.6–10.

——— (2007) *The 17th Central Committee Congress Report*, pp.9–15.

China Technology Development Strategy Research Group (2008) *Report of Regional Innovation Capability of China*, Intellectual Property Publishing House, pp. 54–79.

Dahlman, C.J. (2007) 'China and India: Emerging Technological Powers', *Science and Technology*, Spring, Vol. 23, No. 3, p. 44–53.

Das, B.S., Nikhil Chandra and Pramanik, Alok Kumar (2007) 'Strengthening SMEs to Make Export Competitive' *Journal of Business and Technology*, Vol. 2, No. 1–2, pp. 54–64, http://mpra.ub.uni-muenchen.de/7800/.

Dosi, G. (1988) 'Sources, Procedures, and Microeconomic Effects of Innovation', *Journal of Economic Literature*, Vol. 26, No. 3, pp. 1120–71.

Edquist, C. and B. Johnson (1997) 'Institutitons and Organisations in Systems of Innovation', in C. Edquist (ed.) *Systems of Innovation: Technologies, Institutions and Organizations*, Pinter/ Cassell Academic, London and Washington, pp. 257–61.

Eichhorst, W., S. Profit, and E. Thode (eds) (2001) *Benchmarking Deutschland: Arbeitsmarkt und Besch¨aftigung*, Bericht der Arbeitsgruppe Benchmarking und der Bertelsmann Stiftung, Springer, pp. 55–7, Berlin Heidelberg New York.

Freeman, C. (1995) 'The National Innovation System in Historical Perspective' *Cambridge Journal of Economics*, Vol. 19, No. 1, pp. 41–60.

────── (1987) *Technology Policy and Economic Performance: Lessons from Japan*, Pinter Press, London, pp. 20–35.

Furman, J. L., M.E. Porter and S. Stern (2002) 'The Determinants of National Innovative Capacity', *Research Policy*, Vol. 31, No. 6, pp. 921–33.

Goldstein, M. and N. Lardy (2003) 'Two-stage Currency Reform for China', *Asian Wall Street Journal*, Vol. 12, No. 9, p. 3.

Government of India (2003) *Quick Results: All India Census of Small Scale Industries 2001–2002*, Development Commissioner (Small Scale Industries), Ministry of Small Scale Industries, New Delhi.

Gu, S. and B. Lundvall (2006), 'China's innovation system and the move toward harmonious growth and endogenous innovation', *Innovation: Management, Policy and Practice*, Vol. 8, No. 1, p. 4.

Ho, Kate and Katharina Luban (2004) *National Innovation Systems: A Case Study of South Korea and Brazil*, Coursework for Economic and Public Policy of Technology, University of Edinburgh, School of Informatics, p. 2.

Hongxing, Zhang and Xi Cheng (2005) 'Model and Evaluation Index System of National Innovation' *Statistics Research*, Vol. 7, pp. 20–3.

ITU (2006). *World Telecommunications Development Report 2006*, International Telecommunication Union, Switzerland, Geneva, pp. 37–8.

Ken Guy, Wise Guys Ltd. (2003), Policy Workshops in the First Cycle of the EU Initiative on the Benchmarking of National Research Policies, Co-organised by the European Commission and Germany, Finland, Malta, and Slovenia, p. 1.

Kohl, R. and J. Elmeskov (1998) *The OECD Jobs Strategy: Progress Report on Implementation of Country-Specific Recommendations*, OECD, pp. 8–12.

Krueger, A. (2002), *Economic Policy Reforms and the Indian Economy*, University of Chicago Press, Chicago, IL.

Lardy, N. (2003) 'The Economic Rise of China: Threat or Opportunity?', *Federal Reserve Bank of Cleveland*, Vol. 1, pp. 26–30.

Liu, X. and S. White (2001) 'Comparing Innovation Systems: A Framework and Application to China's Transitional Context' *Research Policy*, Vol. 30, No. 6, pp. 1091–114.

Lundvall, B. (1992) *National Systems of Innovation, Towards a Theory of Innovation and Interactive Learning*, Pinter Publishers, London, pp. 50–2.

────── (1988) 'Innovation as An Interactive Process: From User–producer Interaction to The National System of Innovation', in G. Dosi (ed.) *Technical Change and Economic Theory*, Pinter Publishers, London, pp. 44–9.

────── (1985) *Product Innovation and User–producer Interaction*, Aalborg University Press, Denmark, pp. 78–9.

Min, Hua (2006) 'Economic Development Model Comparison between India and China', *Fudan University Transaction*, Vol. 6, pp. 36–50.

Mu, R. and W. Qu (2008) 'The Development of Science and Technology in China: A Comparison with India and the United State', *Technology in Society*, Vol. 30, pp. 319–29.

Narayana, M.R. (2004) 'Determinants of Competitiveness of Small-scale Industries in India', *The Journal of Business in Developing Country*, Vol. 8, p. 142, http://dcmsme.gov.in/ssiindia/census/sumryres.htm

Nasierowski, W. and F.J. Arcelus (2003) 'On the Efficiency of National Innovation Systems', *Socio-Economic Planning Sciences*, Vol. 37, No. 3, pp. 215–34.

Nasierowski, W. and F.J. Arcelus (2000) 'On the Stability of Countries' National Technological Systems' in S.H. Zanakis, G. Doukidis and C. Zopounidis (eds) *Decision Making: Recent Developments and Worldwide Applications*, Kluwer, Dordrecht, pp. 313–15.

Nasierowski, W. and F.J. Arcelus (1999) 'Interrelationships Among the Elements of National Innovation Systems: A Statistical Evaluation', *European Journal of Operational Research* Vol. 119, No. 2, pp. 235–53.

Naubahar, Sharif (2006) 'Emergence and Development of the National Innovation Systems Concept, *Research Policy*, Vol. 35, No. 4, pp. 745–66.

Nelson, R. (1993) *National Innovation Systems: A Comparative Analysis*, Oxford University Press, New York, pp. 78–9.

Organization for Economic Cooperation and Development [OECD] (1999) *National Innovation System*, Paris, pp. 9–15.

OECD (1998) *National Innovation System*, Paris, pp. 14.

OECD (1997) *National Innovation System*, Paris, pp. 7–11.

Porter, M. (1986), *Competition in Global Industries*, Harvard Business School Press, pp. 14–19.

Porter, M. E. and S. Stern (2002) 'National Innovative Capacity', in *World Economic Forum: The Global Competitiveness Report 2001–2002*, Oxford University Press, New York, pp. 198–213.

Polt, W.C., Rammer, H. Gassler, A. Schibanny, and D. Schartinger (2001). 'Benchmarking Industry-science Relations: The Role of Framework Conditions', *Science and Public Policy* Vol. 28, No. 4, 247–58.

Qingrui, Xu (2000) *Research Development and Technology Innovation Management*, Higher Education Publishing House, pp. 413–20.

Qin, Chang (2006) *Science and Technology in India*, Science Press, pp. 210–25, Beijing.

Romer, P. (1990) 'Endogenous Technological Change', *Journal of Political Economy*, Vol. 98, No. 5, pp. 71–102.

Sibal, K. (2006) Presentation in the World Economic Forum, 10–11 September 2006, during his visit to China.

Tata Management Training Centre, (2006), Innovation in India: Recent Trends, unpublished, pp. 45–56.

Yanhua, Lian (2006) 'Suggestions for Development of National Innovation System', *Science and Technology Management Research*, Vol. 1, pp. 17–19.

Yasheng, Huang and Tarun Khanna (2003) 'Can India Overtake China?' *Foreign Policy*, Vol. 137, July–August, pp. 76–8.

Yasmeen (2004), 'Science Education on a Slippery Path, India Together', October 2004, http://www.Indiatogether.org/2004/oct/edu-science.htm

Xiaoping, Zheng (2006) 'Review of National Innovation System', *Science and Technology Management*, Vol. 24, No. 4, pp. 1–5.

Xie, Yong (2006). 'The Most Undervalued Universities', *China Nan Fang Daily News Paper*, 5 July.

3
Perspectives on China's Integration with the World Economy[a]

HIREN DOSHI

Tango of the Dragon and the Elephant[b]

When choosing between two evils I always like to take the one I've never tried before.

— **Mae West**

For much of last 1000 years what India and China had in common was the fact that they were the richest nations on earth. In 1500 AD, their combined GDP commanded 25 per cent of world's total GDP. However, the last decades of nineteenth century saw both the countries go through disastrous periods, partly eclipsed by famines and earthquakes and partly due to the emergence of imperialist Europe and America. By mid-twentieth century both countries saw a gradual decline in their socio-political and economic well-being. China's fortune reversal started with Deng Xiao Ping coming to power in 1978 and institutionalizing the market economic policies. India adopted that path in early 1990s. Since then both the economies have been growing at break neck speed. China has done better than India in its ability to attract foreign investment and develop infrastructure suitably for export-led low-cost manufacturing economy while India has largely been a domestic consumption story with success in knowledge and services industry.

There have been numerous visits by senior politicians across the border which is recognition of the growing importance and necessity of improving the bilateral economic and political relationship between the countries. The bilateral trade between India and China has increased 30 fold in the last decade. Last year, the bilateral trade touched USD 18 billion and an aggressive goal of USD 50 billion is set to be reached by 2010. These numbers might seem low looking at China's overall trade numbers but the trajectory seems to be moving upward on a fast track. China, which is currently the second largest trading partner of India may replace US to be the largest trading partner within the next few years.

A number of Indian companies have set up operations in China. Few years back it used to be an event, but now it is a regular affair. Similarly, Chinese companies have recognized the potential India has to offer in the infrastructure market and are making the necessary investments in that segment to get some piece of the action. Indian companies have invested in industries like pharmaceuticals, IT, electronics, engineering goods, auto components and diamonds. The bulk

---

[a] These pieces are reproductions of newspaper articles so data sources are not cited everywhere.
[b] First published in *Financial Express*, 17 January 2007.

of export from India is still commodity based but the growth is increasingly becoming broad based spanning multiple industries. Most of conferences now invariably talk about China and India in the same breath. And that means there is always a question of choosing one over the other—India or China?

I think it's going to be India and China together, who will create an Asian century. Even the perception at the local business level has changed considerably in last few years. There are hordes of business delegations traveling across the boundary to understand the strengths of each country and figure out ways to gain from each other in an era of globalization. China is no longer considered a threat by local businesses in India.

Indian companies have taken advantage of Chinese strengths in manufacturing and market, Chinese companies have responded with equal vigor. Huawei has already invested USD 100 million in India in research and development and has committed further USD 150 million. Their revenue from India was around USD 300 million last year. Considering India to be an important market, Haier had set a revenue target of USD 65 million last year. They have struck local alliances with Whirlpool and Voltas and more strategic alliances are on the cards. By 2010 Haier aims to be among the top 3 brands in India.

While Indian companies investing in China might have received more press coverage due to the kind of industries involved, Chinese companies have been playing in segments of strength, such as, infrastructure. Apart from the private sector, there has been action in the public sector too. We have seen the two governments moving from competition to cooperation in important sectors such as, energy after realizing that they both share common challenges and goals and mutual cooperation is going to be in the best interests of both the countries.

In one of its reports, MasterCard pointed out that instead of viewing China and India as competitors, it is more important to understand the China–India business synergy. The new generation of joint India–China companies will change the competitive landscape of global business.

China Pays the Price for Structural Reforms[c]

There are some remedies worse than the disease.
— **Publilius Syrus**

The last three decades have seen many emerging economies starting to bloom and unleash their potential while integrating with the world economy. Different cluster of regions have been at different levels of development depending on the set of policies they chose to pump the growth engines with. The outcome of these polices have both implicitly and explicitly determined the level of integration with the rest of the world and the collateral damage suffered in the process of development. Many developing countries are still grappling with the legacy of decisions taken by patchy regimes with long lasting socio-economic implications. It will take decades to undo some of the damage the countries have suffered in the process of development. Let us take the case of China.

[c] First published in the *Financial Express*, 21 February 2007.

In the course of 25 years between 1978 and 2003, China's economy grew by an average annual rate of 9.4 per cent with its GDP, foreign trade and foreign exchange reserves jumping from USD 147.3 billion, USD 20.6 billion and USD 167 million to over USD 1.4 trillion, USD 851.2 billion and USD 403.3 billion, respectively. China now is the world's sixth largest economy and the fourth largest trader. Many experts predict that China will be the second largest economy by 2020 and topple US to take the honours by 2050, if not sooner, while being able to continue the juggernaut. China has earned a distinct reputation of being the manufacturing factory of the world and has managed to attract some 500 companies to participate in this miracle.

China entered WTO in December 2001 and opened its door to the world to view China not just as a factory but also as a lucrative market consisting of 300 million Chinese middle class with their rapidly rising purchasing power. This served well for the multinational corporations (MNCs) looking at alternatives to keep growing despite the slowdown in US economy and stagnation in Japan. The GDP per capita increased from USD 60 to little over USD 1650 over the last 25 years. The rise is even more impressive if we account for Purchasing Power Parity. China has accumulated the largest foreign exchange reserve in the world owing to large trade surpluses and influx of steady foreign direct investment year after year. It accounted for third of the growth in global GDP in the last decade. All this has come not without a price. Price, which the current government is seriously concerned about. It has recently started acknowledging the need to undo or at least put a stop to adverse socio-economic implications arising from the nature of the growth.

China's rise as the world's manufacturing hub was primarily due to availability of a low cost production base. After entry into the WTO, China has introduced market reforms for many products, but it still tightly controls the cost factors for production such as land, energy, capital and labor. Land is owned by the government in China and is often offered at a low or no cost to attract investments in manufacturing and infrastructure development. This has also resulted in over-investment in infrastructure sector and high dependency on exports to maintain growth. Trade surplus for this year are expected to cross USD 200 billion, up from USD 177 billion last year and with more than USD 1 trillion dollars, China now carries the world's largest foreign exchange reserves.

Energy prices including, oil, gas and electricity, are tightly controlled and a glaring example of this is that the oil prices in China were half than some of its Asian neighbors when the prices of crude oil shot to USD 80 a barrel in world market. Distorted capital allocation is one of the most significant implications of distorted growth economics. Due to high savings rate in China, the Chinese banks are flush with funds, but they also suffer from serious bad debt which is predicted by some experts to be as high as 30 per cent of China's GDP. This is a result of absence of credit risk based loans pricing and government's strong influence in business affairs of domestic banks. Owing to this, the small and medium enterprises were denied cheap access to funds to compete on equal footing in market with state-owned enterprises or SOEs. This has curtailed development of small and private enterprise culture which is very important in any vibrant developing economy.

China's artificially controlled exchange rate pegged to United States dollar (USD) until now has left Yuan (Chinese currency) highly undervalued. This issue has attracted unwanted attention from countries running into high trade deficit with China and also accusing it of dumping goods at artificially suppressed prices. Labor movement across the country was controlled tightly by Hukou mechanism to avoid burdening the urban areas and thereby creating artificial under-employment. This forced the illegal migrant workers to accept lower salaries without any social benefits to settle down in cities. China's unit manufacturing labor costs in 2003 were just 3 per cent of that in US.

Developing countries whose main focus is on infrastructure development, tend to spend less money elsewhere. In case of China, the basic education in rural areas has fallen victim to this vicious obsession with over-investment in a few sectors. This has long term implications and may present structural problems when China moves from current predominant manufacturing to eventual services-led growth in the economy. China abandoned its medicare and old-age pension system from mid-1990s. Households started saving more to protect themselves against future health uncertainties. With few varied and risk free investment avenues, all savings were channelled to bank deposits. Banks used this money to subsidize the inefficient SOEs thereby affecting the returns that were earned through the common man's deposit. In spite of China boasting of its highest per capita GPD among developing countries, its household wealth to GDP ratio is among the lowest in the world. China spends only 3 per cent of total government spending on social welfare.

Environment is the biggest hit and is one of the most serious problems faced by China. Many Chinese cities feature regularly among the top ten polluted cities in the world. With the projected industrial growth rate, China is well positioned to surpass US as the highest emitter of green house gases in the world. China is highly dependent on coal and oil for much of its industrial power needs. This dependency will continue unless strict environmental and emission standards are implemented and enforced in the near future.

The *gini* coefficient, which measures income inequality, is an appropriate measure of efficiency with which the population shares the country's spoils. This coefficient increased sharply from 0.33 to 0.47 in the last 25 years. This demonstrates that the new found wealth amassed by China in the last three decades have been cornered by select few leaving hundreds of millions still in poverty. This wide income gap combined with illegal land extortion by corrupt officials has given rise to growing tensions in rural areas. China witnessed some 65,000 recorded protests due to social unrest last year which shows a marked increase from the officially reported numbers, even few years back. The Chinese top think tank is well aware of the need to address this critical issue and has initiated a series of measures to turn into reality the dream of a 'harmonious society' laid down by the present Chinese President.

To credit the present government, steps have been taken, over the last few years, to carry on reforms on many of the areas mentioned above. In the last couple of years, the government has taken strong action to curb the real estate market from artificially inflating the economy. Measures have been taken to check the proper use of land for industrial development. Restrictions have been put on foreigners' ability to purchase residential property. Government has also pumped in hundreds of billions of dollars to help the state owned banks clean up their balance sheet and start becoming accountable by divesting stake and encouraging foreign participation through investment and management expertise. Yuan has been pegged to a basket of currencies and restrictions have been relaxed to let it appreciate gradually. It surpassed Hong Kong dollar for the first time in the recent past and is well on its way strengthening further. Labor movement restrictions for white collar workers have been relaxed to some extent but there is much that remains to be done to avoid exploitation of some 300 million rural workers who are expected to be moved to cities in the next decade.

Some initiatives have been taken to build pension and social welfare systems, but the coverage is patchy. Currently only a few urban areas have systems of full protection and only 40 per cent of eligible urban dwellers opt to participate in the government subsidized pension plan. The situation is grimmer in the rural areas where government does not contribute to a basic pension plan and participation in the rural cooperative medicare scheme is a mere 10 per cent. For the first time in the 11th Five Year Plan (2006–10), the government stressed the importance of quality along with quantity of output. A renewable energy law came into effect from 2006 and goals of efficient usage of power and water have been set.

Much of the growth China has witnessed in the last decade was due to undivided and relentless focus on investment and export-led industrialization. Local officials were promoted based on the investment they were able to attract and the growth figures they turned in for their respective provinces. This led to a blinkered view of development with the evil baggage of adverse socio-economic implications carried along for years. China needs to continue maintaining at least 8 per cent GDP growth rate to maintain the momentum and create employment for millions of rural workers who will migrate to cities soon. The 16th Central Committee of the CPC concluded its 5th Plenary Session in Beijing on 11 October 2006. The plan emphasizes the need to adopt a more scientific approach to development with the underlying theme of building a strong foundation for a harmonious society. The plan has made all the right noises in local and foreign media and this time round the intention is of putting people ahead of growth. How much of this plan turns into reality in the oncoming years remains to be seen. Nonetheless, the Chinese government does face a tough act of balancing growth and distribution to ensure undistorted growth for future generations.

US China: Maintaining a Fine Balance[d]

Those who invented the law of supply and demand have no right to complain when this law works against their interest.

— **Anwar Sadat**

It was a busy time for US companies playing host and laying out their products for display as the Chinese went on their annual shopping spree across 24 cities in US. This has become one of the annual rituals between the two giants, partly to bring sanity to the highly one-sided trade numbers and mostly to cool down the rising tempers of US political and business faction that has developed a habit of blaming all the woes of the US economy on the artificially deflated Chinese currency and slow pace of market reforms in China.

The Chinese business delegation led by the Vice Minister of the Ministry of Commerce, Ma Xiuhong had announced deals of more than USD 4 billion and this took place just before the scheduled government talks in Washington later to discuss prickly issues such as trade deficit and undervalued Chinese currency. The value of the deals signed constituted a mere 2 per cent of the total trade surplus that China runs with US. More deals in the agriculture sector such as cotton and soybean may be announced in coming weeks once the details are hammered out, but the number won't exceed 5 per cent of the yawning deficit of more than USD 230 billion last year that US carried in favor of China. Companies in computer software, telecommunication, aviation and semiconductor industry such as Oracle, HP, Microsoft, Qualcomm, Cisco and Boeing stood as the biggest beneficiaries. These are the same companies which considered China as a

---

[d] First published in the *Financial Express*, 16 May 2007. The article should be read keeping in mind the context of the international economy in 2007.

core to their business growth strategies and still have significant presence in China. Most of the money eventually found its way into the Chinese market through manufacturing or research and development investment.

These transactions were primarily business in nature and did not materialize just because of political pressure. In fact most of the deals may have been just bundled for announcement during this symbolic 'trade correction' trip and would have been struck anyway in the normal course of business. This seemed to bode well for both sides. This helped the Chinese government to pull off a successful visit by the senior Chinese government official typically following the shopping trip and that implied a sense of temporary victory for the US protectionist faction. Looking few months down the road and we would see the Chinese picking up its cheque book for yet another 'buying mission' to US, once the protectionist sentiments build up steam again.

More recently US have consciously moved much of its negotiation with China on trade issues from bilateral to multilateral forums. On 9 April 2007, the US government announced that would file two formal complaints against China with WTO, alleging that China is in breach of WTO rules for enforcement of Intellectual Property Rights and restriction on market access for foreign media products. This complaint was supported by data from Motion Pictures of America that US media companies lost more than USD 2 billion in 2006 as a result of easy availability of counterfeits and restriction on supply of legitimate ones. In February 2007, US had lodged another formal complaint with WTO. This time under attack was the unfair subsidy that the Chinese government extends to several export oriented industries. Following this complaint was a landmark ruling by federal court that the US department of commerce has the legal authority to impose anti-subsidy tariff on goods made by foreign companies (read Chinese companies) that receive unfair government incentives in form of subsidies. The significance of this ruling was that it came in spite of China being a non-market economy. Although the immediate impact of this ruling will hurt the glossy paper industry, it can soon have wide ramification across many industries.

Lifting the trade battle a notch higher in international forum such as WTO, gives US higher ground and better leverage in pressurizing the Chinese government to act fast or face similar protests from other developed economies. This also helps them muddle politics and business issues which can then be traded to garner Chinese support on political issues such as Darfur and North Korea in exchange of more time to appreciate the Chinese currency and implement market reforms. More than trade deficit, there is domestic political pressure and a general inability on either side to appreciate the constraints imposed on their counterparts by domestic situation realities. Bush administration was under increasing pressure to take more concrete action to reduce the trade gap with China. Unless the Congress saw visible signs, his authority to renew the trade pact agreement (TPA) would not be upheld by the Congress (which is now controlled by the Democrats) when it was due to expire in July 2007. And with 2007 being the presidential election year, scoring points by bashing China seemed tempting and irresistible. However, the reality is that US needs China as much as China needs US. Peoples Bank of China (PBOC) financed one-fourth of US current account deficit. US wanted China to continue buying the US government paper to maintain low interest rate in order to avoid recession.

On the other hand, the Chinese government made it abundantly clear in the past that it would institutionalize reforms on the basis of Yuan, provide access to financial services market and implement IP protection mechanisms 'gradually' when it would feel that the market is ready rather than under foreign pressure. They face a challenge to time this well so as not to shake the maturing economy or cause upheaval in social stability in an already fragmented socio-economic fabric. China also needs to continue its growth momentum to generate enough jobs to spread the wealth and keep social unrest under check. While domestic consumption in China is on the rise, most of the growth is expected to come from investments and export-led industries. The figures of dynamic export growth in the last five years confirm this theory.

It is not unknown that more than 60 per cent of Chinese exports are transacted by MNCs through their subsidiaries or JVs manufacturing operations in China. Any move which makes Chinese exports more expensive could hurt US MNCs more than Chinese companies. This could have a disconcerting effect on the US economy which has been remarkably resilient in the face of the slowing housing market and weakening consumer spending. Even if one were to assume that appreciation of Chinese currency will help correct trade imbalance with China in long run, corporate America has moved far too ahead on a one way street of outsourcing manufacturing and to some extent services to be able to bring those jobs back to US and still be competitive in the global market. Businesses would be swift to find an alternate destination such as Vietnam or India to move manufacturing from China and US would still run a pretty healthy deficit on its balance sheet.

Increasingly, the Chinese government has been proactive in de-risking its overdependence on exports to US. The first action was in July 2005 when it un-pegged its currency from USD and instead pegged it to a basket of currencies. In 2006, China remained European Union's (EU's) second largest trading partner and displaced the US as the largest source of EU imports. According to Chinese statistics, EU continued in its role as China's first trading partner (ahead of both the US and Japan). China is smartly negotiating bilateral free trade agreement with the Asian neighbors at scorching pace and seeking market economy status. The US will still be the most important market for China for foreseeable future and the trade imbalance will only grow wider.

Recent studies by The World Bank show that China is moving up the value chain and does not just assemble imported products with little value addition. Domestic products in Chinese export are on the rise and this is one of the primary reasons of increase in Chinese trade surplus with the rest of world in recent years. Improvements in quality of Chinese made intermediate products have forced even the foreign manufacturers in China to source products locally to make their supply chain more efficient. China's net export contributed an estimated 3.3 per cent to China's GDP growth in the second half of 2006, up from 2 per cent from the first half. Rise in export has accelerated even more in the first few months of this year. The World Bank also highlights that the pickup in China's export growth hasn't been matched by similar growth in export of other Asian economies. This may be happening on two counts. Firstly, China may be making the most of the intensifying competition for international export market. For instance China's export growth to sluggish US economy was growing at 25 per cent during later part of 2006 and early 2007 when similar statistic for its Asian neighbors slowed to 5 per cent. Secondly, improvement in Chinese internal supply chain has gradually replaced import of intermediate parts from neighboring countries. For instance, while China's bilateral trade with India has increased at a brisk pace touching USD 35 billion, the surplus which was in India's favor until 2005 has now moved the Chinese way and is rising rapidly.

If this trend is any indication, Asian countries will soon find their way into the itinerary of Chinese shopping trips to quick fix the China's trade imbalances.

Getting a Piece of the Chinese Economic Pie[e]

Just when you get really good at something, you don't need to do it anymore.

— **William P. Lowrey**

After being in works for the last 13 years, the Standing Committee of National People's Congress finally passed the new Anti-Monopoly Law. The new law came into effect from 1 August 2008. This is one of the many important policy changes (for example, uniform taxation system, new labor law) which the government has undertaken in line with its strategy to promote China as a market economy on the world stage. Prima facie the law reads 'As well as anti-monopoly checks stipulated by this law, foreign mergers with, or acquisitions of, domestic companies or foreign capital investing in domestic companies' operations in other forms should go through national security checks according to the relevant laws and regulations'.

The new law intends to subject foreign acquisitions of Chinese companies to national 'economic' security checks to safeguard against creation of monopolies detrimental to consumers and market. It defines monopoly in three situations a) when an undertaking reaches a monopolistic agreement b) when an undertaking abuses a dominant market position and c) when an undertaking forms an undertaking cartel. It goes on to define seven types of agreement as monopoly agreement allowing seven exceptions which are basically to encourage agreements concerning improvement of technology, research and development of new products, improvement of product quality, protecting the environment, increasing efficiency, and so on.

The initial reaction from representatives of EU and American Chambers of Commerce in China was quite euphoric that the new law will create a level playing field between foreign and domestic companies ultimately benefiting the Chinese consumers. But that was quickly followed by concerns and questions. How will the law be implemented? Will the law impede their ability to bring more money into the country to gain a bigger share of the market.

With China opening up its economy as per agreement with WTO, foreign companies have pumped in billions of dollar to get a piece of action in the growing Chinese market. Industries such as retail, banking, insurance, automobile and consumer electronics have seen most of the action and are now likely to be the most watched under the new law. It will prevent foreign companies from using their global financial muscle to essentially buy away competition. Foreign companies which already hold a dominant market position will face an uphill task of seeking approval for further growth through acquisition. It will help create a level playing field for domestic companies to operate in the market.

A closer look at the law reveals that this may actually be beneficial to foreign enterprises, opening up strategic markets which are currently under tight grip of the monopolistic state owned enterprises. Since it's a double edged sword, local companies which have maintained monopoly in the market through protection of local government can also be exposed to increased competition going forward.

The most interesting dimension of the new law is that it brings the 'administrative monopolies' within its grasp along with 'commercial monopolies'. It means, that the state owned enterprises

---

[e] First published in the *Financial Express*, 26 September 2007.

supported by local provincial government that indulges in unfair trade practices due to monopolistic market conditions will come under increased scrutiny by the anti-monopoly commission which is being setup under state council to be the regulating body governing this law. It is a known fact that the most damaging monopolistic behavior comes from government abuse of administrative power in the economy but there was no political will to deal with it in the last two decades and hence the delay of 13 years in passing of this new law. Europe faced similar problems of protectionist state in the middle of the last century and they had to establish the European Economic Community (EEC) to counter some of those problems although with limited success. These are valuable lessons from history which the Chinese can learn while implementing the new law.

Last year the state council had released a list of strategic sectors in which the state would retain control. These mainly consisted of military, power, telecom, aviation and shipping industries. The new law will no doubt be used to block unpopular foreign acquisition of domestic brands or companies, which is detrimental to growth of domestic industry. But at the same time, the new law also has an entire chapter that protects the foreign enterprise from local protectionism in China, specifically prohibiting administrative agencies and public organizations from abusing their power. The law also does not state that a foreign enterprise will be treated any differently from the domestic enterprises except for the strategic industries falling under national security list or circumstances where national security is concerned. Until the new law is fully understood, large deals involving purchase of state assets would be kept under tight wrap until the deal has the blessings from the top and the mergers and acquisitions (M&A) activities will be mostly concentrated in the mid-market avoiding the radar of the new law.

China is not the first country to implement such a law and China already had basic security check system for Foreign M&A (for example, Carlyle's bid for Xugong) but the previous law was only to regulate deals exceeding USD 100 million. European Union has had this for quite sometime and uses it effectively to prevent monopolistic behavior (for example, Microsoft's anti-trust case). Recently EU referred China's International Marine Container's bid to acquire Berg Industries for review and as a result the bid was pulled out by the Chinese. Back in 2005, CNOOC's sensational bid for Unical was withdrawn by the Chinese after it raised national security concerns in the US.

By passing this law, China has demonstrated its confidence and maturity in adopting international policies and regulatory framework. It shows its confidence in being able to attract foreign investment in spite of a level playing field with domestic industry. This is even more significant when combined with the fact that almost 20 per cent of foreign investment in 2005 was due to foreign mergers and acquisitions. China has also increasingly started to take a more assertive stance in the global arena, be it trade dispute with US or the recent spate of mass recalls of substandard Chinese manufactured goods. Under the able leadership of President Hu and Premier Wen, some of the new policies are clearly directed to create a harmonious society and uplift the rural population out of poverty, seek a more energy efficient growth and keep environmental pollution under check. However, most of this doesn't align with local government's philosophy of 'growth at any cost' hence the real challenge for the central government would be in garnering support from local provincial government in implementation of these laws.

China, More Than the US is a Driver of the World Economy[f]

Do not compute the totality of your poultry population until all the manifestations of incubation have been entirely completed.
— **William Jennings Bryan**

A number of economists anticipated the possibility of the US economy sliding into recession last year. The implication for the global economy may vary from a fundamental shift in pattern of trade and material flow to a new currency regime where Asian currencies are expected to play a significant role. Alan Greenspan, last month said 'the odds of hard landing of US economy have increased as consumer spending may slowdown due to decline in house prices'. Similar assertions have been made by likes of Richard Syron of Freddie Mac to Lawrence Summers of Harvard University.

After 16 years into the current cycle of US trade deficit, which began in 1991, the trend has reversed marking a fundamental shift. For the past two decades, US mainly bought and borrowed while rest of the world sold and saved. The US was considered to have the safest and most liquid financial market and consequently it was the recipient of the global excess savings. It may be in the interest of Japan, China, Russia and Europe to maintain surpluses against US in long run as they tackle the serious demographic changes expected to occur in the next few decades. The US current account deficit which hit an all time high of 6.8 per cent at the end of 2005 of GDP was down to 5.5 per cent earlier this year. Instead of depending heavily on the US economy as global growth engine, the world economy could start to become more evenly balanced. No other country seems to have benefited from the seemingly insatiable consumption by the US consumers than China. There is an interesting and ironical connection between US consumers and China. To pay for these imports, the US has to attract USD 2.1 billion in foreign investment every single day.

Since China opened its economy three decades ago, its economy has been growing at blistering pace. It has clocked more than 10 per cent average GDP growth rate for the last 30 years, which is higher than what most developed economies witnessed during their growth years. America was one of China's most important export markets. Exports kept the factories humming and provided employment to thousands of unskilled and semi-skilled migrant rural workers. To maintain the competitive edge in exports, China pegged its currency to US dollars. To maintain its peg and keep the interest rate low, it started accumulating massive foreign exchange reserves by mopping up foreign currency in circulation. This was in turn invested in dollar denominated assets, mainly US government bonds. While in theory, foreign central banks investing in US government bonds and thereby funding the budget deficit signifies the strength of US economy, this has now reached a stage where more than 40 per cent of national debt is owned by foreigners. The long-term interest rates which are driven by government bond pricing are now controlled by foreign central banks, mainly Japan and China and mortgage rates are directly linked to government bond yields and long-term interest rates.

Increased housing prices was one of the important underlying factors in strong consumer spending and resultant above average growth of US economy since the recession of 1991. With

---

[f] First published in *Financial Express*, 24 October 2007. All data and time periods mentioned should be interpreted keeping that publication date in mind.

the turmoil in credit market and meltdown in housing prices, the consumer spending was almost certain to slow down. Furthermore, the dollar has been hammered in the last 10 months which has trigger fear of higher interest rates and inflation if the foreign central banks decide not to invest in US treasury bonds any more. Recent data shows that long-term capital flows measured just USD 19 billion in July 2007 as compared to USD 91 billion the previous month. Soaring interest rates have increased mortgage rates making borrowing for home more difficult and thereby decreasing the demand for new homes. It is estimated that every 6 per cent drop in dollar value reduces American income by 1 per cent. Coupled with reduced consumption this was enough to nudge US into recession.

It brought shock waves to markets in China, one of the largest trading partners for US. However, the reality was quite different. The Shanghai stock exchange composite index crossed 6000 marking a new high with the price-earnings ratio based on historic profits touching almost 50. Most agreed that this was a bubble in the making but many others predicted that market could still rise before it turned south since historically NASDAQ and Nikkei saw their PE ratio reach well over 100 at their peaks.

China, which has traditionally punched below its weight, has now started playing a much bigger role in the global economy. This year China, at market exchange prices, will contribute more towards global GDP growth than the US. While the fate of US economy is downbeat, the fate of the world's economy may now also hinge on the strength of Chinese economy. China now has enormous influence over economies of virtually every country in the world so it is of great importance to understand the levers which control the Chinese economy. While there are many factors which have the potential to slow down the Chinese economy, singularly, none may be significant enough to cause any substantial damage.

The primary threats are formation of asset bubble, surging inflation, slump in exports to US and over investment. The share prices have more than doubled this year and more than quadrupled since 2005. It is without doubt a bubble waiting to burst but the implication may not have significant impact on the economy. Bulk of the shares is still held by the government through state owned enterprises and the remaining value of the tradable shares is only 35 per cent of its GDP. This accounts for only 20 per cent of household financial assets which may not adversely influence the consumer spending in the event of the market downturn. A nastier impact of fallout in stock market would be in corporate profitability. According to a study done by Morgan Stanley, more than 30 per cent of profits reported by listed companies came from share price gains and other investment income. A stock market crash immediately impacted the corporate profitability and made borrowing from bank more difficult curtailing future investments.

Housing market crash could also have more negative impact on the consumer sentiments and spending since the housing ownership in urban China is almost at 75 per cent. However, barring a few cities, the housing price has been growing quite moderately in relation to the growth in GDP and there is no sign of any bubble in the housing market.

China has gradually shifted its export focus from US in favour of EU. The growth in exports to EU in the last quarter has outstripped growth in exports to US by a factor of 3. While export constitutes 40 per cent of China's GDP, it only contributes to 25 per cent to the growth of GDP. The growth in Chinese economy is increasingly driven by domestic consumption rather than external dependency. The slowdown in US consumer consumption may shave off half a percent of China's GDP growth, but not enough to have any material impact on its already scorching growth rate. Instead it may actually help the Chinese government to cool off the overheating economy. It will further help reduce the burgeoning trade deficit with US, which is often used as a weapon by US to pressurize the Chinese government to appreciate its currency faster.

Surging inflation is another thing that keeps the Chinese think tank awake. The consumer price index shot upwards to 6.5 per cent last month and is at an all time high for this decade. A peculiarity of this surge is that almost all of it has been caused by increase in food prices. Excluding food, which accounts for a third of basket, inflation is at a tame 1 per cent mark. China has withstood far worse situations in late 1980s when the inflation skyrocketed past 25 per cent so the current spike may not cause any serious damage if kept in check. Government has already taken measures to control the prices for products like oil, water and power, by freezing any rise for rest of this year.

The Chinese economy is at a critical juncture where high savings and investment rates are coupled with soaring asset price and upward pressure on inflation and currency. It will be interesting to see how the Chinese economy fares in a fundamentally rebalancing world economic order.

Bilateral Trade Agreements Come in Handy[g]

If nobody uses it, there's a reason.

— **Jane Bryant Quinn**

Recent flurry of bilateral and regional trade agreements brought the issue of multilateral versus bilateral trade agreement (BTA) to the forefront in a fundamentally shifting global economy. Some of the BTAs concluded are Japan–Thailand and US–Korea Foreign Trade Agreements (FTAs). Japan has shown interest in FTA with US in response to US–Korea agreement. There are 220 such odd agreements in existence today and are expected to scale up to 400 by the end of this decade. Let's step back to understand the role played by such agreements in fostering free global trade in a globalizing world. With the establishment of General Agreement on Tariffs and Trade (GATT) after World War II, the multilateral approach was the preferred method of trade liberalization. The WTO was brought into existence after GATT to fix the anomaly resulting from special treatment allowed under GATT for its member nations to subsidize production, agriculture, and export and limit market access.

This practice ultimately resulted in decrease in commodity food price, distortion in global agriculture trade and frustration from non-subsidized agriculture exporting nations. One of the noble objectives of WTO was to eradicate this trade distortion and improve food prices thereby improving the welfare of the farmers. The Uruguay Round launched during 1986–94 touched issues ranging from agriculture, Intellectual Property Rights (IPRs), technical barriers to trade and few more. Since the Agreement on Agriculture was just an interim agreement while the final goal was full liberalization, it was agreed that negotiation would resume in 1999. The Doha Development Round (DDR) was launched in Doha in 2001 followed by subsequent rounds of negotiation. One of the thorniest issues dividing the developed and the developing world was the issue of agriculture subsidy even though its share of the world trade was less than 8 per cent. Due to deadlock in negotiations, the discussion was brought to a halt in July 2006 until the meeting of US, EU, Brazil and India in Potsdam, Germany, in June 2007 post which the discussion have come to a halt again.

[g] First published in the *Financial Express*, 19 December 2007.

With globalization comes the possibility of buying and selling goods and services anywhere in the world. If this is left to market forces alone, it can create distortions in development patterns and vulnerability to foul play by a few. To harness the true benefit of globalization there was a need for an organization which represented all societies and ensured that both developed and developing countries benefit equally in the era of globalization. Hence, WTO was formed on basis of multilateral trading system. While no one denies the benefits fostered by the existence of such a multilateral trade agreement, in reality, it has been difficult for the developed and developing countries to agree on the end game.

A direct consequence of the slowdown in Doha Round was resurgence of regional trade agreement in form of FTAs and bilateral trade agreements. Foreign Trade Agreements, many of which are bilateral, are arrangement in which countries give each other preferential treatment in trade by eliminating tariffs and other barriers on goods. Each country continues its normal trade policies with other countries outside the FTA. One of the advantages of bilateral agreements is that countries can choose when to enter into agreements. US and Canada were ready to start the FTA process in the mid-1980s. Mexico followed a few years later and the US–Canada FTA was folded into the North American Free Trade Agreement (NAFTA). The Dominican Republic–Central America–United States Free Trade Agreement (CAFTA-DR) was negotiated in 2004–5 when the US and other countries decided to share economic and foreign policy benefits. A US–Korea FTA would not have been doable 10 years ago. Regional or BTA also has an advantage in dealing with intractable trade problems over the WTO which usually caters to the lowest common policy denominator.

In theory a 'Global Trade Agreement' is supposed to be an ideal solution in terms of resource allocation, economic welfare and economic prosperity. The next best solution is the regional trade agreement which lowers the trade barrier among members without having to lower barrier for non-members. However, finding systemic issues such as rules of origin, anti-dumping, subsidies are best left to be resolved within a multilateral trade agreement.

World Trade Organization supports existence of such regional agreements as long as they are transparent and help deepen trade and economic liberalization without raising the trade barrier for non members. They should not create ways for trade diversion resulting in imports from inefficient supply bases. There are many reasons for the momentum that regional trade agreement received in recent past. One of the reasons is that it can be negotiated quickly since limited number of parties are involved and can charter into areas such as investment, competition, IPR, labor standards, environment provisions, and so on—some of which are only given broad brush treatment in WTO agreement. Regional agreements also help developing countries to experiment with domestic reforms, regulatory policies and to provide an opportunity for the domestic market to learn how to cope with limited foreign competition before a full onslaught in a multilateral regime. A developing country negotiating such an agreement with a developed country can also expect non-trade preferential benefits such as development assistance and freer market access and gain a point over other competing WTO members.

It is well known that Asia has emerged as a key player in global trade ecosystem. The World Bank expects the global economy to grow at a much faster pace in the next three decades as compared to the previous three as large developing countries such as India and China witness high growth and integrate with the rest of the world at an unprecedented pace. The share in the global output of developing countries is expected to increase from present 5th to a 3rd in the next 25 years.

While integrating with the global trade and production system, Asian economies have also deeply integrated regionally. Intra-regional trade in East Asia makes 55 per cent of the region's total trade which is up from 35 per cent, back in 1980s. This is a result of the conscious effort by Asian governments to embark on closer monetary and financial cooperation after the Asian financial crisis and initiatives such as Association of Southeast Asian Nations (ASEAN) Surveillance Process, Chiang Mai and Asian bond market. Compared with US and Europe, Asia was a latecomer in the pursuit of regional trade agreement or FTAs as an instrument for trade policy. The ASEAN was the only significant regional trade pact in existence before 1998. Since then there has been a dramatic proliferation of FTAs and there are more than a dozen in existence in East Asia today and twice that number is already under negotiation. This uptick was also a result of dissatisfaction with the progress on global trade talks and 'left behind' syndrome. Such a complicated mesh of overlapping regional and bilateral agreements has led to the 'Asian noodle bowl' effect and the overheads to manage plethora of complex rules, such as rules of origin, can easily defeat the efficiencies expected from such agreements. Further, if the transaction costs are high, it can eventually result in decrease of FDI and trade.

Regional trade agreements and FTAs have kept the torch of trade liberalization burning in spite of breakdown in discussion on global trade agreements. This is of paramount importance as the world experiences a paradigm shift in its trade pattern and protectionist sentiments are expected to strengthen further. Regional trade agreements are here to stay and were given their due importance by including the issue in the DDR agenda. However due to the amount of time and attention diverted to the pursuit of regional trade agreement, the commitment to conclude a successful global trade agreement will take some time to come into shape. Whether a regional trade agreement acts as building block or as Jagdish Bhagwati puts it, as a 'stumbling block' to the global free trade regime remains to be seen. In the immediate future, for the successful co-existence of multilateral and regional trade agreement, it is important that the latter enhances the benefits of the former and compliments rather than substituting it.

Wal Mart Increases its Hold on China[h]

I don't care what people think of my poetry so long as they award it prizes.

— **Robert Frost**

The last decade has witnessed a gradual shift in the world economic order of which the last five have particularly seen a shift of focus from the developed to the developing economies. Many factors led to this state of affairs, some which occurred in the natural course of history and some others were man-made as a result of changing world business dynamics. The rise of China was one and the rise of Wal-Mart was another. The China story is well written, followed and acknowledged by everyone around the world. That China touches everyones life in one way or the other is a reality accepted by all. The initial fear of China was replaced by anger which has now been further replaced by acceptance as the reality sinks in that China is here to stay. While China stole the limelight in popular press, the story of the rise of Wal-Mart remained untold outside the American

[h] First published in the *Financial Express*, 6 February 2008.

press and business circles. However Wal-Mart has been and will continue to be an important player in sustaining the Chinese manufacturing supremacy and a crucial link tying these two big forces.

In January 2008 Wal-Mart celebrated approval of its 100th store in China, since its entry into the Chinese market in 1996, in the presence of secretary Carlos Guitierrez from US Department of Commerce and Vice minister Jian Zengwei from China's ministry of commerce. Coinciding with the celebrations in Beijing, celebrations elsewhere marked the opening of the new Wal-Mart super-center in Loudi in Hunan province. This store represents Wal-Mart's inroads into smaller Chinese towns and is one of the 23 new Wal-Marts opened in China just last year. This number may pale in comparison to more than 4000 stores which Wal-Mart meticulously operates in US, with over 2800 more in Argentina, Brazil, Canada, China, Costa Rica, El Salvador, Guatemala, Honduras, Japan, Mexico, Nicaragua, Puerto Rico and the United Kingdom. But this represents an important milestone in the nature of the relationship between China and Wal-Mart. China, which was always a low-cost sourcing destination for Wal-Mart is now being viewed as the biggest opportunity for Wal-Mart to repeat what it did in US. China has the seventh largest retail market in the world and is expected to climb to number five, just behind Germany and ahead of France by 2010. The retail market in China grew by 13 per cent in the second half of 2007 over a base of USD 650 billion.

'The secret of successful retailing is to give your customers what they want,' Sam Walton, the founder of Wal-Mart, wrote in his autobiography. 'And really, if you think about it from the point of view of the customer, you want everything: a wide assortment of good quality merchandise; the lowest possible prices; guaranteed satisfaction with what you buy; friendly, knowledgeable service; convenient hours; free parking; a pleasant shopping experience.'

Today, Wal-Mart is a global company with more than 1.9 million associates worldwide and more than 7000 stores and wholesale clubs across 14 markets. Wal-Mart clocked USD 348 billion as revenue in FY2007 and recorded sales of more than USD 90 billion in Q3 of FY2008. Wal-Mart serves more than 180 million customers weekly. Wal-Mart is not only one of the largest private employers in the US, but also in Mexico and Canada.

Next year Wal-Mart expects to add 48 to 49 million square feet globally, which is an increase of 6 per cent in FY2008 over FY2007. During each of the following two fiscal years, Wal-Mart expects to increase square footage between 48 million and 52 million square feet, an increase of 5 to 6 per cent. To put this in perspective, in FY2005, India had a mere 21.5 million square feet of space in malls across the country which, some reports state has increased to 50 million square feet by end of 2007.

Wal-Mart alone is responsible for around 10 per cent of US trade deficit with China. Seventy per cent of the products sold on Wal-Mart's shelves is made in China. Wal-Mart has moved its global sourcing headquarters to Shenzhen, a city transformed from a sleepy fishing marshland into a world class role model city in just over a decade. Ten years ago Shenzhen's main port did not exist and today it is on verge of becoming the third busiest port in the world. Of the Wal-Mart's more than 6500 global suppliers, experts estimate that as many as 80 per cent is based in China. And this figure can go up significantly if you include the suppliers of Wal-Mart suppliers based outside China. If Wal-Mart was a country, it would figure among the top ten trading partners for China.

Wal-Mart has reversed a century old tradition that the retailer depends on the manufacturer. Now the retailer is in the driving seat and can easily drive its manufacturer or supplier out of business at the drop of a hat if it cannot compete on cost and quality with thousands of global manufacturers dying to be on the suppliers list of the largest retailer in the world called Wal-Mart. Wal-Mart deliberately keeps its vendor list short so that it can have more control over its operations and cost structure. It is estimated that Wal-Mart may have 60 per cent of the world's largest factories churning out products which would be sold on Wal-Mart's shelves.

China is the largest exporter to the US in virtually all consumer goods categories and Wal-Mart is the leading retailer of consumer goods in US. So uncanny and strong is the mutual dependency between China and Wal-Mart that it has been called the 'Ultimate Joint Venture' by some. Wal-Mart's dramatic rise in overseas production and sourcing was a result of landmark changes in public and global trade policies supported by bipartisan consensus for the last twenty five years. Wal-Mart has reached such a level of sophistication in its international sourcing that it is always one step ahead of its competitors in either new product development or in sourcing the same product for a nickel less and thereby doing justice to its motto of 'everyday low prices'. The impact of the rise of Wal-Mart in US on other US-based retailers and manufacturers bears striking resemblance to the impact of rise of China as a manufacturing force on other Asian manufacturing-exporting countries. A few went out of business and others had to find a way to survive within the realms of the new eco-system. The remaining had to be contented with focus on niche products at the cost of growth.

While partnering each other through this economic juggernaut, both have also been the target of backlashes on the question of cost of growth and practices employed to reach this end state. Many social groups have been active in propaganda of anti-Wal-Mart sentiments in the society. Wal-Mart has been accused of being responsible for thousands of job losses in US manufacturing, paying low salary to its employees, and providing inadequate healthcare and other benefits. It has been questioned for not paying enough attention to child labor violation by its low cost suppliers, discriminating against women and not doing enough for the environment. Similarly China has been on the receiving end on issues ranging from artificially suppressing its currency to be export competitive, and human rights violation by stripping peasants of their land and thereby livelihood without adequate compensation to create large export processing zones, to having a single minded focus on growth at the expense of environment and other adverse socio-economic consequences.

4

A Comparative Study of State Response to the Educational Needs of Informal Settlers in Indian and Chinese Cities

AMITA BHIDE AND YANG YAO

Most people in the world perceive democracy and authoritarianism to be two polar ends of state governance. However, reality is far more complex and has many more continuities than is commonly understood. Accountability of a government can best be understood through peoples' experiences, especially of those who challenge the straitjackets of the system—planned cities, urban–rural dichotomy of citizenry—through their movement and settlement patterns. Informal settlers in cities like China and India represent one such group. While migrating to the city and making it their home and workplace, they posit a challenge to the system. The responses of the state to their needs, therefore, have the potential to provide an understanding of the way the state works in reality.

This chapter is based on intensive fieldwork on the government's educational provisions to informal settlements in Mumbai (India), and to migrant communities in Rui'an (China). Education is the most important vehicle for marginalized families to escape from poverty and climb up the social ladder. Educational provisions thus are a test of the government's accountability to the people. The institutional settings are very different in India and China. In India, the Constitution places the right to free movement as one of the fundamental rights that people should have. Therefore, it is within the local governments' mandate to accommodate the needs of migrants and to provide them basic services. In other words, it is a *procedural* requirement placed on the government. In China, the right to free movement is blurred by the household registration or hukou system although the Constitution pledges equal rights to every citizen. Because of the hukou system, recipient cities are not obliged to provide any service to migrants; hence, decisions to provide education to migrant children are driven not by law but by the government's desire to be seen to be performing well.

The provision of education to migrants in both countries depends on the legitimacy of the government. In India, legitimacy of the government comes from preset procedures regarding elections, laws and other regulations placed on the government. This is *procedure-based legitimacy*. In China, legitimacy of the government comes from its ability to continuously deliver development outcomes to the population. This is *performance-based legitimacy*. Neither kind of legitimacy automatically leads to accountability. Procedure-based legitimacy may produce a passive government, and performance-based legitimacy may produce a selective government, that is, a government that caters to the demands of those who contribute to its performance in a direct way. Our aim is to find hints for a set of institutional arrangements from which a procedure-based performing government could emerge.

The chapter is organized as follows. The two initial sections provide background information on India and China's educational systems, respectively, and elaborate on the role of the government in the system. This is followed by case studies in Mumbai and Rui'an, respectively. The key findings from the fieldwork are summarized and explanations provided for them. These findings are used to elaborate our formulation of the two kinds of legitimacy. The last section concludes the chapter by way of pointing out possible routes to a procedure-based performing government.

INFORMAL SETTLEMENTS AND EDUCATIONAL PROVISION IN INDIA

Informal Settlements and Policy Responses in India

In India, slums are an inescapable part of the urban scenario. Almost 42.6 million people live in slums and constitute 15 per cent of India's urban population (GoI 2001). The rate of urbanization in India is about 4 per cent while the rate of increase in slum population is 6 per cent. In more urbanized states such as Maharashtra and Tamil Nadu, the trend of slum formation is as high as 20–5 per cent (GoI 2001).

Slums began to appear in India around the World War II when there was a tremendous housing crisis (Swaminathan and Goyal 2006). They became a feature of major cities in India in the post-independence period but the overall proportion of people in slums was less than 10 per cent. Till the 1970s, slums were generally seen as aberrations in the overall, planning and governance and were sought to be cleared and replaced with better housing. The current strategy landscape, as indicated by the National Slum Policy, however, declares: 'Slums are an integral part of the urban fabric'. This complete reversal of the policy approach is, no doubt, a product of the scale of the issue and the impending crisis.

The very concept of a 'slum' is crucial in this regard. The earliest conceptions of slums are those from the 1950s, and coincide with the adoption of a clearance approach.

A slum may be described as a chaotically occupied, unsystematically developed and generally neglected area which is over-populated and overcrowded with ... neglected structures. The area has insufficient communications, indifferent sanitary arrangements, and inadequate amenities for the maintenance of physical and social health ... of human beings and the community. There is a general absence of social services and welfare agencies to deal with the major social problems of persons and families ... who are victims of biological, psychological and social consequences of the physical and social environment. (Seminar on Slum Clearance May, 1957)

The continuities and differences between this and the more recent definitions of slums are noteworthy. The 2001 Census of India which enumerated slums as a distinct habitat adopts an administrative approach to classifying slums. Thus slums are areas which are: (a) declared as slums by governments (b) newly notified areas and (c) possess 60-70 households or 300 people living in '*kuccha*' structures, in unsafe, substandard habitats devoid of human values.

The Draft National Slum Policy (2002) adopts an 'inclusive' approach to defining slums which can comprise 'all under-serviced settlements', be they unauthorized developments or villages within urban areas in the periphery. Such an inclusive approach, based on an examination of the standard of housing stock and services, disregards variables in emergence of locality, and the contribution of residents to state treasuries. It expresses the reality of Indian cities where deteriorating housing and infrastructure are no longer limited to a few areas but are more diffused.

It is to be noted, however, that the above-mentioned conceptions of slums are largely determined by 'outsiders'. They are based on criteria which can be rectified through the provision of better services and housing. Viewed in this manner, the distinctive feature of slums as opposed to regular neighbourhoods in cities is their inception as unauthorized, spontaneous settlements. They represent the only way for the poor to gain a foothold in cities.

The policy discourse on slums is, however, far removed from the above perspective. It has, in retrospect, been an ongoing flux between the 'dual-city' and 'slumming-city' perspectives.

The dual-city perspective (to borrow terminology used by M.N. Buch) is one that perceives slums as an unintended part of the city and hence, to be tolerated and serviced to some extent. In the Indian context, this perspective took root in the 1970s in the form of Environmental Improvement of Urban Slums (EIUS) Programme. It is also followed in a host of other initiatives for slum upgradation, improvement of sanitation as well as the norms for the Member of Parliament /Legislative Assembly/Corporator Local Area Development Schemes. The major facets of this approach are:

1. Tolerance of slums as settlements of the poor: Slums are seen as problems or challenges but there is a simultaneous recognition that these are the only option available to the poor. Typically, most programs designed under this approach grant recognition to some slum settlements based on certain criteria.
2. A dateline approach: This is a result of the above dilemmatic approach to existence of slums and slum dwellers on the basis of their existence in records such as voters' lists or slum surveys at a particular base year. In Mumbai, the cut-off date was 1 January 1995. The date line served multiple purposes. First, it offered the right to slum dwellers to be in the city prior to the cut-off date. Second, it perpetuated a system of patron-based, popular politics dependent on the local elected representatives attempting to cultivate vote banks. It also served as a tool of manageability for urban administrators. The emergence of middle class activism in cities is largely attributed to being a reaction to this approach.
3. Provision of basic services, albeit with dual standards: The tolerance of slums is expressed through a provision of basic services such as water, electricity, toilets, drains, internal roads and so on. The EIUS in 1976 was based on a ratio of 1 toilet seat per 100 families but the current ratio is 1 toilet seat per 50 persons. The earlier supply-led approach is increasingly giving way to a demand-led approach with recognition of community contribution towards inception and upkeep of services. However, the standard of services continues to be inferior to the official citizenry. For example, the current norm for water supply to residential areas in Mumbai is 120 litres per capita per day; for slums, it is 80 litres per capita per day. There are also tremendous gaps between official norms and the actual situation on ground.

To conclude, the dual-city perspective accepts the existence of slums as a part of the urban landscape and suggests ways to improve the conditions. Some of the most progressive projects emerging from this perspective are the Slum Upgradation Program which improved services and leased out land to cooperative societies of slum dwellers and the Slum Networking Program (SNP) experiments in a few cities which proposed an integrated package of basic services with tenure, led by demands of local communities. The very strength of the dual-city perspective that is, its acceptance of 'slum' as a housing option of the poor often threatens to split at the seams due to the duality it perpetuates. Verma (2002) analyses the experience of the SNP in Indore, and its inability to check the residents' vulnerability to environmental crises and evictions. Geeta Dewan

Verma suggests that this acceptance of duality is, in fact, a perpetuation of the inequity promoted by international funding agencies in alliance with NGOs and certain arms of the government.

The slumming-city perspective based on a critique of the dual-city approach looks at the master plan as a tool to effectively integrate all segments of urban society, including the poor. It strongly advocates the creation of adequate spaces for the poor in the integrated, long-term vision of the city; so that services and entitlements are equitable in nature (Verma 2002). In Indore, for example, a few slum settlements were integrated into the master plan of the city, thereby ensuring permanent tenure for the residents and establishing their equal rights to amenities as citizens. This has subsequently been attempted in a few other Indian cities.

There are few takers for the Master Plan Approach, in spite of its compelling arguments. The reasons for this emerge from multiple perspectives: one obvious reason, of course, as Verma suggests is the real-politik of funding—NGOs on the one hand and the vote bank politics on another. Second, the experience of urban planning in India has not been accommodative of the poor (Banerjee 2002). Spaces for the poor which exist as reservations for 'housing the dishoused' are far less in proportion to need and even those are often appropriated by others (Fernandez 1993). The poor, are therefore, compelled to 'encroach' on lands that are either considered unfit for habitation, or are low priority for development (Panwalkar 1992). Often, the ground for eviction is laid when these low priority lands are developed through the efforts of residents and the potential land value of the region is enhanced. (YUVA 2003). Moreover, the greatest undermining of planning is occurring today because it is being increasingly hijacked by corporate interests (Benjamin 2000). The critical question is whether planning can offer solace to the poor whose foothold in the city is precarious, based on an unplanned settlement. The land that they hold coupled with their votes represents their sole negotiating power.

In some ways the tussle between the Master Plan Approach and tolerance is a clash between the ideal and the practical, the desirable and the 'do'able. Tolerance, practised in a patchy way, can unleash several problems. Tolerance of slums has paved the way for tolerance of encroachments by upper classes, the crumbling of governance, and proliferation of narrow-interest politics—a phenomenon that Verma describes as 'slumming India'. Delhi, Ulhasnagar and several other cities epitomize this condition.

The necessity for integrative, planned actions has never been felt more, even from the point of view of the poor. The Jawaharlal Nehru National Urban Renewal Mission (JNNURM) mandates a budgeted provision of basic services and housing development for slum dwellers. Provisioning for the urban poor is also an integral part of other sectoral programs such as health and sanitation.

A very real question pertains to how the informal settlers experience the state in their everyday lives. Does a democratic system ensure responsive governance? Does it generate services that are appropriate to the needs of people? Are its functionaries accountable to the citizens? What kind of goals does this system set for itself and how are these achieved? The answers to these questions constitute some of the on-ground experiences of the state that matter to people and it is these that are sought to be compared with the experiences in Chinese cities.

Educating Children in Slums

In India, free and compulsory education of all children up to 14 years is a Constitutional mandate. Elementary education is a subject on the concurrent list, that is, a responsibility shared by the central and state governments. While these two tiers act as policymakers and financiers of education, urban local bodies contribute as providers of education and also regulators of the private sector (in case of elementary education).

The role of urban local bodies as providers of elementary education is one that dates back to the colonial rule. Thus, primary education is a subject under the Mumbai Municipal Corporation Act 1888. It was envisaged as a public school system till the 1960s when the grant-in-code was established by the state government, recognizing the contribution of the private sector in education.

While urban local bodies remain a significant provider of education, the private sector has emerged as a major player. In Mumbai, for example, while 280 (21.9 per cent) primary schools are run by the Municipal Corporation, the rest are privately operated. This proportion is even higher at the secondary level. More importantly, the municipal system of education has emerged as the dominant option of educating urban poor children.

In general, urban areas score much better than rural areas in terms of access to educational facilities. According to the PROBE report (1999), the gross enrolment ratio (GER) at the primary level is 100 in urban areas while it is 81 in rural areas; at standard V to VII, it stands at 83 and 59, respectively. Literacy is seen to have a positive correlation with the level of urbanization. However, these aggregate indicators often disguise the nature and level of disparities vis-à-vis education. These disparities are reflected in levels of literacy, participation in schooling in poor pockets and in the educational profiles of slum areas and vulnerable groups.

The municipal education system in Mumbai is among the better ones in terms of infrastructure, as compared to that of several private schools. Over 90 per cent schools have their own building, drinking water, separate toilets for boys and girls, and playgrounds. The student–teacher ratio for primary levels is 53.38 students per teacher and compares well with that in private schools (50.5 students per teacher). Yet the dropout rate (proportion of children who leave schooling halfway) for standard I is 7.19 per cent and increases to about 63 per cent by standard VII.

Several studies have attempted to understand the causes of such wastage. A prime set of causes pertains to migration and household poverty. A 2002 study by Deshmukh Ranadive concludes that children's participation in schooling is affected by cost-benefit analysis by parents (Deshmukh 2002). If the costs concomitant to schooling are high and the benefits accrued after 8–10 years of education are perceived to have little value, the child is likely to be withdrawn from school. A study identifies parents' education and belonging to a woman-headed household as key factors affecting poor children's ability to attend school. Gender differentials also contribute significantly to low educational access and participation (Ramachandran 2003).

The experience of several NGOs suggests that the number of children in high-risk situations (working children, children on streets and in jails, children of sex workers, children in denotified tribes) is on the rise in urban areas. These children constitute the majority of the out-of-school children. The number of out-of-school children in the age group 3–14 has been estimated to be about 2,00,000 in Kolkata and 1,00,000 in Delhi (Ramachandran 2003).

The nature of the situation on ground has been captured very well in a survey by PRATHAM (2003) in Mumbai. In non-slum areas, practically all children attend pre-school and go on to primary school. In settled slums too, the demand for education is high. Less than 10 per cent of the children were out of school in these areas. Chronically backward pockets vis-à-vis education are found in specific areas and population groups: pavement dwellers, residents of unauthorized colonies, construction workers, and tribes. The percentage of out-of-school children in these groups is as high as 40 per cent, as estimated in 1998.

It is important to create a more flexible educational strategy that responds to the specific realities of each vulnerable group. Several civil society organizations are engaged in such efforts and the state has come out in support of such a strategy through the multi-pronged approach of the *Sarva Shiksha Abhiyan* (Campaign for Universalization of Education).

Systemic Determinants of Elementary Education

The focus on creating physical access to schools diverts attention from the systemic issues that lead to wastage in already existing schools. The urban scenario in India is one where physical access to a school is not a critical issue. There is a primary school available to 95 per cent children within a distance of 1 km. The correlation of percentage of urban population with the presence of a middle/high school was positive till the 1971 Census. However, since 1981 (-0.25) to the 2001 Census (-0.27) the correlation has been negative. This indicates that the growth of urban population has led to increased pressure on the basic amenities of education. Shortage of school seats thus, remains an issue within urban areas. In Delhi, for example, as per Development Plan norms, a primary school should be available for every 2500 population thus necessitating about 2976 schools to provide for the educational needs of the current population. However, there are only 2412 schools (Hazard Center 2000). In Mumbai too, it is estimated that the current availability of schools is 1 per 5000 population. The issue of access is thus, not entirely straightforward. The available schools are often characterized by overcrowding. The physical location of schools across busy roads and highways and their absence in interiors of slums also makes access difficult. Leaking roofs, broken windows, unclean toilets are common observations in the schools that exist.

Added to this is the issue of low achievement levels. Estimations of standard III and IV students who do not possess the numeric or literacy levels expected of their age ranges from 18 to 33 per cent. As noted by educationist Vimala Ramachandran: 'Physical access is just one dimension. The backward and forward linkages that create a meaningful environment where every child not only goes to school but also benefits from schooling are critical' (Ramachandran 2003). Disregard for these linkages results in irregular attendance or even dropping out.

Often the assumption is that it is the lack of resources that makes municipal schooling so unattractive. Current statistics reveal that while private unaided schools spend about Rs 225 per child per month, municipal schools spend Rs 578.5 per child per month (Kabeer, Subrahmanian, and Nambissan 2005). Why is the quality of education so poor then?

The context of poverty and its facets have a critical role in creating an environment where education is *disincentivized*. The slum child sees little relevance of the curriculum in day-to-day life. The presence of demoralized youngsters who may have completed elementary education or dropped-out and who are unemployed or underemployed creates a vacuum of identifiable role models and leads to a general disinterest towards formal education.

Investment in meaningful education thus has to be accompanied by an investment to improve this environment. Is the system (the teachers, administrators, peoples' representatives, civil society organizations) equipped to deal with these challenges? How do these actors interface, what kind of a system do they produce, and what changes do they seek? These questions are explored in the case study.

MIGRATION AND EDUCATIONAL PROVISION IN CHINA

Migration Policies

Though China launched economic reforms in 1978, led by rural reform that dismantled the commune system, restrictions over rural–urban migration were prevalent. At a personal level, urban residents did not want to share the high-quality life with their rural counterparts, while at the governmental level, local governments worried about additional costs for infrastructure demanded by a non-stop influx of rural population (Zhao 1999). Nevertheless, the expansion of the non-State sector and the export sector continued to draw migrants into cities, especially after 1992 when the second wave of economic reforms started. This subsection provides a brief introduction to the migration policies implemented by the Chinese government since the 1950s.

Rural–urban segregation in China was strictly instituted following the famine in 1959-61. Policymakers were so concerned about the shortage of food in urban areas (Wu 1994; Zhao 1999) that they restricted the mobility of the population in the 1960s. The methods included creating a high opportunity cost for migration by tying income to participation in collective farm work, and establishing the so-called hukou system (Zhao 1999). The government tied the farmers to the land because of the continuous need for cheap agricultural products for the industrial sector to achieve the goal of a capital-intensive industry.

From the introduction of the hukou system till the early 1980s, specific principles were developed to guide internal migration: rural to urban permanent migration was strictly controlled and usually prohibited; movement from towns to cities and from small to big cities was limited; and movement from large to small towns or from urban to rural locations was encouraged (Goldstein and Goldstein 1985). A modification of migration policies was carried out during the mid-1980s, following the small town strategy advocated by advisors like Fei Xiaotong (Fei 1985). Rural residents were permitted to 'leave the land but not the village' (*litu bu lixiang*) and 'enter the factory but not the city' (*jinchang bu jincheng*) (Wong and Huen 1998).

The year 1985 witnessed the launch of new initiatives. New regulations were promulgated in July that specified that all migrants over the age of 16 who move to and stay in an urban area for longer than six months needed to apply for a 'temporary residence permit' (*zanzhuzheng*), and people conducting business and staying for a long time in a given city should get a 'living away from home permit' (*jizhuzheng*) (Wong and Huen 1998: 976). Rural residents were now allowed to live away from their native cities, and the movement of floating population was finally legalized. However, migrants with such permits were granted neither food rations nor housing allocation, and their children could not enter urban schools. Local governments still failed to meet the basic needs of migrants in urban areas, which explained the unpopularity of these permits. Not many people actually migrated as a result. With the approval of the Regulations on Resident Identity Card in September 1985, rural residents got their own personal identity documents for the first time, instead of being registered collectively. Even so, migrants to cities and towns still faced unequal treatment.

Probably due to such a strong appeal of bonafide urban residency from huge numbers of migrants, local officials in many cities eventually found a way to meet the demand. In 1988, local governments of Lai'an and Quanjiao counties of Anhui province initiated the practice of selling urban hukou by charging migrants a certain fee (Wong and Huen 1998). By 1992, almost all provinces had launched similar schemes, with the price varying from a few thousand to tens of thousand yuan (Ibid). Within that period, migration was becoming such a significant social phenomenon that the government felt it necessary to interfere with and restrict migration (Huang and Pieke 2003). Till 2000, the central government encouraged rural-urban migration to some extent, but post-1995 many local governments in major cities strengthened controls on migration to tackle lay-offs and unemployment in urban areas (Ibid).

Migrants from rural to urban areas were partly, if not completely, denied equal rights for job hunting, housing, children's schooling, social security and so on because they were not registered urban citizens. Local governments in major cities were originally justified in providing neither housing nor schooling for migrants (though they contributed to the economy of destination cities by working and taxation), simply because local governments' responsibilities were supposedly restricted to their registered citizens. Zhao (1999: 782, n. 30) discusses an example of Beijing in the mid-1990s:

Beijing People's Government stipulates that any institution or person leasing housing to non-Beijing residents must obtain a house-leasing certificate from the district or county government and renew the certificate annually. The house ... must be privately owned and must be certified by the police bureau for meeting safety standards. An affidavit must be filed with the police bureau and family-planning agency in which the owner of the dwelling agrees to be responsible for preventing any crimes that may be committed in the house or apartment as well as for above-quota births, and they must pay a fee equivalent to 2% of the annual rent'.[1]

This regulation applies even today. Therefore, the hukou system not only serves to restrict population mobility—especially from rural to urban areas—but also provides an excuse for deprivation of migrants' rights as compared to urban residents.

In the heyday of persecution, people on the streets who looked like migrants were frequently stopped by police patrols in cities for checking of identity cards and temporary residence permits. If the migrants failed to produce these on the spot, police would take them into custody immediately, sometimes beat them up, and then send them back to their hometowns. This conflict between migrants and urban police in China came to a climax in 2003 when Sun Zhigang was beaten to death in Guangzhou. Sun, a 27-year-old college graduate, was mistaken for an undocumented migrant because he failed to show his temporary residence permit. He was taken into custody and beaten to death. This incident led to widespread protests all over China which ultimately led the government to abolish the Regulation on the Custody and Deportation of the Urban Homeless and Beggars on 1 August 2003 (Zhao 2005: 289, n. 3). Since then, government policies towards migrants have become more tolerant.

Government Policies Towards Migrant Children in China

In the past, migrant children were denied entrance into urban schools, even for basic education. Since household registration connects almost all basic rights of people, including school enrolment, with resident status, schooling policies gradually evolved along with the reform of hukou system. In spite of the experiments of selling urban hukou, no actual reform measures were taken until the mid-1990s.

Then, a unique type of *lanyin hukou* (blue chop household registration[2]) came into effect in Shanghai and Shenzhen in 1993 and 1995, respectively (Wong and Huen 1998). It represents an intermediate status between a rural hukou and a permanent urban hukou. Children with a lanyin hukou were eligible for nine-year basic education in Shanghai, though they had to pay much higher tuition fees than local children if they wished to pursue education after graduating from junior high schools. Specifically, before June 1996, migrant children had to return to their places of origin for higher education since they were denied entrance into universities in Shanghai. Since then, senior high school graduates are allowed to take the university entrance examination in Shanghai though they are still barred from municipal funded universities. The denial of access to higher education in destination cities exerts a profound impact on migrant children. Since high school education, or even basic education, varies in content as well as style of examination between provinces—especially between eastern provinces and those in the middle or west— the denial of the right to take the university entrance examination in destination cities usually offsets the merits of better senior/high school education there. Local governments receive no funding from the

---

[1] See Beijing People's Government, *Beijingshi waidi lai jing renyuan zulin fangwu zhian guanli guiding* [Regulations on house leasing to non-Beijing residents], 1995.

[2] Sometimes translated as 'blue stamp household registration' in the literature.

central government for the schooling of migrant children. Hence, these children are expected to pay a prohibitive tuition fee in senior high schools in destination cities which drives them back to their places of origin.

Educational entitlements that came along with lanyin hukou in Shenzhen were only slightly different from those in Shanghai. Children under the age of 16, with both parents holding *lanyin* status, enjoyed the same right to education as permanent urban residents, though this right excluded education above technical school, namely higher education in universities. Also, if only one parent was a lanyin hukou holder, the children within the same age limit could register for lanyin status in accordance with the state policy of hukou transfer (Ibid).

It seems that lanyin hukou had great merits but only 261 such applications were approved in Shanghai in the year when it was started (Wong and Huen 1998). The reason was simple; the cost of application was too high. Consider one common condition under which people could apply for such a hukou in both cities. In Shanghai, 'people who buy a domestic-sale commercial flat for a minimum of 400,000 yuan measuring 80 sq. m. are qualified for applying for a blue chop hukou' (Ibid: 981), while in Shenzhen, there was a particular category of so-called 'flat-purchase blue chop household registration (*goufang lanyin hukou*)' (Ibid: 984). It is apparent that this type of lanyin hukou is essentially for the rich and skilled elite and targets the upper class which is a very small proportion of the migrating population. This device is biased against the poorer and less educated/ unskilled majority of rural migrants who are originally attracted to cities because of the existing wage differentials. Although lanyin hukou helped to break the strict segregation of the traditional hukou system, there is still a need for genuine permanent urban residence for migrants.

The central government has been reforming the hukou system. By March 2007, twelve provinces, autonomous regions or municipalities, including Hebei, Liaoning, Jiangsu, Zhejiang, Fujian, Shandong, Hubei, Hunan, Guangxi, Chongqing, Sichuan and Shaanxi (excluding Beijing and Shanghai), abolished the distinction between rural and non-rural hukou and granted these two groups the same status of resident hukou. Regarding the education of migrant children, after many changes in policies, the State Council's Suggestions on Carrying on Efforts of Compulsory Education of Migrant Children in Urban Areas (*Guanyu jinyibu zuohao jincheng wugong jiuye nongmin zinv yiwu jiaoyu gongzuo de yijian*) were issued in September 2003. The main focus of the circular is maintaining the same standard of tuition fees for all students, whether or not they possess an urban hukou.

An important reform measure to provide better access to basic education for migrant children involves complete elimination, or at least partial reduction, of school fees. It is well-known that migrant children have to pay a 'temporary schooling fee' (*jiedufei*) because they lack urban hukou. This is charged to offset part of the financial responsibility of local governments in destination cities towards educating migrants.[3] In Zhejiang province, for instance, jiedufei varies from an average of 300 yuan per semester for primary schools to 600 yuan per semester for junior high schools. This severely aggravates the economic burden of migrants. The jiedufei in Zhejiang might be regarded as typical; for instance, Shandong province also followed a criterion of 300 yuan per semester for primary schools and 500 yuan per semester for junior high schools before some of its cities gradually abandoned jiedufei. Since 2003, following the State Council Circular, some provinces,

---

[3] It is noteworthy that jiedufei does not apply only to migrant students. Any student who attends a school outside his/her own school district is charged. In fact, jiedufei has become the most important source of income for many good schools because it is very high. Migrant students pay jiedufei because they do not have local hukou and thus are automatically regarded as attending schools outside their own school districts.

TABLE 1: ELIMINATION OF JIEDUFEI FOR MIGRANT CHILDREN IN SELECTED PROVINCES/MUNICPALITIES

(UNIT: *YUAN*)

Provinces / Municipalities	Cities / Districts	Status	Time	No. of primary schools	No. of junior high schools
Beijing		Required	Pre- Sept. 2002	500	1000
		Reduced	Sept. 2002	200	500
		Eliminated	Apr. 2004		
Shanxi	Taiyuan	Eliminated	2004 Fall		
Liaoning	Shenyang: Heping district	Eliminated	2004 Fall		
Jilin	Changchun	Eliminated	2004 Fall		
Jiangsu	All	Eliminated	2004 Fall		
Zhejiang	All	Required		300	600
Fujian	Xiamen	Required		480	780
	All	Reduced			
Shandong	Jinan	Eliminated	2004 Fall		
	Weihai	Eliminated	2004 Fall		
	Qingdao	Eliminated	2004 Fall		
	Others	Required		300	500
Henan	All	Eliminated	2004 Fall		
Hubei	Yichang	Eliminated	2004 Fall		
	Wuhan: Hanyang dist.	Eliminated	Sept. 2005		
	Xiangfan	Eliminated	Sept. 2006		
Hunan	Xiangtan	Eliminated	2004 Fall		
Guangdong	Shenzhen	Required		400	700-900
Sichuan	Changdu: Jinniu dist.	Eliminated	2004 Fall		
	All	Eliminated	Nov. 2006		
Yunnan	Kunming	Eliminated	2004 Fall		
Shaanxi	All	Eliminated	2004 Fall		

Sources: Various provincial and municipal government announcements.

major cities and certain districts of metropolises have gradually eliminated jiedufei. They charge the migrant children the same tuition fees as local children. For example, Beijing lowered jiedufei from 500 yuan to 200 yuan for primary schools and 1000 to 500 for junior high schools in September 2002, and abandoned it in April 2004 (Table 1). What is more, the municipal government decided to provide funding for schools according to the actual number of registered students (including migrant students), instead of only students with local hukou. Provinces including Jiangsu, Henan, Shaanxi, major cities including Changchun of Jilin, Taiyuan of Shanxi, Kunming of Yunnan, Xiangtan of Hunan, Jinan, Weihai and Qingdao of Shandong, Yichang of Hubei, and urban districts such as Heping district in Shenyang of Liaoning, and Jinniu district in Chengdu of Sichuan all announced the abolition of jiedufei for basic education of migrant children before 2004. Hanyang district in Wuhan of Hubei and Xiangfan of Hubei abolished jiedufei in September 2005 while Sichuan province did the same in November 2006. It should be noted that some other cities lowered jiedufei, but did not totally abandon it, such as Xiamen of Fujian declared a reduction of about 960 to 1,560 yuan in total fees for migrant children's basic education in primary and junior high schools. Nevertheless, there are some cities, as in Fujian, especially those with huge numbers of migrants, which still ask schools to collect jiedufei from migrant children, and even increase the amount. In 2004, there was a big debate in Shenzhen of Guangdong on whether jiedufei, which was 400 yuan for primary schools and 700–900 yuan for junior high schools, should be abandoned. However, Shenzhen did not abandon jiedufei, due to financial problems and an overwhelmingly large number of migrant children in the city.

Also, the critical requirement for producing various certificates, before migrant children could be admitted into urban schools has been relaxed. In the past, schools demanded both parents' identity cards, temporary resident permits (*zanzhuzheng*), working contracts longer than at least six months, certificate of transfer issued by the Bureau of Education from the place of origin, and sometimes children's cards of immunity. Though some destination cities adhere to these conventional requirements, since 2003, schools in cities such as Rui'an of Zhejiang have started accepting certificates of any form which attest the child's migrant identity.

In 2001, Zhengzhou initiated a reform of hukou system and a majority of rural residents who wished to migrate into the city were given the approval, together with their children, upon fulfilling conditions such as purchasing an apartment measuring 56 sq. m. or more. Since 2005, in Guangdong, children whose parents possess residence permits for three years can directly participate in the national entrance examination for universities. Compared to the introduction of lanyin hukou in the mid-1990s, reforms in later years have successfully led to a decline in conditions demanded from migrants and the hukou system has been made more relaxed. These measures have facilitated more convenient access for migrant children to urban schooling, which is better than rural education, thus attracting surprisingly large rural population into cities.

Despite these encouraging changes, one has to realize that the policies actually implemented vary from province to province and even from county to county. Also, migrant children's education is still crippled because of the ultimate restriction that they have to go back to their home province to take the university entrance exam. Since every province has a fixed quota for high school students to go to university, a nationally coordinated policy is needed to solve the problem.

THE MUMBAI CASE STUDY

Mumbai, the financial capital of India, mirrors several contradictions characterizing the Indian urban landscape. Prime among these is the co-existence of elite settlements with slums. Slums comprise over 60 per cent of the current population of the city. They are located on public as well as private lands comprising a little over 7 per cent of the land mass. Economic pressures bring migrants to Mumbai daily from different states (current estimates are about 400 immigrants per day). Given the fact that the supply of public housing has been almost non-existent for the past decade and the private sector is engaged in value-added construction, the entire supply of housing to the low income segments operates through informal markets (Mumbai Metropolitan Region Development Authority or MMRDA 1995).

Dharavi, located in the central part of Mumbai, is one of its oldest and largest slum settlements. Its current population is around 3,759,660. It houses six municipal constituencies and forms a major population block of one state assembly (akin to a province in China) constituency. The 85 Nagars (townships) in Dharavi comprise of highly diverse population groups in terms of caste, ethnicity and economic profiles. Thus, Kumbharwada (potter settlements), Koliwada (fisherfolk settlements) have village-like traits of large joint family housing cum work units, open mixed use spaces while others like Social Nagar and Kunchikorwe Nagar are dominated by certain ethnic groups. Areas like Transit Camp are cosmopolitan and highly commercial.

The lack of basic infrastructure in Dharavi is indicated by the fact that of a total area of 1282 hectares (ha), 1.90 ha is open space, 1.4 ha is taken for institutional space (colleges, hospitals and so on) and 2.5 ha is devoted to public amenities such as toilets, community halls and so on. Settlement density is very high, that is, approximately 4000 persons per acre and most tenements are 150 square feet in size.

Dharavi is an economic hub, providing the production base for several industries—leather, readymade garments, readymade foods—besides housing the processing of certain goods, for example, embroidery and production of low income market commodities like pots and toys so on. A large number of these industries operates from home-based units. Estimate of the economic output from Dharavi is around Rs 4000 crore annually.

The number of children of school-going age in Dharavi is about 1,500,000. There are five municipal schools, all having units that teach in 5-6 different mediums of instruction. Altogether, these schools cater to 240,000 children. A significant number of children attend grant-in-aid schools located outside Dharavi. The intake capacity of these schools has remained static for the last ten years. The shortfall has been filled by the emergence of private, unaided schools in Dharavi both recognized and unrecognized. A study of one of the schools, Dharavi Transit Camp Municipal School, reveals several contradictions in terms of access to quality elementary education (author's research).

The Transit Camp School houses six schools providing instruction to 40,000 children in six different languages. It has standard I to VII. Maximum enrolment is in the English medium school (1270 children) and the minimum is in the Telugu School (179 children). According to the prevalent norm of a student–teacher ratio of 40:1, there should be about 100 teachers in the school but the current number is 69. An analysis of medium of instruction indicates that the maximum shortage is in the English medium school (15 teachers against an expected number of about 30) while the Marathi school (Marathi is the local regional language and the official language of Mumbai corporations) has excess teachers (21 against the required 14-15). These variations indicate that the distortions in teacher-student ratios are even greater than those seen in averages.

The infrastructure is fairly good. Classrooms are spacious, well-ventilated and well lit. There is a good playground and drinking water available. However, there are only 15 toilet seats in working condition in the school. Several of the classrooms do not have adequate seating arrangements and children have to sit on the floor. There are four non-aided, recognized schools operating from the premises of the Transit Camp School; they utilize rooms rented out by the Corporation. There are two other private, unaided schools in the vicinity of the Municipal School. The private schools began operations from the premises in the mid-1990s. They educate about 3000 children. Two of the schools run English medium classes from kindergarten to standard IV, while the other two are English–Urdu schools at the secondary level. These schools charge fees ranging from Rs 70—Rs 100 per month. The children have to bear the expenses of uniform, teaching materials and so on.

An interaction with several parents from Dharavi revealed some interesting findings. Most parents consider the municipal schools as a last resort as education provided here is inferior in quality. The advantages of private schools over the municipal schools are: continuity of education from kindergarten to standard X, English as the medium of instruction, more attention paid by teachers and the management. On the other hand, municipal schools are seen to be very poor in teaching-learning and the administration and teachers are non-responsive.

The profiles of families whose children study in municipal schools were identified through interviews with parents and teachers. These include single parent and single earner families, families engaged in uncertain and precarious livelihoods, and families that are affected by crises and pressures of various kinds. They perceived the support (uniforms, textbooks, notebooks, tiffin, water bottle and so on) received from the municipal school as extremely helpful. They expressed helplessness about the quality of education received, though they seemed aware of the issue. While some saw the teachers and headmasters as non-responsive and unaccountable, others were inhibited by their own 'ignorance'. Some parents reported that their children in standard III and IV still did not know how to read and write

Discussions with teachers from the municipal school reveal the following issues: vacancies and excessive student ratios, burden of administrative and other duties, and the disinterested student and parent population. Teachers from adjoining private schools were quick to point out that their clientele was also located in the same communities but they did a better job of teaching, in spite of having inferior infrastructure.

Apart from the parents, several industrial and NGOs active in the field of education and outreach officers of the education department of the municipal corporation are also important stakeholders. One NGO-Education First (name changed) is active in this area. It has attempted to improve the quality of education through provision of preschool education, support classes, libraries, and campaigns to engage teachers in improvement of education. Two outreach officers and one special campaign officer for the universalization of primary education are expected to work together with NGOs to ensure 'every child in school and learning' (a slogan of the Corporation). An indication of the actual divergence is revealed by the fact that while the survey conducted by the NGO identified 630 out-of-school children in the 6–14 age group; the special campaign officers were not able to trace these children and could initiate only two classes of remedial learning covering 40 children.

The campaign for universalization has introduced a new forum and new actors in the system of education. This is the Education Committee which has representatives of teachers, parents, local community organizations and NGOs, and is presided over by the corporator (elected representative to the municipal corporation). The Committee is expected to establish a system of local accountability and undertake measures to improve access and quality of education. In practice, the Committee consists of very few representatives and even fewer who actually take an interest in the school.

In the Transit Camp School Education Committee, the corporator hardly attends the meetings; however, the contracts for improvement works are routed through him. Two members of the committee are entrepreneurs of the private schools in the vicinity; hence, the direction of their real interest is questionable.

There is a complex interrelationship between the stakeholders in elementary education for slum dwellers. This leads to a system that works at cross-purposes, moving away from the ideal of a public school system. Available evidence suggests that the infrastructure generated through the decades is now being handed over to a private system of education. The procedures of representation, the dynamism of civil society, the voice and agency of the people are inadequate by themselves to create an educational system responsive to their needs; rather they are being forced to find solutions outside it.

THE RUI'AN CASE STUDY

Rui'an, located on China's south-eastern coast, is a county in Wenzhou, a city in Zhejiang province. It has a population of 1.16 million of which one-fifth are migrants. It is one of the top 100 counties in the country in terms of economy size. In 2005, the urban per capita disposable income was 18,830 yuan or 2511 dollars and the rural per capita net income was 7436 yuan, or 991 dollars. The agricultural sector is very small—accounting for only 4.3 per cent of the city's total GDP although the percentage of population living in rural areas is much higher.[4]

In 2003, the Bureau of Education (BoE) of the Rui'an city government started two programs to improve migrant children's education. One was the 'Sunshine Project', and the other involved issuing 'Educational Subsidy Certificates' (ESCs) to migrant children. The Sunshine Project was a comprehensive program aimed at integrating migrant children into the local community. The ESCs were designed to subsidize the educational costs of children from extremely poor migrant families. These two programs caught the attention of the nation and were dubbed 'the Rui'an Experiment'.

This section is based on our field work. We review the Rui'an experiment and provide an evaluation of its performance and use survey data to evaluate the effects of ESCs on migrant children's academic performance. Then, we discuss the government's rationale behind the experiment and compare Rui'an with Beijing and Yueqing.

THE SUNSHINE PROJECT

The essence of the Sunshine Project is to provide *tongcheng daiyu* (literally meaning 'to treat migrant children the same as local children'). Three major policies have been implemented.

- **Opening local public schools to migrant children**. Rui'an does not have local private schools or migrant schools, that is, private schools set up by migrants for their children. This is quite different from most other cities where migrant children attend migrant schools. Rui'an used to have migrant schools, but the government closed them and asked migrant families to send their children to local public schools. It is noteworthy that except for a few exceptions, migrant schools are for-profit schools and charge tuition fee somewhat equivalent to jiedufei charged by public schools. There were two reasons that Rui'an opened up public schools to migrants. On the one hand, population growth in Rui'an, as in other coastal cities, has been slowing down in recent years. The situation is aggravated by large-scale emigration to developed countries. As a result, the student population has declined and many schools have excess capacities. The BoE was under pressure to maintain teachers' employment and enrolling migrant children was an effective way to solve the problem. On the other hand, the Bureau, especially the chief, Ye Yaoguo, was keen to provide equal educational opportunities to migrant children.
- **Mixed classes for migrant and local children**. This policy was implemented after much debate within the bureau and among school teachers. Most migrant families are poor; their children wear cheap clothes and have bad habits. In addition, migrants come from all over China and their lifestyles are in many ways different from local customs and culture. Lastly, most migrants work as floor workers in factories and do not have time to take care of their children's studies. Many of them are not well educated and cannot involve themselves in their children's education even if they want to. As a result, migrant children are a difficult group to teach. Thus, there was strong pressure on keeping local and migrant children separate. However, Ye Yaoguo insisted that it was imperative to have mixed classes for the assimilation of migrant children into the local community. Towards the end, he started a 'One Family' campaign within

---

[4] All the numbers are sourced from *Rui'an Xinwen Wang* (Rui'an News Network) and are available at www.66ruian.com.

the city school system. Schools organized activities to educate teachers and students that local and migrant children belong to the 'same large family'. After years of continuous efforts, local and migrant children are now treated as equals. The relationship between local and migrant children has improved although frictions do exist.

- **Equal opportunities for all children.** The lack of a local hukou means that migrant children are not automatically entitled to benefits provided to local children. Even in Rui'an, migrant children need to pay jiedufei. This is an incentive for schools that admit migrant children because 40 per cent of the jiedufei is given to schools while 60 per cent is included in the BoE budget. The Rui'an BoE has tried to treat migrant children and local children equally in other aspects. For example, schools are asked not to discriminate against migrant students in registration, selection of outstanding students for awards, and miscellaneous charges for books and school activities. In interviews, several principals told us that many migrant children have shown outstanding performance in local and national academic competitions.

Educational Subsidy Certificates

About 35,000 students, or one-fifth of the total number of students in Rui'an's elementary and middle schools are migrant children, many of whom come from poor families. Some local students also come from poor families. Since 2000, Rui'an has been providing ESCs to local students from poor families. The aim is to help poor families to pay for their children's education. Each school gets an ESC quota from the BoE before the semester. Poor students are identified by their class teachers and recommended to the BoE. When the new semester begins, students on the list are given the ESCs. Their parents can use these certificates to pay the school fees. The amount of one ESC is 400 yuan.

In 2003, the Rui'an BoE began to extend ESCs to migrant children. In 2006, 1000 migrant students and 6000 local students received ESCs. The ratio of migrant and local recipients is lower than the ratio of migrant and local students in the student population. However, this is a symbolic gesture by the Rui'an government to make the migrants feel a part of the local community.

More substantial benefits are provided for vocational education. The Chinese government is actively promoting vocational education for middle school graduates. In Rui'an, there are a dozen

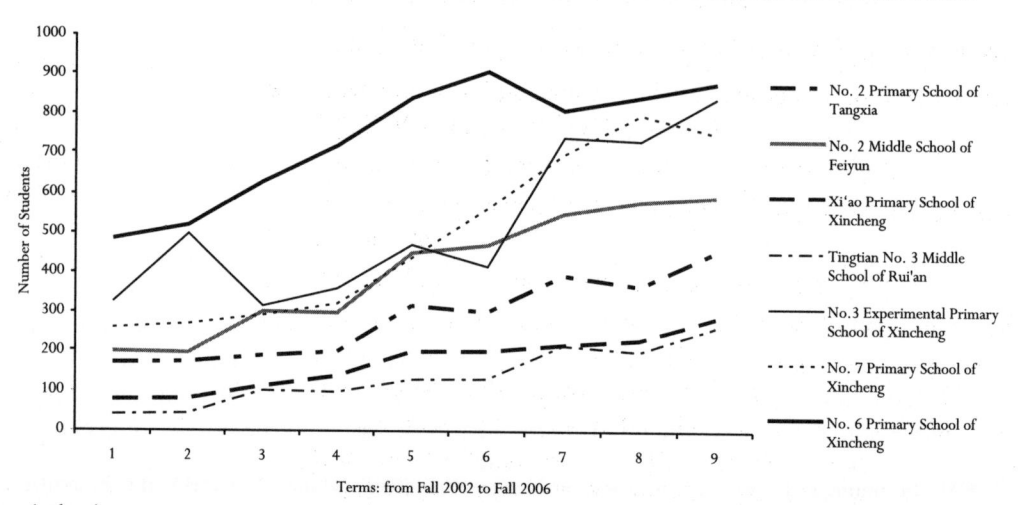

Figure 1: Growth of Migrant Students in Seven Rui'an Schools, Fall 2002 to Fall 2006

Source: Authors' survey.

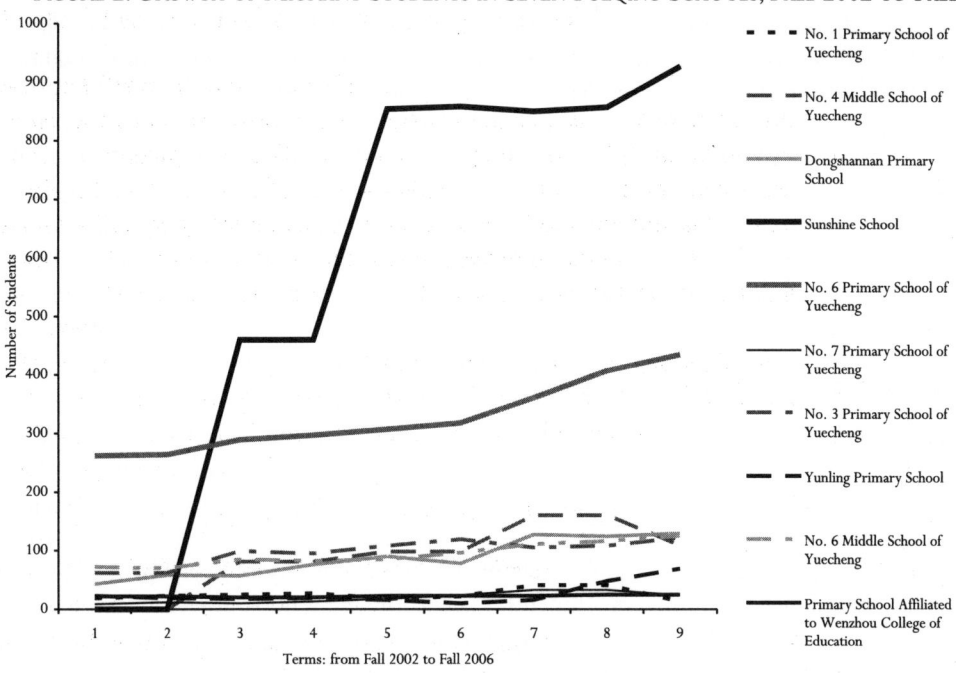

FIGURE 2: GROWTH OF MIGRANT STUDENTS IN SEVEN YUEQING SCHOOLS, FALL 2002 TO FALL 2006

Source: Authors' survey.

TABLE 2: EFFECT OF ESCs ON STUDENTS

	Monthly family income (yuan)	Change of average score (per cent)	Change of homework time (minutes)	Change of time spent on household chores (minutes)
Students without ESCs	1094.34	−1.31	22.0	−5.0
Students with ESCs	928.14	0.58	5.0	7.0

Note: The changes are for the period: Spring Semester to Fall Semester of 2006.
Source: Authors' survey.

public and private vocational high schools. The BoE figured out that it was costly to establish new public vocational high schools or expand existing ones. Instead, it proposed to provide direct subsidies to students who chose private vocational schools. The plan was approved by the mayor and the City People's Congress. Each student choosing to attend a private vocational high school gets 1000 yuan toward his/her tuition. The average cost for a three-year vocational high school education is about 9000 yuan, so the subsidy is substantial.

This plan treats migrant and local students equally. It has a much larger impact than subsidies provided to elementary and middle school students. Since migrant children cannot take the university entrance exam in the recipient province, it does not make any sense for them to complete high school education here. There are three options for migrant families with school-age children. The first, for those having high expectations for their children, is to move back to the home province so that the children can take the university entrance exam there. The second, for those having low expectations for their children, is to stop their children's education. And the third, for those wanting their children to get a decent workshop job, is to send their children to vocational high schools. Many migrant families left their home provinces a long time ago and it is impractical for them to go back. Also, it has become increasingly difficult for a middle school graduate to find a job in the coastal areas. Thus, the third option has become extremely attractive for migrant families. In fact, many migrants hope to get local hukou through the efforts of their second generation. Like many other small and medium cities, Rui'an allows migrants to obtain local hukou as long as they buy a house or an apartment. With their children added to the rank of wage earners, it is possible for a migrant family to afford a small old house or apartment. Thus, getting vocational education for its second generation will serve as a bridge for a migrant family to become 'local'. Giving ESCs for vocational education is the first step by the Rui'an government to help migrants realize this dream.

EFFECTS OF THE SUNSHINE PROJECT AND ESCs

The first effect of the Sunshine Project and ESCs is an increase in the number of migrant students in Rui'an's elementary and middle schools. Figure 1 shows the growth of migrant students in seven schools between the fall semesters of 2002 and 2006. It is evident that 2003, when these programs were started, was the starting point for fast growth in all the schools. This can be contrasted with Figure 2 that shows the case of seven public schools in the nearby city of Yueqing that has not introduced any program to help migrant students. Except for one school, others in Yueqing did not experience any fast growth during the same period of time. In fact, except two schools, all other schools in Yueqing had a small number of migrant students. Yueqing's economic growth has been equal, if not higher than that in Rui'an, and it has a higher per capita income. Therefore, the contrast is not a result of different rates of economic growth but different government policies.

The other effect of Rui'an's programs is the improved academic performance of migrant recipients. A sample of 191 migrant children from six schools—three primary schools and three middle schools—in January 2007, was asked questions about their involvement in ESCs, their academic performance, time allocation after school, and their family backgrounds. Among the 191 students, 34.5 per cent received ESCs in the fall semester of 2006. Table 2 compares students with and without ESCs.

The table shows that students with ESCs come from poorer families. Compared with the 2006 spring semester, their average score increased by 0.58 per cent in the fall semester while students without ESCs had a drop of 1.31 per cent. However, over these two semesters, students without ESCs increased their daily homework time by an average of 22 minutes and reduced time for household chores by 5 minutes, whereas students with ESCs increased homework time by only 5 minutes and increased time for household chores by 7 minutes.

THE POLITICAL ECONOMY OF THE RUI'AN EXPERIMENT

The Rui'an experiment is unique among Chinese cities. Rui'an is a rich city; in 2006, the BoE had a budget of 500 million RMB. While 400 million was used to pay teachers' salaries, 100 million was spent by the bureau on school construction and designated programs. However, the higher income is not responsible for the success of the Rui'an experiment. Yueqing is as rich as Rui'an, but it does not have any pro-migrant policy.

There were extensive debates when Ye Yaoguo first proposed the Sunshine Project and extension of the ESCs to migrant students. He gave three reasons in support of the programs, all of them related to the interest of the local population and government.

The first reason was that extending benefits to migrant students was a requirement of the central government to build a 'harmonious society'. This concept has been proposed by the Hu Jintao and Wen Jiabao government to conceptualize its vision of future China. In the last thirty years, China has made tremendous economic progress, but has also accumulated problems in economic and social equity and environmental protection. The Hu-Wen government is trying to 'put a human face' on China's fast economic growth. A harmonious society is one where people live with each other in a harmonious way; that is, a society where economic and social justice is adequately addressed, and the environment is taken care of.

His second reason was more practical and won the hearts of local business people. He told the People's delegates that providing equal education to migrant children was good for Rui'an's economic growth. In the short run, providing decent education to migrant children would attract qualified migrant workers. Like other coastal cities, Rui'an has a shortage of qualified workers. In the long run, educating migrant children would be good for Rui'an's future. The shortage of skilled workers is likely to continue in Rui'an. Local kids prefer staying at home than going to work in a factory as floor workers. To maintain high economic growth rates, Rui'an needs skilled workers from outside. The second-generation migrants can be a good source of workers. Their parents were farmers and becoming a skilled worker was perceived as a step up for the family.

The third reason was that providing education to migrant children would keep them off the street. Having children in school is one way of keeping them away from crime. Indeed, Rui'an is much safer than other cities in the Pearl river delta. What Ye Yaoguo did not tell the delegates was that providing education to migrant children was also important in keeping jobs for teachers.

The Rui'an experiment is a performance-driven effort aiming more at gains of the society than delivering equitable treatment to migrants per se. Often equity is depicted as a matter of justice. The harm of such an approach is that the issue of equity is framed in the debate on who gets what and how much. The Rui'an experiment shows us that equity can be efficiency enhancing. That is, treating people equally in access to education has the potential to enlarge the pie for the society to share. It is a common good rather than a favor handed to a portion of the population.

However, to make this line of argument work in reality, visionary leaders are required. Politicians usually tend to be short-sighted because their tenure is limited and quick results are more important for their survival in office. However, the gains associated with education are slow, thus, we often observe that education policies are not on the radar of policymakers. Indeed, the emphasis on performance in China often leads to the neglect of, and discrimination against, migrants in terms of their children's education. Beijing is a case in point.

A Comparison with Beijing

Among Beijing's 14 million residents, 3.834 million were migrants (at the end of 2006).[5] There were about 500,000 children among the migrants: 34.3 per cent of them were born in Beijing, and half of them were in compulsory educational ages (6 to 16 years old).[6]

The public school system is officially open to migrant children but the threshold is high. First, migrants need to pay high jiedufei. Second, migrant children need to take entrance exams, which many of them are unable to pass. Third, migrant families are required to present five certificates before registering their children with the school—personal identification card, temporary residency card, migration registration card, marriage and birth card, and employment

---

[5] *2006 Beijing Statistical Report of Economic and Social Development*, Beijing Statistical Bureau, December 29.

[6] *2006 Beijing 1% Migrant Population Survey*, Center for Population and Development Studies, Renmin University, June 2007.

registration card. While most migrants possess the first two, they seldom obtain the latter three cards because they are not legally required. In addition to these institutional barriers, the education offered by Beijing public schools is not suitable for migrant children. In Beijing different textbooks are used from those in migrants' original provinces. This creates a problem when migrant children return to their home provinces to take entrance exams for high schools and colleges—this is, of course, linked to China's quota system for college entrance. As a result, only 53 per cent of the migrant children are in public schools.[7] The rest attend private migrant schools.

It is estimated that there are about 300 migrant schools in Beijing—all of which are private.[8] These schools have gone through very hard times to survive. Even as late as 2006, the Beijing Municipal Government waged a campaign to shut down these schools despite the central government's call for establishing a harmonious society. Almost all migrant schools rely on student tuitions to finance their operations.[9] Most schools offer their teachers low salaries and schoolowners make only a small profit at the end of the year.

The Beijing Municipal government has tried to regulate private schools through certification. However, only 62 certificates had been issued by June 2007. Changping district on the northern outskirt of downtown Beijing has performed the best—issuing 16 certificates, one-third of all the migrant schools in the district. In contrast, Haidian district has issued only two certificates although it has the largest number of migrant schools. District governments often subsidize certified schools, usually by providing used desks and chairs from public schools. The Changping district government has even provided several schools free land for extending their school buildings.

Overall, Beijing has done poorly in providing affordable and quality education to migrant children. Population growth in Beijing has slowed down and many public schools are facing the problem of not having enough students. However, the municipal government prefers to consolidate schools rather than opening them up to migrant children. This is consistent with Beijing's objective to develop a knowledge-based economy. Such an economy does not need low-skill labor. Raising the bar of public schools for migrant children is a strategy by the government to drive out migrants. The contrast between Changping and Haidian districts reflects the different aspirations of the two districts. Haidian is headed towards building hi-tech industries while Changping still has a large rural population and is in the middle of defining its status in Beijing's overall development plan. Thus, the local economic conditions and aspirations of local officials decide whether migrant children get educational opportunities comparable to local children.

PROCEDURE BASED VERSUS PERFORMANCE BASED LEGITIMACY: AN INTERPRETATION OF THE MUMBAI AND RUI'AN CASE STUDIES

China presents a model of growth of urban settlements where freedom of movement was curtailed through residency permits. Corresponding to these were service structures pertaining to education, health, housing and so on. Increasing emphasis on urbanization as a driving force for development has meant a gradual removal of these barriers to movement. In terms of service structures, the

---

[7] Ibid.

[8] Authors' interviews with school headmasters.

[9] There is only one migrant school that is registered as a nonprofit school. It gets substantial support from donors as well as from the government.

acceptance of migration is difficult. Education is one of the first services to have shown some signs of opening to migrants, especially in provinces where migrant workers are highly needed. This process is gradual; a large proportion of migrant children are serviced by private schools. The other sectors of services remain fairly closed, even now. Overall thus, the Chinese experience is one of moving from non-acceptance of migrants to a gradual, grudging acceptance.

In India, the scenario is complex because outwardly, there are no barriers to movement, or in access to services. Migration of the rural poor to cities in search of livelihood opportunities has been a consistent phenomenon. However, urban bodies have not been able to provide adequate access in terms of housing, health, and education to these migrants, nor have they been able to capitalize on their potential contribution to the city. The consequences of these contrary forces are reflected in the widespread existence and tolerance of slums, the provision of services characterized by dual standards and fostering of clienteles' politics that perpetuates the dependence of these migrants on government institutions and political systems. Thus, while the system provides for a framework of open access, the actual experience is discriminatory.

We provide a summary of our key results and then try to come up with an explanation for the results within a unified framework. This framework is centered at the different sources of legitimacy that the government relies on in the two countries. In India we see *procedure-based legitimacy* whereas in China it is *performance-based legitimacy*. We explain how these two kinds of legitimacy are responsible for the findings in Mumbai and Rui'an.

SUMMARY OF MAJOR FINDINGS

The major findings from the Mumbai case study are as follows:

1. The local government system has limited degrees of freedom for performance.
2. The system of education is over-governed with too many stakeholders and very poor real accountability on the part of service providers.
3. The society has a general demand for education, but the demand is highly diverse and segmented.
4. The intermesh of the above factors produces an educational system for the poor that is characterized by stagnation and wastage.
5. One significant consequence has been the decline of the common school and municipal school systems in the last few years.
6. Introduction of market forces further contributes towards polarized access to education.

The major findings from the Rui'an case study are as follows:

1. China has a highly decentralized system of governance that gives local governments freedom of action.
2. The government system is centered on delivering economic performance.
3. The public education system until recently provided near complete education to all, but has been challenged by large migration.
4. Many local governments have not fully acknowledged the reality of migration.
5. There are large variations in the provision of education to migrant children.
6. Markets step in to fill the gap left over by the public education system.

PROCEDURE BASED LEGITIMACY: WHY ACCOUNTABILITY MAY NOT BE DELIVERED?

At the time of independence, the Indian state took on the challenge of transforming a 'nation' created by colonial rule, and a massive institutional structure of governance crafted by colonial rulers to systems based on democracy and equity. It had inherited a legacy of traditional inequities which were perpetuated by these systems of governance and various conflicting interests that had to be reconciled. This challenge was taken up in parts. While principles of equitable access were adopted, the framework of governance was left intact. The system as it has evolved is that of a 'soft' state which finds it difficult to reconcile the conflicting goals and take hard decisions. There are gaps at every level. However, these gaps also generate several possibilities of spaces that can accommodate, and create possibilities of change at micro-levels. The role of private entrepreneurs and other civil society actors in almost every sector of governance is quite significant. Yet there is diversity in aims, content and nature of actual delivery.

With respect to the educational system, the overall investment in education has never gone beyond 6 per cent of the planned funds. More importantly, the recommendation to implement a common school system was never implemented. The educational system in India is a highly divided one. It differs in terms of providers, standards, and motivations. While the public schools are a significant player in the provision of education, the role of non-governmental institutions is important, particularly in urban areas. The role of the local bodies is thus of a provider and a facilitator and regulator. To compound this, the restricted powers and resources of local bodies imply that educational provision is highly divergent and segmented and has not kept pace with actual needs. The losers in this system are those, whose demand for education is weak and is mediated by their socio-economic vulnerability.

Performance Based Legitimacy: Why Performance May Not Be Delivered?

When it established the People's Republic of China, the CCP derived its legitimacy as the dominant political power of China from its long struggle against imperial powers and its unification of China as an integral and independent country. A strong China has been the dream of several generations of Chinese leaders since the opium war. The painful lesson learnt from China's encounters with western powers in the 1800s has been that without economic power, China could be bullied. Unfortunately, economic growth was interrupted by civil wars and the Japanese invasion. The establishment of the People's Republic gave China a chance to concentrate on economic growth. People from all walks of life rallied around the communist party in the hope of building a strong China. Although socialism was promoted as a national ideology, it was the party's determination to build a strong China that gave people confidence in the leadership. This confidence faltered after the Cultural Revolution led China to the verge of a major economic crush. The restoration of a pragmatic leadership in the late 1970s, with Deng Xiaoping at the helm, finally gave China another chance to pursue its century-long dream of economic prosperity. The 'growth consensus' was built and has since become the norm of the party. Fortunately, China did not miss the chance and has maintained an average growth rate of 9.7 per cent in the last thirty years.

The 'growth consensus' has not only historical roots but also contemporary rationale. Socialism centered on state ownership was once thought to be the key to higher rates of economic growth, but the competition between the socialist world and the capitalist world provided decisive evidence that this version of socialism would not outperform capitalism. The fast growth of the four east Asian Dragons showed China that it was necessary to introduce some elements of capitalism to catch up with the developed nations. However, the introduction of capitalism posed a threat to the legitimacy of the orthodox ideology of the Communist Party. To win popular support from the party, Deng Xiaoping initiated a nation-wide debate at the end of 1978. The debate was not directed at the prudence of having more markets, but was framed as a philosophical discussion about the sources of truth. This proved to be a wise political strategy; it disguised the true intentions under a classical Marxist issue. The conclusion of the debate was that there could be only one source of truth, which was practice. From then on, a wide door was opened to experiments and change.

The collapse of the former Soviet Union and the eastern European communist governments showed the Chinese leaders that communist ideology alone would not guarantee legitimacy of the communist party; the party would have to deliver tangible performance results to the population in order to hold on to power. Even the 1989 Tian'anmen Square incident did not stop the reform efforts. Instead, reforms were accelerated in the 1990s and the growth consensus was reinforced.

Manifestations of this consensus are everywhere, but it is in the area of political promotion that these are most obvious. In China's one-party system, a government official's political fate is not determined by the constituency, but by his/her superiors. Because there are fewer posts at the top, government officials have to enter a political tournament if they want to get promoted: those with better performance records get promoted, and those lagging behind, stay in their old positions or may even be sacked (Zhou 2007). This provides them strong incentives to perform well in their jurisdiction. However, their performance is selective: due to the growth consensus, it is natural for them to concentrate on economic performance and ignore social development. That is, whether an issue is considered by a government official, depends simply on its relevance to economic performance.

This explains why wide variations were observed between Rui'an and Beijing in terms of provision of education to migrant children. Two practical reasons contributed to Rui'an's provision of better education to migrant children. The first reason is related to Rui'an's economic structure. Rui'an is a manufacturing-based city; the share of secondary sector in total GDP was 53 per cent in 2006.[10] Most of its industries are labor-intensive. This industrial structure is not likely to change in the foreseeable future. With declining population growth and general unwillingness of local youth to work in factories, Rui'an has had to open doors to migrant workers. The second reason is related to Rui'an's size—it is a small and growing city.

Beijing has a very different economic structure. Seventy-five per cent of its GDP is generated from the service sector; manufacturing is not the focus of development. In addition, it is already a crowded city and wants to curb population growth. Since directly controlling the entry of migrants is difficult, not providing proper education to migrant children is one way for Beijing to slow down migration into the city. This over-emphasis on economic performance has, however, violated the fundamental right of migrant children to get proper education.

CONCLUSIONS

Both case studies in China and India reveal highly complex educational systems. In terms of ensuring access to elementary education for all, both a democratic system and a non-democratic system are not automatically responsive or otherwise. Accountability structures for informal settlers are weak and mediated by a range of factors from degrees of decentralization and pressures for performing to larger development forces, tolerance of migration in particular cities, demand for education, extent of convergence or otherwise of actions of institutional actors, and availability of resources. The procedure-based system in India is prone to be handicapped by conflicting interests of institutional players as well as various civil society groups. In contrast, the performance-based system in China assigns power to the government and often leads to selective provisions of public goods that fit the goals set by the government. There is ample space for a middle ground that

---

[10] *Rui'an Xinwen Wang* (Rui'an News Network): www.66ruian.com.

combines the merits of the two systems. We need a louder voice from every walk of society to counterbalance government powers in China, and a more competent government to bring conflicting interests together and work towards common goals in India.

REFERENCES

Banerjee, Guha (2002) 'Ideology of Urban Restructuring in Mumbai: Serving the International Capitalist Agenda', paper presented in Taegue University, Taegue, Korea, August 3–19.

Baud, J.S.A., K. Pfeiffer, N. Shridharan, N. Nainan (2006) 'New Forms Of Governance In Indian Cities', (unpublished work), presented at Seminar on Tata Institute of Social Sciences, Mumbai.

Benjamin, S. and R. Bhuvaneshwari (2000) 'Urban Governance, Partnership and Poverty: Bangalore', Working Paper 15, International Development Department, University of Birmingham, Birmingham.

Bhide, A. (2006) 'Civil Society Governance and Partnership: A View from The Periphery', *Indian Social Initiative*, Vol. 28, No. 1, Spring.

Fei, Xiaotong (1985) 'Xiahao Zhongguo Renkou Wenti Zhepanqi' (Play Well the Chess Game of China's Population Issue), in D. S. Ji and Q. Shao (eds) *Zhangguo Renkou Liudong Taishi Yu Guanli (Trends and Management of China's Population Mobility)*, Zhongguo Renkou Chubanshe (China Population Press), Beijing.

Fernandez, F. (1993) 'Evaluation of Relocation Programmes in Metro Manila', expert meeting on Urban Relocation, IHS, Rotterdam, Netherlands.

Goldstein, S. and A. Goldstein (2001) 'Population Mobility in the People's Republic of China', Papers of the East-West Population Institute, No. 95.

Government of India (2001) *Census 2001*, Office of the Registrar General, New Delhi.

Hazard Center (2000) *Citizen's Report on Development Plan of Delhi*, New Delhi.

Huang, Ping and Frank N. Pieke (2003) 'China Migration Country Study' paper presented at the Regional Conference on Migration, Development and Pro-Poor Policy Choices in Asia, Dhaka, June 21–4.

Indian Conference of Social Workers (1957) *Seminar on Slum Clearance 1957*, May.

Kabeer, N., R. Subrahmanian, and G. Nambissan (2005) *Child Labour and Right to Education in Asia*, Sage Publications, New Delhi.

Kundu, Amitabh (2005) *Handbook of Urbanisation*, Sage Publications, New Delhi.

Ministry of Urban Employment and Poverty Alleviation (2002) *National Slum Policy*, Government of India, New Delhi.

MMRDA (1995) *Development Plan of Mumbai Metropolitan Region, 1996–2011*, MMRDA, Mumbai.

National Slum Policy (2002) *Ministry of Housing & Urban Poverty Alleviation*, New Delhi.

Nee, Victor and Peng Lian (1994). 'Sleeping with the Enemy: A Dynamic Model of Declining Political Commitment in State Socialism,' *Theory and Society*, Vol. 23, No. 2, pp. 253–96.

Panwalkar (1992) *A Study of Community and Non-governmental Management of Environment in Mumbai*, MEIP, A Study of Community and Non-governmental Management of Environment in Mumbai, (mimeo), Tata Institute of Social Sciences, Mumbai.

Pratham (2003) 'Status of Education Among Urban Poor Children', Paper presented at All India Mayors' Conference.

PROBE (1999) *Public Report On Basic Education*, Oxford University Press, New Delhi.

Ramchandran, Vimla (2003) *Getting Children Back To School*, Sage Publications, New Delhi.

Swaminathan, R. and J. Goyal (2006) *Mumbai Vision 2015: Agenda for Urban Renewal*, Macmillan India, New Delhi.

Verma, Geeta Dewan (2002) *Slumming India: A Chronicle of Slums and Their Saviors*, Penguin Books, New Delhi.

Wong, Linda and Wai-Po Huen (1998) 'Reforming the Household Registration System: A Preliminary Glimpse of the Blue Chop Household Registration System in Shanghai and Shenzhen', *International Migration Review*, Vol. 32, No. 4, pp. 974–94.

Wu, Harry Xiaoying (1994) 'Rural to Urban Migration in the People's Republic of China', *China Quarterly*, No. 139, pp. 669–98.
YUVA (2003) *A Study of Slum Sanitation Program in Mumbai*, YUVA.
Zhao, Yaohui (1999) 'Labor Migration and Earnings Differences: The Case of Rural China', *Economic Development and Cultural Change*, Vol. 47, No. 4, pp. 767–82.
——— (2001) 'The Role of Migrants Networks in Labor Migration: The Case of China', working paper no. E2001012, China Center for Economic Research, Peking University, Beijing.
Zhao, Zhong (2005) 'Migration, Labor Market Flexibility, and Wage Determination in China: A Review', *The Developing Economics*, Vol. 43, No. 2, pp. 285–312.
Zhou, Li-An (2007) 'Political Tournament and Economic Growth in China' paper presented in the ninth NBER-CCER annual conference, China Center for Economic Research, Peking University, Beijing.

PART TWO

Governing Urban Spaces: Economy, Design, and Governance

5

Urban Development and Governmental Approach

Experiences in China and India

ZONGYONG WEN[a]

It is well chronicled in human history that entire civilizations have sprung up on the banks of great rivers. Water is not only the origin of life but also serves as a means of transportation and trade. Many large cities flourished due to their proximity to the sea such as Shanghai, Tianjin, Hangzhou, Guangzhou, Shenyang, Harbin and Guilin in China, and Mumbai, Surat, Kandla and Kochi in India. Land, with its inherent symbolism of indestructibility, security, absence of mobility and the emotional bond it creates with its people, has special significance for the city that builds itself upon it. The land fosters its citizens while nurturing its local culture. The word 'culture' is in fact, derived from 'agriculture' the cornerstone of settled human life. Therefore, water, land and culture are an integrated whole. The story of urbanization dwells on the evolution of human activity and the influence it wields in leveraging the trinity of water, land and culture in furthering the socio-economic agenda embedded in a civilization.

This chapter is a brief comment on the recent development experiences of urban China placed in conjunction with that of India in the context of the approaches and priorities of their respective governments.

DEVELOPMENTAL PARADIGM OF MODERN CHINA

RAPID GROWTH

China is urbanizing rapidly, consistently delivering double-digit economic growth. Cities are

[a] I have gained both perceptual and rational knowledge about urban development in China and India, two big countries in Asia, through the India China Institute (ICI) research project as well as exchanges of views with scholars from China, US and India. My understanding in this aspect was deepened by field investigations, interviews and personal interaction. I would like to thank the ICI for spearheading this initiative and administering it with such competence. After the first New York conference in April 2006, I have undertaken research on 'Government Practices in Globalization and Urbanization', in conjunction with Partha from India and Yang Zuojun from Hangzhou, China, with who I have formed a cooperative team. In November 2006, I undertook a field trip to India to examine its contemporary culture against the backdrop of its rich traditional heritage. This was followed by another field trip in June 2007, this time to Shanghai, Beijing and Hangzhou in China. My research experience has been greatly enriched by the many seminars, discussions and symposia that I have been a part of.

emerging overnight; tens of thousands of people are migrating into the ever expanding urban areas in search of jobs that big and new cities invariably generate. This has also given rise to the urban middle class nourished by the hectic economic activities that support and perpetuate the city's life. In the past 15 years, urbanization in China has increased from 36.09 per cent in 2000 to 42.99 per cent in 2005, an average growth of 1.38 percentage points each year, thus surpassing the average urbanization speed of developing countries by miles. This momentum of growth is expected to be maintained through the 11th Five-Year Plan period (2006–10).

PAYING THE PRICE FOR DEVELOPMENT

Against the backdrop of globalization and rapid urbanization it is important to assess the price being paid for development. Natural resources in China are being exploited without restraint, with serious consequences for the environment; the gap between the wealthy and the poor is widening; and social stratification in terms of the 'haves' and 'have-nots' is emerging anew. The urban governments in China are ill-prepared to deal with the social and economic obligations of the state within a market economy—they are resorting to short-term strategies to address equity issues related to market forces and conflicts of interest. Consequently, problems are being tackled temporarily within a myopic perspective at the expense of long-term objectives, overall interests, and organic harmony of the socio-economic system.

THE POWER OF THE STATE

In China, the government has always exerted a strong influence, be it the political influence in the planned economy, or economic influence in the market economy. During the transitional period of development of the market system, local governments have assumed economic powers, thus, playing a crucial role in local economic development. Confronted with the dual pressures from peer competition and performance evaluation, many local governments now think that their economy and GDP are not growing fast enough, so they want to push it forward at any cost.

Starting in 2004, the central government, in line with the new situation in China and the world, formulated a series of concepts of sustainable development—'outlook on scientific development', to build a socialist 'harmonious society', 'human factors come first' and 'to build an environmentally friendly and energy-saving society'. Since 2007, the government also shifted the requirements for economic development from 'fast and sound' to 'sound and fast'. In terms of the distribution system, the slogan 'priority is given to efficiency with equality taken into account' has been changed to 'efficiency and equality are equally important'; the concept of green GDP is gaining importance and the notion that 'development is absolute' has been substituted by 'sustainable development'. The government is also concerned with the livelihood of its people and social stability based on the new principle of 'human rights, democracy and livelihood'. The Chinese government has developed the theory and guiding principles suitable for this period of growth and expansion. Thus, the focus has shifted from economic development to overall development. However, this change in ideas will take some time to become completely successful and fully operational. As local governments do not have any model to follow in the application of the new concepts, they will definitely face a number of challenges.

THE STRUGGLE BETWEEN THE OLD AND THE NEW

Amidst rapid urbanization, the conflict between development and protection of traditional culture has become more acute with traditional urban culture losing out due to the priority accorded by local governments to GDP increase and short-term development. Chinese economic and social life is undergoing tremendous change in the struggle between the old and the new.

Take Beijing, for example. This city has a 500 year old history and it integrates elements from imperial cities of different dynasties. Thus, it is a rich historical and cultural living monument. Despite this, the old city walls as well as many courtyard houses and alleys have been torn down and replaced by high-rises. Today's Beijing is so new, and has developed so fast that much of its original culture has been overshadowed by new developments, newer, but not necessarily better. Although valid figures are not available to verify this contention, it is almost certain that not much traditional architecture is left in Beijing. It is not that old houses are devoid of value, but that culture, when locked in competition with the economy, always tends to be the loser in the face of rapid growth of the latter. Economic development brings practical benefits to a section of the society; therefore, it is difficult to curb its momentum especially when it is encouraged by the state policy of 'development is absolute'.

When the issue of protecting old architecture arises, many units are not cooperative, as they believe that preserving old houses constitutes an obstacle to development. Since there is a general lack of respect for traditional culture, conservation work often proceeds without support and understanding.

Improvement of Rule of Law

Governance by law and transparent administration have become the priorities for the government. One of the many (following) laws that have generated immense influence on urban development: the Administrative Empowerment Law, which was passed and implemented on 1 July 2005. Since then, cases involving resettlement and land acquisition by municipal governments have increased year on year, with the local governments sometimes losing cases. This demonstrates that social supervision and citizens' participation can help the government in raising its legal awareness, and governance according to the Rule of Law.

The promulgation of the Property Law on 1 October 2007, elevated the protection of private rights to the same level as protection of public interests. The passing of the Urban and Rural Planning Law on 1 January 2008, guarantees the scientific dimension in urban planning by standardizing procedures and encouraging public participation and supervision.

Democratic Awareness Among the Population

Statistics show that living standards in urban areas correspond to their level of economic development. For instance, if urbanization is lower than 30 per cent, then per capita GDP would be below USD 1000, whereas if the level of urbanization reaches 30–50 per cent, 50–70 per cent, and 70 per cent or above, the per capita GDP would be in the range of USD 1000–3000, USD 3000–7000, and USD 7000 or above, respectively. Similarly, participation in democracy is also linked to economic development. When the average yearly income of a city's residents reaches the USD 3000 level, their democratic awareness increases—they begin to take interest in public affairs and issues such as, environmental protection. When their annual income reaches USD 6000, such citizens demand protection of their rights, access to information, involvement in decision-making and if their rights are violated, they protest. If they start earning USD 9000 per annum, they urge the government to safeguard public interest and seize the initiative to monitor the performance of the government. Only when citizens earn USD 12000 or more can 'relative harmony' be achieved.

Urbanization in China has resulted in many problems, such as displacement and resettlement of peasants to cities, and possible violation of their rights. The per capita GDP in Beijing is about USD 6000 and the urbanization rate is approximately 83.6 per cent, indicating that the rate of urbanization is surpassing the development of the economy. Because of this, economic and social conflicts are becoming more intense and there has been a need felt by the masses to safeguard their rights.

As urban development, which often involves electrification of urban cities, construction of roads, providing public facilities, and looking after the community environment, sometime causes and creates trouble to the residents, which is likely to trigger conflicts. For instance, some residents recently protested the construction of a 220 kilowatt transformer substation by the government on the grounds of noise pollution, radiation and even explosions. They were concerned about their safety and health. Thus, site selection for large-scale public facilities such as transformer substations is problematic for the government. On the one hand, development requires the construction of such facilities. On the other hand, the site chosen for the same is often at conflict with the interest of local inhabitants, thus placing the government in a 'catch-22' situation. Such examples reflect an increased participation of the people in day-to-day governance issues.

Market-led Economy

Under the planned economy, nearly all the investments in construction were made by the government. In the market economy, investment has shifted to multiple modes. Again coming to Beijing, for example, 80 per cent of investment is sourced from channels outside the government, which results in a variety of needs and end products. A case in point is residential housing in Beijing. During the 10th Five-Year Plan period, the total housing area construction comprised 153 million sq. feet, of which commercial housing accounted for 135 million sq. feet, or more than 88 per cent of the total. The size of individual units have become larger, leading to soaring prices and scaring away medium- and low-income buyers. This is a direct result of the market economy. In the 11th Five-Year Plan period, however, the government plans to make some adjustments in housing construction. Of the 123 million sq. feet to be built, affordable and 'two-limit' commercial housing will account for 25 per cent, thus satisfying the needs of medium- and low-income citizens.

It is obvious that the market itself cannot optimize resources. The main reasons for this are: first, monopoly reduces market efficiency; second, market adjustments cannot balance the macroeconomy; third, the incomplete information in the market reduces efficiency; fourth, the market cannot/does not provide public services such as the urban traffic infrastructure, public facilities and parks and green belts; lastly, the market cannot solve the problems of social equality. The problem of providing housing to low-income city dwellers cannot be resolved without the intervention by the government.

Is Cultural Development Being Fostered?

The report submitted to the 17th National Congress of the CPC stated that cultural development and prosperity as well as soft cultural strength should be enhanced. Many historical cities such as Yangzhou and Zhenjiang are trying to promote their unique cultural elements in the face of urban development. This practice has been appreciated widely.

INSPIRATION FROM INDIAN DEVELOPMENT

India is a large and complex country. Some scholars surmise that it is composed of three worlds: the ancient world, western world and the underdeveloped world. The recent ICI research project has provided some crucial insights (even though they may be limited) into various aspects of this big elephant that is India. It seems that India is self-contained, slow-paced, self-contented, mysterious, tolerant and contradictory, all at the same time.

Stable Economic Development

Statistics show that the Indian economy is developing at the rate of 7 per cent per annum, and its cost of development is only half that of China. This implies that India is in a 'high development–low cost' framework, something remarkable for an economic powerhouse. Positioning itself as the 'world office', the Indian economy displays low costs and low consumption while China, which is regarded as 'a world plant', is characterized by high costs, high pollution and low yields. China has a competitive edge in the world in terms of its low prices, high production and high quality, with profits arising mainly from processing fees. As a result, the harder the government tries to promote production, the more acute conflicts may become. It seems that there is something completely incongruous between development and the government's achievements. The question about why it is so difficult and costly to transform the production mode and industrial structure requires further research.

Although India's development concentrates on high-end products, its government is not strong—characterized by low efficiency, limited power and a large, possibly incompetent bureaucracy. The Indian government lacks both effective guidance and control in terms of the development structure. This is why high-rises and 'slums' co-exist in big cities such as Mumbai and New Delhi. Indian infrastructure—backward as compared to that of China, faces the problem of inadequate investment.

Prevalence of Democracy

India enjoys a long-standing tradition of democracy, with many grass roots democratic organizations in rural areas. Generally speaking, an active democracy allows the nation to move forward on the path of stable development with checks and balances in place. This is unlike the case in China where the extra-fast train of development could not be curbed once it began to rush forward. However, there are exceptions to the rule. Stable development and dynamic democracy are often unable to resolve problems, and result in lost opportunities for development, thus harming the interests of the people. For example, a debate on how to revamp a cluster of dilapidated factory premises in Mumbai has been continuing for the last twenty years. According to the original plan, factory owners were to receive one-third of the land gains while the remaining two-thirds were to be used to build affordable houses for medium- and low-income dwellers. After ten years of debates, with no solution in sight, the factory owners took possession of the total land because the government scrapped its plan of building affordable housing for the poor and created a green belt. This was an unsatisfactory result as it compromised the larger public interest.

Human Factors

Most Indians seem to have a resigned and passive outlook towards life. They appear to be contented with their lot in life. They believe in karma and are usually at peace. From Agra to New Delhi to Mumbai, you would see smiling faces everywhere, including the slums. This is a testament to the optimistic attitude of the citizens of this nation. The peace-loving character of Indians was witnessed during the non-violent independence struggle led by Gandhi. On the contrary, Chinese history has witnessed too many revolutions and violent changes of power.

Usually, Indians are active thinkers, who think more than they act, whereas the Chinese have the opposite temperament, 'tending to cross the river by feeling the stones'. This difference in people's character is closely related with the cultural traditions of the two countries.

Respect for Nature and Traditions

The natural environment in India is fairly well preserved, although the drinking water is not of good quality. The filthy and disorderly surroundings are caused mainly because of the improper disposal of household waste. Compared with the industrial and housing construction wastes in China, it is much easier and less costly to treat wastes in India. Man and nature co-exist in a harmonious way in India. Traditional housing is better preserved in India than in China. And traditional lifestyles are still observed in various parts of the country in sharp contrast to China, where the same have been fading away very rapidly in the last 20 years.

DEEPENING THE PROJECT: THE RESEARCH HAS JUST BEGUN

The priorities of a strong government in a country should be: macro-controlling of the economy, providing social services, helping the poor and enhancing employment security, and so on. To enable the selection of rational, ideal and optimistic legislators is the key to ensuring that the government operates in a scientific, democratic and legal manner. Having an accountable and performance assessment system is the legal guarantee to reduce/ eradicate malpractices by government officials. Past experience proves that single-mode of development, unreasonable structure and high energy-consuming operations cannot lead to sustainable development. To sustain the balance across population growth, resources and the environment, a scientific outlook on development is required. This should be accompanied by a move away from a single-mode economy towards a comprehensive mode that encompasses political, economic, social and human factors.

Although interest in India has already become stronger. Discussions with a few Indians have helped open the doors of this mysterious and ancient country, to observe its development as well as its ancient culture. After two years of exchanges, investigation and reflection, two important questions that come to the light:

1. Are China and India following the footsteps of the US on their respective paths to development?
2. Which of the two countries will ultimately win the race of development?

With respect to the first question, I believe that the Chinese have imbibed too much from Americans—urbanization, car culture, highways, overpasses, to hamburgers and Hollywood movies. Our cities have become an experimental ground for foreign architecture and American-style food. As a result, traditional culture is being marginalized. And even the values of our younger generation have been adversely affected. However, it is surprising yet heartening to note that Chinese culture is still full of vitality, and westernization is but something superficial. The country is still deeply rooted in traditional culture.

Is India more prone to western culture, since its language, political system and the mild national character are akin to those prevalent in the West? However, in my opinion, India has been influenced by the West at a much slower rate than China.

As far as the second question is concerned, if China attempts to develop by simply following the West, the country will very soon be surpassed by its competitors. It is traditional Chinese culture that can help this huge country—that has been plagued by myriad hardships—to move forward on the path of sustainable development. Ancient Chinese philosophers had discussed the concept that 'man is an integral part of nature'. But it is only now that the Chinese are beginning to understand this. After the initial years of prosperity of Qing Dynasty, and the subsequent 200 years of shame and suffering, Chinese people ultimately won liberation, peace and stability. Today they are exploring their own way and working hard to achieve a bright future.

6

Land Acquisition and the Protection of Farmers' Interests

The Practice in Hangzhou, China

ZUOJUN YANG

BACKGROUND

The process of urbanization mainly comprises two kind of changes: the first is that agricultural land is used for non-agricultural purposes; the other is that farmers become urban residents after losing most or all of their agricultural land. In China, there has been rapid urbanization since the reform and decontrol policies were adopted in 1978. Since then, the urbanization level in China has increased by about 1per cent per annum and in 2006 it was about 46 per cent. The rapid urbanization process in China has brought about great changes not only in urban areas but also in rural areas and farmers' lives. Like other cities in China, Hangzhou, the capital city of Zhejiang province, has also witnessed rapid urbanization. The urban area has expanded and urban population has increased rapidly. However, discouraged by China's strict policy of agricultural land acquisition, many agricultural collective bodies set up their own factory buildings, zones or commercial official buildings on their own land by attracting outside investment without resorting to a legal land acquisition process. The secondary or tertiary industry activities bring greater benefits to the collectives than traditional agricultural activities. However, this kind of land repurposing by village collective bodies does not consider the overall rational land-use layout. As a result, the land along the urban fringe areas or urban roads has been occupied for farmers' residences, factory buildings and other commercial uses, interspersed with the isolated agricultural pockets. There is a very interesting aerial view of farmlands around Hangzhou—the agricultural land is in the form of a square with rows of farmer-homesteads which are small houses. Such land repurposing in addition to the legally acquired land has created a situation in which the amount of agricultural land around the urban area has dropped sharply. The so-called contradiction between rapid urban development and limited land space has become more serious, and many urban development projects have had to be delayed or canceled due to lack of land.

Hangzhou is a small city considering its administrative scale. However, to meet the needs of rapid urbanization, the administrative region of Hangzhou has been continuously enlarging in the past two decades. Prior to 1996, Hangzhou city had an area of only about 450 sq. kilometer. In 1996, three towns from northern Yuhang and southern Xiaoshan were assimilated into Hangzhou which released about 233 sq. kilometer land for urban development. This situation lasted for about five years. In 2001, the boundary of Hangzhou was enlarged from 683 sq. kilometer to 3068 sq.

kilometer, which gave Hangzhou a chance to create an overall plan for urban development and agricultural layout. According to Chinese law, all the administrative region adjustments must be approved by the central government. As China has adopted a very strict policy on agricultural land protection, it becomes imperative for each city to preserve a certain amount of land as basic agricultural land. With the enlargement of the administrative boundary, many agricultural lands around the urban area have become susceptible to acquisition by the central government. In line with the land protection policy, the so-called agricultural land protection can be extended to more remote agricultural regions through what is known as trade of agricultural land quota. However, this kind of urban expansion mechanism has created three major problems. The first is that many villages in urban fringe areas have gradually been swallowed by the city in the process of urban sprawl, creating what are now popularly called 'urban villages' in many developed cities. Second, the legal or illegal land acquisition process has led to the construction of illegal buildings by farmers to gain economic benefits. As the need for rental houses began to increase, farmers in the urban fringe areas built more houses to let out at low rents to the floating population. A number of the so-called 'village' illegal buildings were built in these areas. The third problem is the increasing number of farmers who lost their agricultural land and had to move to the urban area for work. In Hangzhou, the farmers around the urban areas live on the benefits from the collective bodies and house rent. In comparison with the floating farm labor from other provinces, these original farmers are relatively rich and have more time for leisure activities.

To consolidate the urbanization process, in 1999 Hangzhou started a reform called '撤村建居 Che Cun Jian Ju' (which means turning the village into a neighborhood and the farmers into urban residents by acquiring their land). It is regarded as the most important reason behind the fast growth of the urban areas. In order to utilize the limited land resources fully and efficiently, the government stated that only multi-storied or high-rise residential buildings would be allowed when relocating the farmers. The traditional one-farmer-family-one-building policy for farmers' housing was done away with, which meant that the farmers would be relocated to apartments like urban residents. Since the policy was adopted nine years ago, farmers from about 70 per cent of the villages within the Hangzhou Ring Road have been relocated to multi-storied or high-rise farmer apartment blocks. In fact this policy has played an important role in the effective and efficient use of land resources in Hangzhou, and has contributed towards the urbanization process in the city. It is interesting to note that this policy followed the central government land policy and had the support of farmers. Without the farmers' acquiescence, the policy would not have been such a great success. That is why, the Hangzhou government has made great efforts to protect the farmers' interests in the entire urbanization process, especially in terms of solving the housing, working and livelihood problems of the farmers who lost their land.

RELATED NATIONAL LAWS

The urbanization process is, in fact, the process of agricultural land being acquired for urban development while the farmers themselves are transformed into urban residents. For the process to proceed smoothly, the farmers must not be passive participants but be active beneficiaries of the process. There are many problems that confront the urbanization process in China, but the primary problem concerns the protection of the interests of farmers who lose their land during the process. There is a requirement of national laws that can safeguard the interests of farmers during the land acquisition process. There are several laws which have clear articles or sections related to the protection of farmers' interests. For example, the Constitution of People's Republic of China, the Property Power Law, the Urban and Rural Planning Law, the Land Administration Law, and so on, have separate articles or sections that emphasize this issue and also have some clear requirements and restrictions on the local government. According to Article 10, section 3 of the Constitution of PRC, 'the country can acquire the land for the public interests based on the law requirement'. This is the basic law that grants power to the central and local governments to acquire land in public interest. However, it also gives room for differing perspectives on what is public interest, which sometimes causes conflict between the farmers and the government.

According to the Property Right Law, section 4, 'the country, collective bodies and private property right and the property right of other obligee are protected by the law, and no institution or person can violate their rights'. Also, the Land Resources Administration Law has similar articles and sections on the protection of rights. Sections 45–50 of the Law prescribe the approving authority, process and allocation and compensation of land acquisition. For farmers, the land resource is their source of livelihood and their guarantee to a basic quality of life which either provides income directly or from the potential added values of their properties. All these functions of land resources are lost once the land is acquired 'for public interests'. Hence, the law requires that necessary and sufficient compensation be paid to village collective bodies to which the farmers belong. In order to safeguard the interests of individual farmers, Section 49 of the Law prescribes that 'the village collective body of which land is being acquired should publicly declare the inflow and expenditure of the funds received as compensation for the land acquired. The members of the collective body should have full access to such information and under no circumstance should the compensatory funds be diverted to any other purpose without the consent of all members'. With the growth of urban spaces, the value of land has increased very rapidly in recent years, and while the standard of compensation for land acquisition is established by laws and regulations, land reservation by the village collective body for redevelopment becomes an inevitable choice of both the collective body and the government. Thus, the land reserved by the village collective for village development during the land acquisition process ensures that most of the added value of the land is reserved for the farmers. Thus, farmers who have lost most of their land can still receive stable incomes from the land reserved for them.

RELATED POLICY AND REGULATION OF THE GOVERNMENT

Under the national laws, many policies and regulations have been instituted by different levels of government in China, in order to protect rare land resources and the interests of the farmers. Though the basic policy and regulations of land resource protection are the same, there are variations in local policies and regulations in different cities based on different land situations. For example, land-use policy and regulations in Hangzhou are different from cities in middle and western China as they have relatively less land available and the land there is more suitable for agriculture.

THE LAND ADMINISTRATION POLICY OF THE CENTRAL GOVERNMENT

The basic requirement of the land administration policy of the country is to protect national arable land to ensure food security of the country. The land acquired for urban development must comply fully with urban planning and land-use planning, and must be used efficiently. According to the land administration policy, any piece of basic arable land acquired for urban development must be approved by the Ministry of Land Resource Administration. The land reserved for the relocation of farmers' housing should also be decided in accordance with urban planning and land-use planning, and if these buildings occupy the arable land, the land use application must be approved by the Ministry of Land Resource Administration, or by the provincial government.

CHE CUN JIAN JU (撤村建居) IN HANGZHOU

Though Che Cun Jian Ju in Hangzhou has evolved gradually year by year in the past nine years, there are four basic policies:

1. **Land Sale Policy**: One of the most important steps in land acquisition is relocating farmers' houses. Usually the farmers pay only about 900 RMB yuan per sq. meter floor area for the new housing, and the difference between the farmers' payment and the real cost of the building is subsidized by the local government. In Hangzhou, each urban district government has set up an institution called the Farmer Housing Building and Management Center. In order to balance the cost of farmers' housing buildings, the Hangzhou government has a policy which authorizes each urban district center to find a piece of land suitable for real estate development from where the center generates funds for building farmer-houses.

2. **Housing Demolition and Compensation Policy**: As most of the acquired land has some farmer homes or village factory buildings on it, it is the responsibility of the central government to provide compensation before clearing the land. According to the Housing Demolitions and Compensation Policy, the compensation includes not only the cost of the building but also the cost of interior and exterior decoration of the same, based on evaluations by an independent property evaluation company. The central government cannot break the building and clear the land for new development before the farmer or village collective body approves the evaluation. An interesting phenomenon is seen in Hangzhou: one can easily find out which piece of land is to be acquired soon by observing if there are any new but unnecessary decorations on the exterior.

3. **Housing Relocation Policy**: According to this policy, the floor area of housing allocated is decided according to the number of family members. The farmer housing allocation standard is an average of 50 sq. meter floor area per family member for families relocated to multi-storied buildings, and an average of 55 sq. meter floor area per family member for families relocated to high-rise residential buildings. The one-child family is regarded as a four member family in housing relocation.

4. **10 per cent Reserved Land Policy**: This policy ensures the future development of the village and the farmers after most of their land has been acquired. According to this policy, the former village collective body can retain 10 per cent of the total land acquired for urban development. The exact location of the reserved land is decided by urban planning and land-use planning in order to ensure that this piece of land can be used for real estate or some other development purpose, which will be carried out by the village collective body. The farmers can share the benefits of these developments for as long as these developments are profitable and fetch good returns. According to the policy, this 10 per cent reserved land cannot be sold in the real estate market but is owned collectively by all members of the village.

INTRODUCTION OF *CHE CUN JIAN JU* IN HANGZHOU

Che Cun Jian Ju has been in operation in Hangzhou for about nine years. After so many years of functioning and varied experiences associated with the project, Hangzhou has a proper mechanism in place to effectively and efficiently deal with the problems.

BASIC CONCEPT OF THE PROJECT

The project of Che Cun Jian Ju is to repeal the rural status of a village within the administrative jurisdiction of Hangzhou where the average arable land is less than 0.1 mu or 66.7 sq. meter per villager or the total arable land is less than 20 mu or 1334 sq. meter and give it the status of a neighborhood. Thereby the former village becomes an urban neighborhood with a collectively owned economic body or company to manage the public properties of the village, and the villagers become urban residents of the neighborhood with an urban *hukou*, that is, become registered urban households. They form a part of a special urban population who will live on the interests from their former collectively owned properties and rent from their spare houses. Though only a few of them will be able to find new jobs they will still have a stable and financially secure life.

Basic Goals and Objectives of the Project

The following are the fundamental goals of the project:

1. To promote urban development.
2. To improve the administrative institutions in the urban fringe regions.
3. To make full and efficient use of land resources and explore new spaces for urban growth.
4. To ensure that all villagers who become urban residents enjoy the same services as other urban inhabitants: employment opportunities, education, medical care, tap water and sewage, gas supply, and so on.
5. To make sure that the new residential buildings have the same construction and service standards as that of the urban areas.

The Current Living Condition of Villagers in Urban and Fringe Areas in Hangzhou

After many years of urban development, the villagers in Hangzhou, especially those living in the so-called 'urban villages' or in the urban fringe areas, comprise of a special population in Hangzhou. An understanding of their living condition is essentially linked to the success of the Che Cun Jian Ju project:

- Housing: The villagers live in 3–4 storey isolated buildings—usually one-family-per-one-building. These are not constructed by any building company but by laborers hired from within the families of the village.
- Employment: Only some of the villagers are still engaged in agricultural activities, especially vegetable growing and tree or flower planting for making the urban areas green. The rest try to find work in the urban service sector or just stay at home.
- Income: Most income of the villagers is earned from giving out their spare rooms on rent. The average family income is about 3000–5000 yuan per month. Other income includes the interest from the collective-owned properties, and temporary work in factories or other jobs in the city.
- Living conditions: Most of the villagers in Hangzhou enjoy a good life in comparison with village laborers from other provinces who find jobs in the city. Most of the families are able to access and utilize urban infrastructure services.

The Problems of the Existing Farmers' Buildings

The existing farmers' buildings in the urban villages or the fringe areas of the city represent, to some extent, the economic development and power of farmers in this city. These isolated 3–4 storey buildings with similar exteriors are not well- planned or well located.

1. **Densely located buildings:** There are basically no layout plans for the villages so construction looks haphazard. Anyone starting their own family can apply for land to build their house. Usually the piece of land allotted is about 100 sq. meter and the building can be 3–4 stories tall. There is no clear plan defining sites for construction of new buildings. The only principle for site selection is to ensure that the land is vacant and is not reserved as basic arable land. As there is no building code in the villages, the buildings stand cheek by jowl without enough space or greenery; there are safety issues and sanitary problems. However, the interior of these buildings is modern and well-equipped. As these buildings are usually 3–4 stories high, the floor area ratio is relatively low and land is not utilized efficiently.
2. **Lack of proper roads:** Very little land is available for road improvement. There are no proper roads within the village—only paths between buildings. The residents are unhappy that there are only one or two roads, 5–7 meters wide, that are the main roads for a village with more than a thousand farmers.
3. **No land-use plan:** Within the village, factory buildings and warehouses including those that produce, store or release hazardous items are interspersed with residential buildings. Land-use is chaotic, in sharp contrast to the urban region around.
4. **Lack of education facilities:** The villages usually follow a traditional village layout, without a center park, a kindergarten, primary or middle school, and so on. Children have to walk long distances to attend schools located in urban areas.
5. **Lack of public facilities:** As there is no overall plan for the development of villages, the public facilities—electricity, telecom, gas, tap water and sewerage—remain inadequate.
6. **Vulnerability to floods:** Since adjacent urban land has been developed using cement and steel, these lands are elevated and in comparison, the villages have sunk. Because the farmers' houses were usually built without meeting the anti-flood standards of the urban region, these buildings are vulnerable to floods and during heavy rains, the village can sometimes resemble a pond.

CASE STUDY OF CHE CUN JIAN JU: XINTANG VILLAGE REDEVELOPMENT PROJECT IN JIANGGAN DISTRICT

GEOGRAPHIC LOCATION

Under the Che Cun Jian Ju Project, 41 villages were chosen as the first group of experimental villages to be rebuilt. Xintang village being one of the villages, located in Pengbu town in Jianggan district in Hangzhou has three major urban roads surrounding it. Further, Subway line 4 is planned across the western side of the village. Xintang is about 3.5 kilometer from the new urban center and 5 km from the existing urban center. As Hangzhou is now implementing its new version of the urban Master Plan, the development focus is shifting from the area around the west lake to the more spacious area along the Qiantang river. Xintang happens to be located in a very advantageous geographic location in this strategic shift of urban development of the city (see Figure 1).

EXISTING SITUATION OF THE VILLAGE

The existing farmers' residences are mainly located to the south of Genshan road, a trunk road in

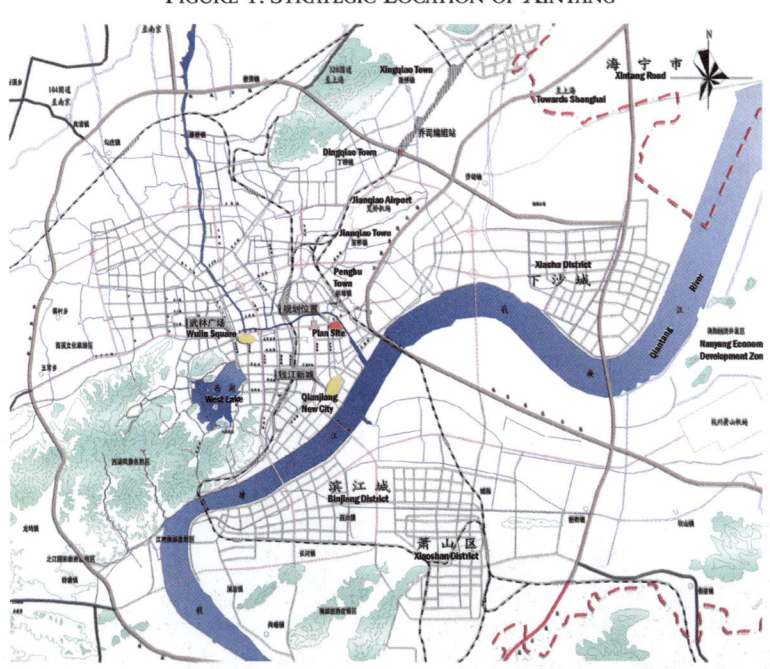

FIGURE 1: STRATEGIC LOCATION OF XINTANG

FIGURE 2: AERIAL PHOTOGRAPH OF XINTANG VILLAGE

Hangzhou which runs from west to east through the heart of the city. The area covered by farmers' residences is about 16.87 hectares. It has a total of 956 farmer households with 3042 persons, of which 1482 persons are urban residents but have lived in this area for many years. Apart from the residential buildings, there are several factories and warehouses in the southern part of the village which collectively belong to all Xintang farmers. These factory buildings and warehouses are the only collectively owned property and are an important income source for the farmers. The total floor area of these buildings is about 42,000 sq. metre (see the aerial photograph of Xintang village in Figure 2).

Like other villagers in Hangzhou, farmers in Xintang were allowed to build their own residential buildings before the Che Cun Jian Ju policy was enforced. From Figure 3 we can see that the farmers' residential buildings here are typical of urban village residential buildings in Hangzhou; 3–4 storey buildings are constructed side by side without adequate space in between for movement or public services. This is in sharp contrast to the surrounding urban areas. Farmers here are not involved in agricultural activity but own small businesses (self-employed) or work in factories or other service sectors.

FIGURE 3: TYPICAL URBAN VILLAGE RESIDENTIAL BUILDINGS IN HANGZHOU

THE REDEVELOPMENT PROJECT OF XINTANG VILLAGE

The aim of the Xintang Redevelopment Project through Che Cun Jian Ju is to transform this area into an urbanized area with efficient public facilities. Through legal procedures, the village status of Xintang is now canceled and all Xintang villagers now have the status of Hangzhou urban residents with access to all the benefits of ordinary Hangzhou urban residents for example, life insurance. However, all the land in Xintang except that reserved for relocation of residential buildings for villagers and future economic development of the new community is being acquired by the government for real estate development or other purposes.

The interests of the farmers of Xintang community are being fully protected by several means during the redevelopment. As stated above, the farmers are getting land for relocation of their houses and land for the future development of the community. They are also entitled to compensation for land acquisition (including the cost of the land and compensation for the demolition of their former residential buildings). However, as the Che Cun Jian Ju policy requires, the new houses for the farmers are no longer going to resemble the previous one-family-one building of 3–4 stories but apartment buildings similar to those in urban residential neighborhoods. The families are going to be relocated into the new farmer apartments with a space of at least 200 sq. meter or more, based on the family size. These farmer apartment houses are being constructed by the Jianggan District Farmer House Building Center (JDFHBC) and distributed to the farmers at 900 yuan per sq. meter which is much lower than even the building cost. In practice, one family gets two apartments with a total floor area of more than 200 sq. meter and one apartment is then leased out. Recently, the Hangzhou government agreed to give these farmer apartments the status of commodity houses, which means that the apartments distributed to the farmers are likely to receive the same value as houses in the real estate market and can be sold at any time without extra fees such as land-use fees. Through these means, the interests of the farmers are now protected and the urbanization process is speeding up with little resistance from the farmers.

As for clearing of the land in Xintang village, the farmers are getting compensation for their buildings (including the value of the building, plus the value of internal and external decorations, and even the trees and plants in the garden). It is estimated that about one million RMB yuan is going to be given as compensation to families with isolated 3–4 storey houses in Xintang village.

THE LAND-USE PLAN OF THE PROJECT

Before all the ideas can be realized in Xintang community, the land-use plan for the whole area is being prepared by the Hangzhou Urban Planning Bureau. After careful site visits and analysis, the tentative land-use plan is being prepared for the Xintang community and presented to the farmers. The farmers or the new urban residents of the community are mainly concerned about the land for relocation of the apartments and the 10 per cent land reserved for future development. The JDFHBC will also present observations on the land-use plan in terms of financial balance or building feasibility. After receiving consent from the community, the Urban Planning Bureau of Hangzhou will submit the land-use plan to the Hangzhou government for approval. As soon as the Hangzhou municipal government approves the land-use plan, the redevelopment project of Xintang community can be carried out (Figure 4).

FIGURE 4: LAND-USE PLAN OF XINTANG COMMUNITY

Impact of the Redevelopment Project of Xintang Village

Through careful land-use planning and management, this project is proving to be successful—meeting the needs of urban development and also ensuring a secure future for the effected households at every step. Most importantly, this redevelopment project is proving to be economically successful with little resistance from farmers. Many families have been relocated into the newly built farmers' apartments and this area is fast developing into a new urban neighborhood.

The Relocation of Farmers: There are 956 families, with 3042 persons, including 1482 non-farmers, in Xintang community. The number of farmers who are being relocated—1866 when a one child family is counted as a four member family. As per the relocation policy, farmer families are allotted 55 sq. meter of space per family member, while for non-farmers the floor area allotted exactly matches that of their former homes. Sites C and D (about 7.41 hectares) (see Figure 5) have been set aside for farmers' residences to be constructed by JDFHBC. According to the planning management of the two sites, the total floor area permitted is 170,500 sq. metre. This can accommodate 3100 farmers (given the standard of 55 sq. meter per farmer). After relocating the 1866 farmers, 67,870 sq. meter floor area which is still remaining may be used for the relocation of non-farmers in the village who will be relocated according to a different standard. Thus, the permitted floor area on sites C and D can accommodate all 956 families of the Xintang community, including farmers and non-farmer urban residents. The relocation of the families is the first and

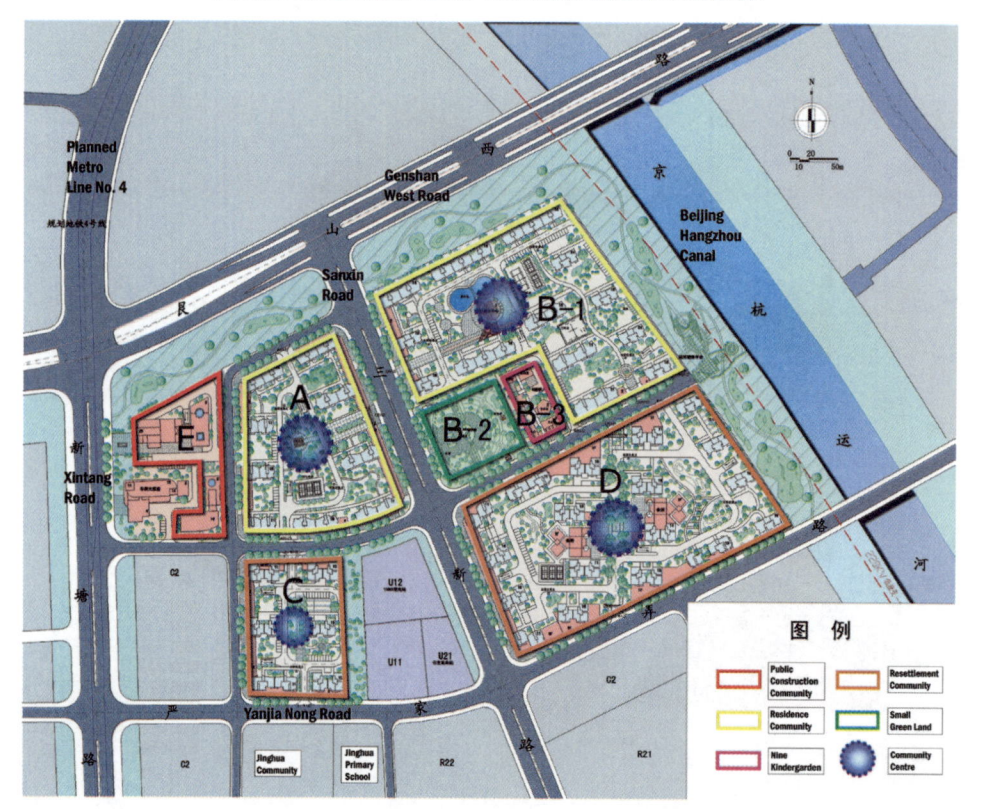

FIGURE 5: DETAILED LAND USE PLAN: SITE ALLOCATION

most important step in the redevelopment project. According to the Che Cun Jian Ju policy, site B which is about 4.45 hectares is going to be sold in the land market by the JDFHBC in order to pay for the balance costs of farmers' houses. It is estimated that site B can bring the central government about 600 million RMB yuan which is enough to subsidize the relocation of the 956 families of the Xintang community. Sites A and E are going to be cleared by Hangzhou Land Reserve Center under the Land Management Bureau and then sold in the land market for real estate purposes. The money thus collected by the Hangzhou municipal government is to be allocated to the infrastructure development in the whole region.

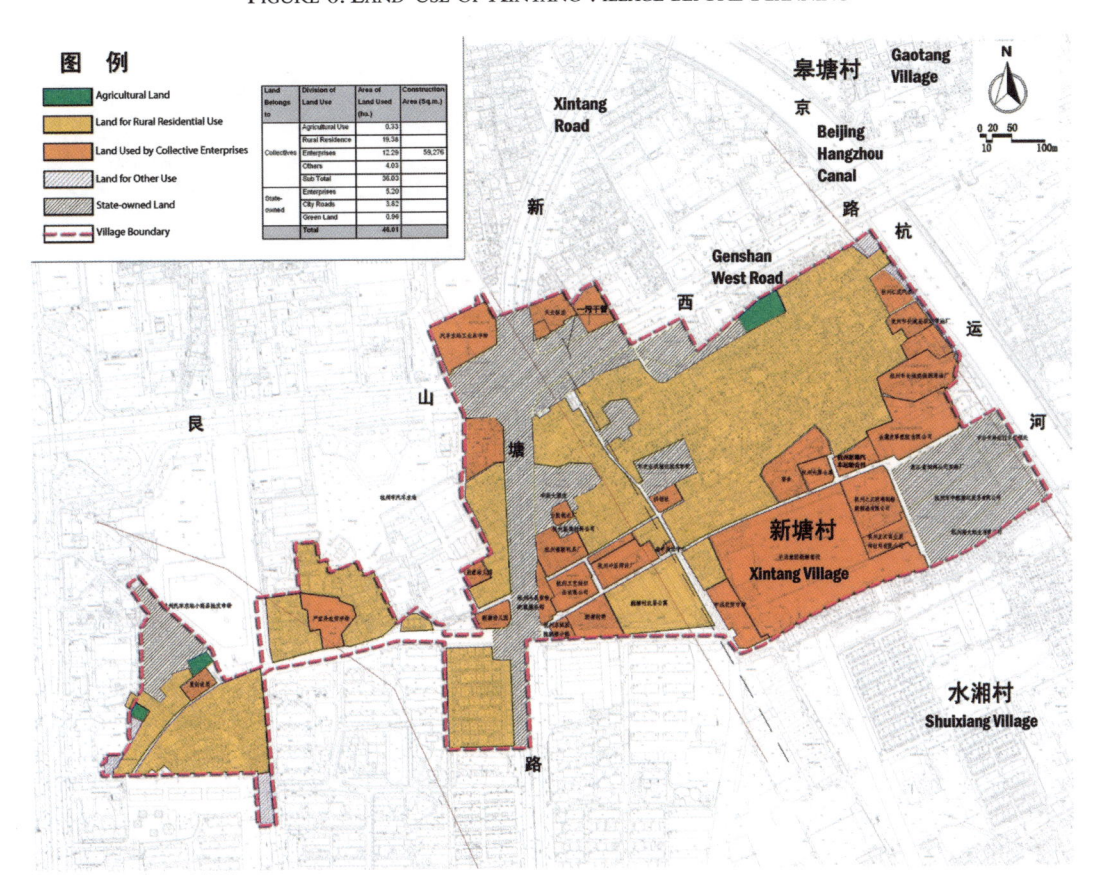

FIGURE 6: LAND-USE OF XINTANG VILLAGE BEFORE PLANNING

The Reserved 10 per cent Land for Future Development: As Xintang village had only 59.6 mu or about 4 hectare arable land left before the redevelopment project, the 10 per cent reserved land for future development of the community (owned by the community) is 6 mu or 4000 square meters, and is going to be used only for commercial or other profitable uses (see the blue rectangle lot in Figure 7).

Therefore, only 5.97 mu or 4000 sq. meter land is to be reserved. This piece of land will belong to the new Xintang community, and can be used for commercial or any other profitable use. The revenue from the development of this piece of land will be shared by all the previous farmers who are now urban residents. They can have the red share of the property each year.

FIGURE 7: LAND USE FOR XINTANG VILLAGE AFTER PLANNING

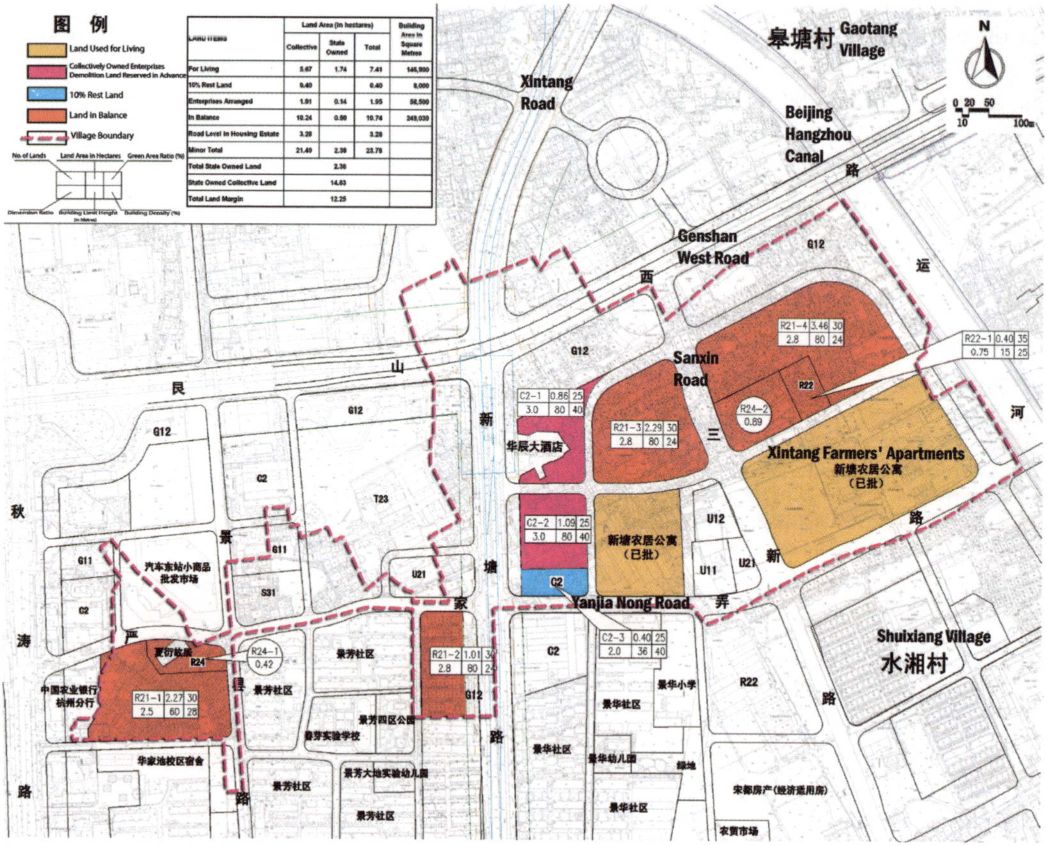

LAND ITEMS	Land Area (in hectares)			Building Area in Square Metres
	Collective	State Owned	Total	
For Living	5.67	1.74	7.41	146,800
10% Rest Land	0.40		0.40	8,000
Enterprises Arranged	1.81	0.14	1.95	58,500
In Balance	10.24	0.50	10.74	249,030
Road Level in Housing Estate	3.28		3.28	
Minor Total	21.40	2.38	23.78	
Total State Owned Land	2.38			
State Owned Collective Land	14.83			
Total Land Margin	12.25			

The Relocation of Buildings in Xintang Community: Before Xintang village lost its status as a village, there were buildings, mainly factories and warehouses, on about 42,000 sq. meter of land. The ownership of these buildings was with Xintang Economic Development Cooperation, which is now collectively owned by all farmers. According to the policy of Che Cun Jian Ju, these buildings should be relocated to the redevelopment project in order to protect the interests of farmers. In the land-use plan, a piece of land of about 1.95 hectares is earmarked for the relocation of these buildings. According to the plan, 58,500 sq. meter floor area can be built on the land—larger than the floor area previously owned by the village. And the newly relocated buildings are going to be a source of income for all farmers of the new Xintang community.

The Xintang project is about two years old. For this, a detailed master plan is being prepared by the Urban Planning Bureau of Hangzhou. The development of Site C in the first phase of the relocation is complete and the farmers are going to be soon accommodated there. Site D, in the second phase of the relocation, is now under construction. (See Figures 8–12.)

FIGURE 8: MASTER PLAN OF XINTANG COMMUNITY

FIGURE 9: BIRD'S-EYE VIEW OF THE XINTANG COMMUNITY

FIGURE 10: APARTMENTS COMPLETED

FIGURE 11: APARTMENTS UNDER CONSTRUCTION

FIGURE 12: COMPLETED APARTMENT IN XINTANG

CONCLUSION

Land acquisition is an inevitable component of urbanization. This is especially true in China which has experienced a very rapid urbanization process in the last three decades. Like many cities in China, Hangzhou also witnessed fast urban growth in last three decades. A large amount of arable land in fringe areas of Hangzhou has been acquired from the villages, and thousands of farmers have become new Hangzhou urban residents. However, during the urbanization process, Hangzhou has relied on a practical means of urbanization—Che Cun Jian Ju. During this process, the interests of the farmers and the villages have been protected to the maximum extent, and therefore, land could be acquired with less resistance from farmers. The practice of Che Cun Jian Ju in Hangzhou has proved to be a successful and effective way of urbanization, while protecting the interests of the farmers.

To conclude, urbanization must not involve only the expansion of the urban area but must protect farmers' interests. If farmers lose their land during the urbanization process and become new urban residents without adequate skills to earn their livelihood in the urban landscape, several problems are bound to arise. Rapid urbanization that takes place at the expense of the farmers cannot be sustained.

7
Silicon Valley in Paradise
Wiring the Urban Water Body of Hangzhou, China

BRIAN MCGRATH

Civic boosters in Hangzhou, China, cleverly combined northern California's famous high-tech corridor with the popular saying in China that the city is 'Paradise on Earth to establish Silicon Valley in Paradise' as a concise slogan that brands the city for tourism and economic development (Hartford 2002). The Southern Song Dynasty (1127–1279 AD) capital is considered to be one of the most scenic cities in China due to its site between the Qiantang river, the Grand Canal and West Lake with its mountain views. But it is a recent embrace of the information economy that fuels its leaders' evocative urban branding which leverages the city's physical charms. This chapter interrogates the metaphor of the brand, as it offers an even more promising urban model than that of a beautiful global high-tech office campus development with lake and mountain views. Rather, Silicon Valley in Paradise offers the basis for a new urban design model for ecological development in China, which combines an ancient sensibility to create a new urban metabolism around an intricate ecosystem of water, land and cultural relationships.

HANGZHOU

The city of Hangzhou—which literally translates as 'city across the water', has always been defined by socio-hydrological relationships; politically, economically and aesthetically. Located near the mouth of the Qiantang river, the completion of the Grand Canal in the beginning of the seventh century made Hangzhou accessible to both the Yangtze and Yellow rivers. The canal ensured the city's strategic economic and political position, first as a sea faring market town, a regional capital, and later as the Southern Song Dynasty Imperial Capital. The city's most prominent feature, the infamous (now) West Lake, has appeared in mythologies, poetry, songs and paintings over the centuries, and caters to a huge domestic tourist market today. Even after the capital was moved to Beijing, the 'Ten Scenes of West Lake' inspired poets and artists as the city was transformed from Imperial Capital to scenic retreat. Now, branding Hangzhou as Silicon Valley in Paradise, economic planners are tuning the ancient landscape to the digital age as the city leverages its physical charm towards a high-tech future.

This essay focuses on the environmental, social and experiential possibilities of mixing 'Silicon Valley' with 'Paradise on Earth', beyond its obvious civic branding appeal. A scientific literature search reveals scores of environmental problems and ongoing ecological monitoring in West Lake, the Grand Canal, the Qiantang river as well as in the headwater mountain area which nourishes the rapidly developing agricultural delta. The growing economic disparities and massive displacement and migration of both farmers and waterways are a coupled socio-natural problem that needs to be fully addressed by the promise of a high-tech paradise. This research is part of a larger research question concerning sustainable urbanization and development in India and China in a networked world. Can these two ancient cultures with rich traditions of skillful environmental design bypass the most severe environmental problems of western industrialization to create a socially and environmentally resilient (urban) future?

WATER BODIES AND URBAN DESIGN IN CHINA

Chinese cities are designed with great emphasis placed on the position of the city in relation to the flow of air and water, and the experience of those (flows) over time by human actors in the city. Cities are located to the south and east of mountains with fresh water flowing from the northwest through the city and draining to the southeast. This reflects the geography of the country as a whole with the Tibetan and Mongolian plateau to the north and east, and the Pacific Ocean and the China Sea to the east and south. With mountains to the west, and West Lake as a fresh water reservoir, Hangzhou is ideally situated to the east of the Lake, draining to the Qiantang river to the southeast, and there is a rich archive of paintings, poetry and songs which reflects a deep appreciation of urban bodies in relation to the water body.

China's history has to a significant extent been defined by its two great rivers: the Yellow river which runs 2400 miles from the Central Asian mountains through north China to the Yellow Sea near Tianjin, draining an area of 400,000 sq. miles of land, and the Yangtze river which originates in the same general area and courses 2750 miles through the middle of the nation, draining 695,000 sq. miles of land before entering the east China Sea near Shanghai. The Yellow river is not navigable, but it is an important source of drinking and irrigation water. The Yangtze is navigable for hundreds of miles, however, and sea-going ships steam 1000 miles up the river from the sea. The Yangtze also provides irrigation water, and the completion of the Three Gorges Dams project on the upper river may provide as much as one-ninth of China's electrical power requirements (Cole 2005). These two great waterways anchor a huge web of rivers and canals that interconnect the inland and highland provinces to the coast. Hangzhou is closely connected to this system through the Grand Canal, the world's oldest and longest at 1114 miles, connecting the city to Beijing.

China has accumulated 5000 years of technical experience in river and watercourse design protecting and enhancing the ecological functioning of the country's water. About 2000 years ago, Li Bing of the Qin Dynasty instituted the technique of cutting across a low watershed and channeling water of the Minjiang river into the Chengdu plain. This project simultaneously solved the problems of the Minjiang river's regular flooding and the Chengdu plain's drought. Its success was due not only to the construction, but also regular maintenance, the two principles of which are 'to pelican deeply and to build a lower wier', to stabilize the ecological features of the river. Around 1000 years ago, Qian Liu of the Wuyue kingdom dredged the hydrographic net of Taihu lake. This project is a successful example of keeping the ecological features of the watercourses. Some 400 years ago, Pan Jishun of Ming Dynasty led the construction of Gaojiayan Dyke, which retained the water of the Huaihe river to form a great reservoir—Hongze lake with volume of more than 10,000 million cubic meters and used its water to wash the Yellow-Huaihe river of its many silts and mud, thus ensuring that the Beijing–Hangzhou Grand Canal, the economic artery of China, remains unblocked (Yang and Pan 1996).

CONSTRUCTING THE HANGZHOU WATER BODY

Hangzhou is ideally situated embracing West Lake at the foothills of large mountain ranges to the west. The Qiantang river is to the south and east of the core of the city, just before it widens to form an estuary to the northeast. The Grand Canal is just one of the thousands of excavated watercourses that crisscross the fertile flood plain between the Qiantang and Yangtze deltas. During ancient times much of Hangzhou was covered with water—people needed boats to get from one place to another. The area of the modern city of Hangzhou was a shallow bay which appeared and disappeared with the ebb and flow of the tidal waters of Qiantang river. The city occupied new land constructed by shifting silt between the Qiantang river and dredging a mash to create West Lake (Chen 2003: 23). Historical maps record the shifting outline of the city in relationship to the fluidity of river flooding and lake silting up over time.

In the late sixth century, the Grand Canal was extended south from the Yangtze river. The first city walls were built in 606 AD. There were ten gates which were associated with the material flows that passed through them: fish were brought in at North Pass Gate; silk was available out of Moat Dyke Gate and Gen Hill Gate; horse riding was popular outside Sunward, Phoenix Hill Gate; salt was available outside Spiral Shell Gate and Quiet and Peaceful Gate; vegetables were taken in at Grass Bridge Gate and Riverview Gate; wine was transported at Tide Awaiting Gate; firewood came in at Clear Ripples Gate; boating started from Surging Waves Gate; pilgrimage was made via Qiantang's Seawall Gate; manure was carried in and out of Peaceful and Tranquil Gate; and finally, Spring Celebrating Gate. Also, in the Tang Dynasty (618–907 AD) six wells were diverted to make available drinking water from West Lake to the city. Fertile soil led to the development of many agricultural products including mandarins, oranges, sugar cane, rice, cotton, rape, hemp, flax, and so on. Hangzhou's silk industry was established in the seventh century, but the leading product was tea (Chen 2003: 16 and 17)

Between the tenth and thirteenth centuries Hangzhou served as the capital of the tributary kingdom of Wuyue (907–78 AD) under the Five Dynasties [907–60 AD] (Chen 2003: 15). During this time a prosperous mercantile economy developed with international trade via sea connections to Japan, Korea and India. Later, Hangzhou became the Imperial Capital of the Southern Song Dynasty [1127–1279 AD] (Chen 2003: 15 and 23). The population increased at that time to 1.24 million, as the city became the largest in the world. In the late thirteenth century, after the invasion by the Mongols, the capital was moved to Beijing (Chen 2003: 24). Marco Polo visited the former capital city during the Yuan Dynasty (1271–1368 AD) and recognized it as 'Paradise on Earth'.

While lake dredging was neglected during the Yuan Dynasty, the Qing (1644–1911 AD) emperors made Hangzhou their vacation retreat and inscribed steles at the 'Ten Scenes of West Lake', thus inaugurating the city as a leisure and tourist destination. The city was damaged by imperialist powers in the wake of the Opium War [1840–42 AD] (Chen 2003: 25), but has seen a huge upswing in prosperity in recent years, with much capital investment on restoring the landscape and water quality of West Lake. This includes the People's Republic Reforestation Projects; dredging the lake in the 1950's; a river water diversion project to daily flush the lake and sewer interception project in the 1980s, and a complete renovation of the southern perimeter of the lake at the beginning of this century.

QIANTANG RIVER

Hangzhou, while located near the mouth of the Qiantang river, traditionally turned its back to the river and faced the lake. The most compelling characteristic of the mouth of this great river is the tidal bore which regularly appears at the estuary of the river. It is one of the most spectacular bores in the world (Pan, Lin and Mao 2007). There are records of the historical development and use of thousand-year-old tide-prediction tables which give evidence to the long term careful observation of the natural phenomenon of the river (Zuosheng, Emery and Yui 1989).

Tide-prediction tables require an understanding of the relation of the tide to the moon and the sun, as expressed by correspondence of tide heights to phases of the moon and by the lag of high tide after local meridional transit of the moon. Such tables were compiled earlier in China than elsewhere more to satisfy the interests of sightseers of spectacular river bores than for convenience of shipping. Zuosheng, Emery and Yui (1989) used the earliest extant Chinese tables of 1056 AD to compare ancient predictions with those from modern tide tables for the Qiantang river bore near Hangzhou. Today, a new city hall complex faces the river in a dramatic reorientation of the city towards the south, where the new high-tech industry zone is located.

GRAND CANAL

The construction of the Grand Canal in the Sui Dynasty (581–618 AD) triggered the growth of Hangzhou into a major cultural, economic and political center. The Grand Canal links up five great rivers: the Haihe, Yellow, Huaihe, Yangtze and Qiantang. Emperors shipped rice, salt, tea, exotic flowers and birds and grotesquely shaped rocks from east China, while travelling, happy emperors toured east China by boat (Chen 2003: 15–33). China's Grand Canal travels 1114 miles connecting Beijing to Hangzhou. Construction began in 486 BC, but the new Song Dynasty (1127–1279 AD) capital of Hangzhou linked the Canal to the Yangtze river. When Beijing replaced Hangzhou as the capital of the Yuan Dynasty, the Canal reached its final form. The Grand Canal was built for both commerce—transporting rice, tea and silk and government control.

Beginning in the sixteenth century, officials promoted the hydraulic religion of the 'Great King' cult as an adjunct to their administration of the Grand Canal and the Yellow river (Dodgen 1999). In the middle years of the Ming (1368–1644 AD) Dynasty, temples dedicated to the Fourth Son Golden Dragon Great began to appear on dikes and in administrative centers along the Yellow river and the Grand Canal. The Golden Dragon cult originated as an ancestral cult dedicated to an apotheosized Southern Song (1127–1280 AD) patriot from the Hangzhou area. It later became popular with boatmen and merchants who traveled on the Grand Canal. A network of minor canals criss-crosses the entire region between the mouths of the Qiantaing and Yangze rivers, interconnecting farms, villages, minor towns and the cities of Suzhou, Shanghai and Hangzhou.

WEST LAKE

West Lake was thought to have formed first as a lagoon from alluvial sediment from the Qiantang river around 12,000 years ago. Two thousand years ago it was formed by a sandbar built up by the Qiantang river, eventually forming a lake about 1400 years ago during the Sui Dynasty (Ramsay 2005). The lake collected between two fingers of land that jutted into the estuary. First a small bay at the river's mouth, then a small lagoon, finally 1400 years ago, with the help of human settlers, the lake turned into an inland water body. Hangzhou was settled on the alluvial plain east of the lake, which was served by multiple canals as main arteries.

Myths account for a Jade Dragon and Golden Phoenix who ground a dazzling pearl from a pebble. The pearl fell into the earth and turned into a clear lake. The Flying Dragon and the Dancing Phoenix forever stood by as they turned into the hills which guard the lake today. Geographer Zhu

Kezhen (1890–1974) describes the birth and formation of West Lake in great detail. According to him, it is 2.1 miles north/south, 1.7 miles east/west and 9.3 miles in circumference. The lake is fed by natural rainfall and springs from the hill as well as river water. The drainage area 8.1 sq. miles and it is surrounded by verdant hills north, west and south. Two man-made causeways divide the lake into three parts: outer and inner to the west and back to the north.

One natural island—Solitary Hill is located to the north, while three man-made islands were constructed from dredging lake sediments. Solitary Hill was geologically formed by rhyolites from an erupting volcano during the Cretateous period and rose to 125 feet from the surface of the lake (Chen 2003: 74). Springs streams and caves found in surround hills: Tiger Spring, Dragon Well Spring, Jade Spring, Rosy Cloud Cave, Yellow Dragon Cave, Lingyin Stream, Nine Creeks and Eighteen Gullies are among the noted natural features around the lake. Architectural marvels include pagodas and temples (Chen 2003: 37).

Although naturalistic in its scenery, the lake has been continuously manipulated by human actors and agents. Tang Dynasty poet/governor Bai Juyi (772–846 AD) built a stone culvert to release lake water and did the first large scale dredging. During Bai Juyi's two year governorship, the weather took a turn between excessive rain and drought. He tackled the problem through first hand investigation, and dredged the ancient wells and erected the causeway to store irrigation water (Chen 2003: 42). The dike/causeway created an upper and lower lake in order to store water in times of drought. Bai Causeway is the only access from the city to the natural island of Solitary Hill in West Lake. It is a one kilometer long embankment lined on both sides with peach blossoms and weeping willow trees. 'Strolling the willow-shaded white-sand dyke I enjoy the most' (Chen 2003). These landscape and architectural features' main purpose was to connect the various sensing apparatus of human bodies to the variabilities of nature around the constructed water body of Hangzhou.

Su Dongpo (Northern Song, 960–1127 AD) inaugurated further dredging and constructed the Su Causeway during his second term (1089–91 AD) with his 1000 strong dredging team. Su Causeway is 2.8 kilometers long and is comprised of six single arch bridges. The Southern Song Imperial Art Academy Painters created 'Ten Scenes of West Lake', turning civil engineering into art and poetry: 'Spring Dawn at Su Causeway', 'Breeze-ruffled Lotus at Quyuan Garden', 'Autumn Moon over the Calm Lake', 'Lingering Snow at the Broken Bridge', 'Orioles Singing at the Willows', 'Viewing Fish at Flower Pond', 'Three Pools Mirroring the Moon', 'Twin Peaks Piercing the Cloud', 'Evening Bell Ringing at Nangping Hill', and finally, 'Leifeng Pagoda in Evening Glow' (Chen 2003: 36–43).

The Palace Museum in Taipei has an extensive collection of different sets of Ten Views of West Lake'—various interpretations of famous scenic pictures of a landscape near Hangzhou—over the centuries when it was an Imperial retreat. The views are of fog between twin peaks, listening to orioles, appreciating snow and so on. In other words, various places in various seasons, times of days and weather conditions remembered through specific sensations. Instead of static pictures, it was as if the human presence in the landscape was actively picturing a fluid moving nature. The word 'views' is a misnomer—the painting cycles are accompanied by poetry by various artists within structured themes. Views, in the sense of different points of view; multiple, fluid, ephemeral. Capturing fleeting impressions and securing them as embodied memories.

One series is an unfolded album of square folders, with a gold square pasted on the left and the 'view' on the right. There are stamps and calligraphic signatures which add to the layering of the images. Another example is a series of vertical scrolls. The eye looks down—foreground, then across—middle ground—then up—background. Again the painting is glued to the scroll and beautifully framed with different fabric. The stamps and calligraphy again mark another layer on the images. Another album series, and then there appears a long horizontal scroll—a kind of 180 degree panoramic overview of the entire scene. Finally a dark burnt amber series, the most delicate and ephemeral of the series. One leaves the room with such a vivid impression of this place, structured around ten standard views, but with an endless variety of attempts to depict their elusive senses; sounds, fog, subtle feelings.

While the lake silted up during the Yuan Dynasty, dredging revived in Ming Dynasty. Quing emperors expanded lake to present proportions and made many trips and inscribed names of popular scenes marked with steles (Chen 2003: 36). As mentioned above, lake dredging later resulted in the construction of artificial islands in addition to the two causeways. A mid-lake pavilion island was constructed in 1552 AD, while the famous 'Three Pools Mirroring the Moon' is located off an island built in 1607 AD with dredging from the lake. This 'fairy islet' features 'a lake within an islet and an islet within a lake'. In Chinese gardens, water is the soul of gardening. Sixty per cent of this 17.3 acre islet is water. The nine turn bridge offers a different scene with each step; there are actually 30 turns on the bridge—giving the illusion of spaciousness in the tiny park. There are two pavilions along this short bridge which sits low on the water. Walls do not necessarily serve as part of a building, but to hide views—a psychological trick to whet the appetite for the next view (Chen 2003: 47).

Most often the question posed is 'how do the three pagodas mirror the moon?'. The answer to it suggests that they form an equilateral triangle 2 meters above the water, 62 meters long. Each pagoda is hollow with five circular openings. Candles are placed inside and paper covered for the openings creating moon like reflections in the rippling water. The Breeze Ruffled Lotus is a 1699 AD scenic spot moved and enlarged for Emperor Kangxi's visit. Since the 1970s this popular scene has been greatly extended as a big tourist attraction (Chen 2003: 74).

Ruan Gong Islet was built in 1800 from lake bottom silt. Its soil was too soft for the construction of a building, so it became a wildlife refuge. However, in 1982 thin slab construction allowed for buildings, a paved road and 600 flowers and shrubs creating a new tourist attraction (Chen 2003: 51). The historic fish viewing pond has also been expanded enormously since 1949. It is known for goldfish, stream and flowers. However, '…to assemble so many different kinds of flowers in a small area, however, is (more) typical of Western gardening' (Chen 2003: 81–2). The tendency of recent embellishments has been on pictorial beauty, and the desires of tourists to be photographed near the scenery. The more sensory aspects of the design and appreciation of the earlier ten scenes seem often lost today in the crowd of visitors.

WIRED WEST LAKE

Hangzhou continues to be a magnet for tourists seeking manicured nature and urban scenic beauty within the rapidly modernizing China. The local government has embraced the developmental potential of the information economy, particularly networking and internet expansion for a number of years (Hartford 2002). Hangzhou's strategic advantages include a strong foreign trade orientation and a relatively high proportion of population with a good technical education. Zhejiang University, an outstanding center of science and technology education, is the Stanford of the imagined Silicon Valley of technical experts and venture capitalists.

The Yangtze river delta region is characterized by light industry, a strategic export orientation, rural industrialization, foreign/joint venture investments and recent upgrading of regional transportation networks. Hartford speculates that current industries—textile, apparel, machine tools and chemical are likely to find themselves under increasing stress. The policy response is to place Silicon Valley at the center stage in the city's strategy and future vision.

Hartford highlights Hangzhou's path to the information economy from 1995 when it became the third city in China to be connected to the internet in 1995. 'The Informationization Work Leading Group' was established shortly after 1996, and a new High Technology Development Zone was created for startups. It was at this time that the notion of 'Silicon Valley in Paradise' was created, which included an 'infoport' and 'pharmaceuticals port' and Hangzhou Cable Network was tapped to create the broadband transmission network. Hence the city's scenic tourism position was combined with new economic development that scaled down to 'informationized tourism', 'informationized communities' and 'informationized households'.

Historically in China, the design of public and private urban landscapes in relation to water has played a large role in engaging people through periods of cultural change and development. A key research question will be how to create a public environment to link these themes with environmental monitoring and social justice under the theme of "'Wiring the Water Body of the City'. With millions of domestic tourists descending upon Hangzhou every year, how can they take back with them not just more scenic photos, but new environmental knowledge and direct sensorial experience with ecological processes? In addition to the high profile public waterfront parks along the river front, canal banks and West Lake, the study will also examine more humble settings on the periphery where wet rice farming, surface canals and the aquifer, intimately connected to the hydrology of the river, canal and lake, are being replaced by new development and how this transforms the meaning and metabolism of water and place in Hangzhou.

NEW ECOLOGICAL MODELS FOR URBAN DESIGN

Sharon Haar argues that urban design in China has focused more on the metaphor of the ecological city than ecological metabolism. However, I would argue that there is great value to both. Without broad-based popular engagement with urban ecology, all the scientific understanding in the world will not create the change in perception required to connect scenic beauty, sensual pleasure, and sustainable design. Ecologists Steward Pickett and Mary Cadenasso write about the need to combine meaning, model, metaphor to integrate ecology and design, and the shift in thinking about ecology *in* the city to ecology *of* the city. For them, all ecological concepts have a core definition, need to be applied though specific models, and have informal, imagistic content as metaphors. A provocative metaphor that practitioners from both disciplines find compelling can link the ecology *of* the city to urban ecosystem design *in* the city. The metaphorical connotation of any scientific concept allows the idea to be imagined by a wide public as well as to specialists in other disciplines. The ecosystem concept begins with a general definition, which is specified or turned into scientific models which apply to certain situations and collections of organisms found in particular places. A turn from ecology *in* the city to ecology *of* the city would shift the emphasis of West Lake as a scenic resource to the metabolism of the Wired Water Body of the wider Hangzhou region.

An example of a model of ecosystem function is the Hubbard Brook Experimental Forest in New Hampshire, which provided the context for the discovery of acid rain in North America. The ecosystems at Hubbard Brook are delimited by small watersheds, and have limited infiltration with nearly impervious granite bedrock (Likens and Bormann 1995). The small watershed spatial limitation allowed for the study of nutrients and chemistry of the streams draining each watershed. Continuous monitoring of phosphorus levels led to the discovery of acid rain and its affect on the forest ecosystem. (Likens 1992). The third dimension of the ecosystem concept is used in informal or non-specialized communication. People often use the term ecosystem to refer to an area of the world they are interested in simply to identify it as a place, or perhaps more provocatively to assume something about how biological processes in that area work. The metaphorical dimension of the ecosystem concept is often used to connote self-regulation, or a closed network of energy and matter flow (Golley 1993). Using such metaphors of the ecosystem expresses values in the public discourse about environmental policy (Pickett and Cadenasso 2007) and expands the human imagination in appreciation of the intricacies of natural systems.

CURRENT SCIENTIFIC MONITORING OF HANGZHOU'S WATER BODIES

Numerous modern scientific studies have begun which monitor the ecological functioning and dynamics of the powerful Qiantang river, the Grand Canal and West Lake. The Qiantang river includes risk levels of 13 organochlorine pesticides (OCPs) in surface water and sediments. A total of 180 surface water samples at 45 sampling sites and 48 sediment samples at 19 sampling stations were collected (Zhou, Zhu, Yang and Chen 2006). Development impacts on the natural swing of the main channel of the Qiantang river as controlled by the high-water and low-water changes, as well as the impact of large-scale reclamation of tidal flats are being studied (Feng and Bao 2007). Numerical models of the tidal bore on the Qiantang river are being run (Pan, Lin and Mao 2007) and a physical model of the flow field or the Qiantang tidal bore is being constructed analyzing sedimentation (Chanson 2003).

Eleven surface sediment samples have been collected from the Hangzhou section of Qiantang river, the Grand Canal and West Lake to investigate 17 polycyclic aromatic hydrocarbons (PAHs) in aquatic sediment (Zhu, Cai, and Wang 2005). Nitrogen pollution characteristics in the Hangzhou section of the Qiantang river were monitored during 2000–1 (Wu, Yu and Qian 2003). The main sources of the nitrogen were discovered to be sewage and livestock faeces and the over-application of nitrogenous fertilizer in the basin of the Qiantang river.

In spite of the emphasis on new high-tech industry, a dirty industrial legacy haunts paradise's waters. Dunao and Huanxin (1987) discovered higher contents of iron and manganese in confined aquifer along the Hangzhou reach of the Grand Canal. The canal was heavily polluted by PAHs released from factory wastewater. PAHs trapped in the sediment are now the main sources of this pollutant in surface water. The PAHs in Qiantang river were attributed to soil runoff (Chen, Zhu, Wang, Gao, Yang and Shen 2004). Groundwater and soil samples from the Hangzhou reach of the Grand Canal were examined by infrared spectrum and differential thermal analysis. Hydrogeological investigations were also carried out. The higher contents of iron and manganese in water from unconfined aquifer were caused by their release from the heavy soils and the anaerobic environment. This study indicated that internal release of oxygen-depletion materials from sediment maybe the major factor affecting water quality of the Hangzhou section of the Grand Canal (Zhu 2002).

Investigations were conducted to evaluate the contamination level of the Grand Canal and the adjacent hydrogeological systems near Hangzhou (Weng and Chen 2000). The top layer sediment in the Grand Canal serves as a sink to anthropogenic contaminants consisting of heavy metals as well as organic compounds (Zhu, Chen, Zhou, Wang and Wu 2001). Polluted canal water impacts adjacent soil and groundwater systems. The sediment from the Hangzhou section of the Grand Canal, China, was also examined with a potential ecological risk index (He, Zhu, Chen, Tian, and Chen 2002). Release of phosphorus from sediments of the Hangzhou section of the Grand Canal was discovered by Zhu, Chen, Zhou and Qin (2002). Jin, Chen, Wang and Norio Ogura (2003) detected nitrate sources in urban groundwater by isotopic and chemical indicators in Hangzhou City. Concentrations of heavy metals and organic matters vary widely along the canal (Chen, Liu, Zhu, Chen and Tian 2004).

Li, Zhu and Wang (1998) discovered some physical and chemical characteristics of sediment in West Lake that demonstrate that the precursor of West Lake sediment was a bog. Wu and Yu (2001) looked at the long-time ecological effect of eutrophication control measures such as damming, dredging, diluting, establishing and restoring the ecosystem mainly of macrophyte, which was the effective way to control the eutrophication of the West Lake. In 1988, Wei proposed that the current water of the Qiantang river could play a principal role in improving the water quality of the West Lake by studying zooplankton. As a result, river water is now diverted to flush West Lake. Wu, Wu, Jin, Xuan, Li and Meizi (1998) released preliminary studies on the total phosphorus content in the West Lake waterbody before and after introduction of water from Qiantang river.

Ning, Shi, Liu, Chen, Liu and Zhu, Genhai (1989) had investigated the primary production and eutrophication in the waters of West Lake. Pei, Ma, Zhou, Cai and Li (2000) created a dynamic model of algae in West Lake. The model describes the dynamics of the four main algae (cyanophyta, chlorophyta, cryptophyta and bacillariophyta) and zooplanktons in West Lake on yearly time scales. Pei and Ma (2002) later studied the algae dynamic model for West Lake to create a management strategy limiting eutrophication processes in West Lake keeping West Lake clear. However, none of this scientific work, or the new technological solution is legible or visible to the millions of visitors seeking splendid scenery in Hangzhou.

PARTICIPATORY WATER MONITORING

Katshuhiko Takahashi has described two decades of exchange projects between China and Japan to see how local inhabitants are motivated to get involved in monitoring water and its amenities. He describes the conflictual and complex governmental organizations which oversee water resources in China. The State Environmental Protection Administration (SEPA) is considerably understaffed, and its authority must be coordinated with The National People's Congress, the State Council, The State Economic and Trade Commission, Ministry of Foreign Affairs, Ministry of Water Conservancy, Ministry of Construction, Ministry of Agriculture, Ministry of Science and Technology, State Forestry Administration, State Oceanic Administration, Ministry of Land and Resources, China Meteorological Administration, Ministry of Communications and local governments.

The China–Japan Joint Project on Conservation and the Environment and Historic Landscape of West Lake (1993–99) illuminated the mechanisms of eutrophication to local residents and proposed ways to improve the quality and clarity of the lake through public environmental activism. The Joint Project included an environmental program that established an Environment Day with exhibits, lectures and presentations, community activities to clean up the shores of the lake, recreational walks around the lake, nature watching activities, water quality monitoring, and the publication of educational supplements. An Amenity Workshop was held in West Lake between 1996–98 focusing on water monitoring and youth education and exchange. Finally, a Field Museum was planned between 1998 and 2002. These joint China–Japan programs have established local knowledge and monitoring to supplement the twice yearly official monitoring established every March and October.

IS BEAUTY SKIN DEEP?

Forbes recently named that Hangzhou as China's top city for business—proving that in at least an economic, if not in an ecological sense, its beauty is more than just skin deep (Jenny Lu, 2004). In a survey released by the Chinese-language edition of Forbes magazine, Hangzhou surpassed

Shanghai and Beijing and scored highest among Chinese cities in overall business strength. The survey took into account market size, the percentage of workforce with a college degree, the cost of doing business, and transportation infrastructure. Since its adoption of the new open economy in 1992, the study confirmed the success of the Silicon Valley in Paradise campaign in transforming Hangzhou's industrial base from the textiles, silk and machinery to the burgeoning high-tech sector. Hangzhou is now connected by high speed railway to Shanghai in time for the 2010 World Expo. Travel time between Hangzhou and Shanghai has been reduced from two hours by road to less than an hour.

According to Lu, foreign investment has been encouraged by a significant government role in development. Like many other Chinese cities, the Hangzhou government has acted aggressively in recent years to attract new investments. In 2001, Hangzhou's two neighboring cities Xiaoshan and Yuhang were merged into the Hangzhou municipality as districts. With this integration, the city's total urban area has been enlarged from 683 sq. kilometers to 3068 sq. kilometers and the Qiantang river replaced West Lake as the scenic focus for urbanization. South of the Qiantang is the booming Xiaoshan development area, Hangzhou's high-tech zone. In the river's northern side sits the older city area together with the Yuhang district and a new waterfront civic center and park. Spanning the soaring tide of the Qiantang are six gigantic bridges that fully connect greater Hangzhou.

Complementing the lush enhancement of the park on the southern edge of West Lake, Hong Kong's Shui On Land Limited launched a new 'lifestyle destination', *Xihu Tiandi* (Heaven and Earth by West Lake), modeled on the company's flagship development, Shanghai's famous *Xin Tiandi*. The place, with its renovation of historic buildings and new low rise luxury retail around pedestrian plazas has become popular among locals as well as tourists. On a rainy afternoon, one can sip a café latte and enjoy the tranquility of the lake with the city's newly emerged middle class.

With such massive changes at the regional scale and in the commodification of landscape and scenery, how will Hangzhou maintain its intimate connection with its water bodies? The city traditionally embraced West Lake as its symbol of poetic inspiration, cultural enlightenment and environmental health, carefully manipulating and observing its various moods over the seasons. With the expansion of the city over the entire Qiantang river estuary, new remote sensing technology is needed to supplement the close-up observation of the city's water bodies. Zhang and Huang (2005) have analyzed coastal changes using multi-spectral imagery from eight different time periods. The city has also incorporated a high-tech digital urban management system at a micro level, with an army of mobile data recording devices, which tag information on every planted tree, waste receptacle, park bench and street light. This large and small scale and long-term monitoring can be linked to the types of participatory activities begun in the joint China–Japan program. Multi-spectral imagery *senses* the water body of the city giving thermal and reflectivity data in wave bands in the non-visible spectrum. How will these new sensing and monitoring technologies create new 'scenes' to complement the traditional ones that have captured the cultural imagination of the visitors to and citizens of Hangzhou for centuries?

REFERENCES

Chanson, Hubert (2003) *Mixing and Dispersion in Tidal Bores*, International Conference on Estuaries and Coasts (ICEC), November 9–11, Hangzhou, China.

Chen, Gang (2003) *Hangzhou China Travel Series*, Foreign Language Press, Beijing.

Chen BL, L.Z. Zhu, J. Wang, Y.Z. Gao, K. Yang, H.X. Shen and J.K.X. Huan (2004) Vol. 25, No. 1, pp.107–10. (in Chinese)

Chen Y.X., H. Liu, G.W. Zhu, H.L. Chen, G.M. Tian (2004) 'Pollution Characteristics of The Recent Sediments in the Hangzhou Section of the Grand Canal, China', *Journal of Environmental Science* (China), Vol. 16, No. 1, pp.34–9.

Cole, Bernard D. (2005) 'Waterways and Strategy: China's Priorities', *China Brief*, Vol. 5, No.4, February 15.

Dodgen, Randall (1999) *Hydraulic Religion: 'Great King' Cults in the Ming and Qing*, Modern Asian Studies, Cambridge, pp. 815–33.

Dunao, W. and W. Huanxin (1987) 'Higher Contents of Iron and Manganese in Confined Aquifer Along the Hangzhou Reach of the Grand Canal', *Acta Scientiae Circumstantiae*, Vol. 7, No. 3, pp. 279–88.

Feng, Lihua and Yixin Bao (2007) 'The Formation and Evolution of the Xisan Tidal Furrow and the Reclamation of Tidal Flats in Hangzhou Bay', *Journal of Coastal Research*, Vol. 23, No. 4, July.

Golley, F.B. (1993) *A History of the Ecosystem Concept in Ecology: More than the Sum of the Parts*, Yale University Press, New Haven, CT.

Haar, Sharon (2006) *The Ecological City: Metaphor versus Metabolism*, IFoU, International Conference, Beijing.

Hartford, Kathleen (2002) 'West Lake Wired: Shaping Hangzhou's Information Age' in Chin-chuan Lee (ed.), *Chinese Media, Global Contexts*, Routledge, London.

He, Yun-feng, Guang-wei Zhu, Ying-xu Chen, Guang-ming Tian and Hua-lin Chen (2002) 'Study on The Ecological Risk of The Sediment From the Hangzhou Section of The Grand Canal, China, with Potential Ecological Risk Index', *Journal of Zhejiang University*, Agriculture & Life Sciences, Vol. 28, No. 6, pp. 669–74.

Holledge, Simon (1981) *Hangzhou and the West Lake*, Rand McNally, Chicago.

Li, Zhenyu, Yinmei Zhu and Jin Wang (1998) 'Some Physical and Chemical Characteristics of Sediment in West Lake, Hangzhou', *Journal of Lake Sciences*, Vol. 10, No. 1, pp. 79–84.

Likens, G.H. (1992) 'The Ecosystem Approach: Its Use and Abuse', *Excellence in Ecology*, Vol. 3, Ecology Institute, Oldendorf/Luhe, Germany, p. 167.

Likens, G.H. and F.H. Bormann (1995) *Biochemistry in a Forested Ecosystem*, 2nd edition, Springer-Verlag, NY Inc.

Lu, Jenny, (2004) 'Beauty Reigns', Sino Media, http://www.sinomedia.net/eb/v200410/regional-feature.html.

Ning, Xiuren, Junxian Shi, Zilin Liu, Zhongyuan Chen, Zhensheng Liu and Zhu (1989) 'Investigation of Primary Production and Eutrophication in The Waters of West Lake Hangzhou', *Oceanologia et limnologia sinica/Haiyang Yu Huzhao*. Qingdao, Vol. 20, No. 4, pp. 365–74.

Pan, Cun-Hong, Bing-Yao Lin and Xian-Zhong Mao (2007) 'Case Study: Numerical Modeling of the Tidal Bore on the Qiantang River, China', *J. Hydrological Engineering*, Vol. 133, No. 2, pp. 130–8 (February).

Pei, Hongping, Jianyi Ma, Hong Zhou, Jingxian Cai and Gongguo Li (2000) 'The Dynamic Model of Algae in West Lake [Xi Hu] of Hangzhou', *Acta Hydrobiol*, Vol. 24, No. 2, pp. 143–49, Sin./Shuisheng Shengwu Xuebao.

Pei, Hongping and Jianyi Ma (2002) 'Study on The Algal Dynamic Model for West Lake, Hangzhou', *Ecological Modelling*, Vol. 148, No. 1, pp. 67–77.

Pickett, S.T.A. and M. L. Cadenasso (2007) 'Patch Dynamics As A Conceptual Tool to Link Ecology and Design', in B. McGrath, V. Marshall, M. L. Cadenasso, J. M. Grove, S.T.A. Pickett, R. Plunz and J. Towers (eds) *Designing Urban Patch Dynamics*, Columbia University Graduate School of Architecture, Planning and Preservation, Columbia University, New York, pp. 16–29.

Ramsay, Juliet (2005) 'City Lakes as Heritage Settings: West Lake Hangzhou and Lake Burly Griffin, Canberra', Conference Paper from Monuments and Sites in their setting—Conserving cultural heritage in changing townscapes and landscapes, ICOMOS 15th General Assembly, Xian, China, October 2005, http://www.international.icomos.org/xian2005/papers/1-17.pdf.

Takahashi, Katsuhiko (2002) 'Monitoring Water for Improving Amenities in Participating with Local Inhabitants: West Lake, Hangzhou, China', The Precession of the Third World Water Forum, United Nations University Center, 16–17 October.

Wei, Chongde (1988) 'Studies on zooplankton after controlling water pollution in West Lake, Hangzhou', *Transactions of oceanology and limnology/Haiyang Huzhao Tongbao*. Qingdao. no. 1, pp. 72-76.

Weng, H., and Xunhong Chen (2000) 'Impact of Polluted Canal Water on Adjacent Soil and Groundwater Systems', *Environmental Geology*, Vol. 39, No. 8.

Wu, Genfu, Xuechang Wu, Chengtao Jin, Xiaodong Xuan, Li and Meizi (1998) 'Preliminary Studies on Release of Phosphorus From the Sediment of West Lake, Hangzhou', *China Environmental Science*, Vol. 18, No. 2, pp. 107–10.

We Jie, and Zuo-Ming Yu (2001) 'The succession of phytoplankton and the ecological effects of eutrophication control measures in Hangzhou West Lake', *China Environmental Science*, Vol. 21, No. 6, pp. 540–544, 20 December.

Wu, Jie, Zuo-ming Yu and Tian-ming Qian (2003) 'Studies on Nitrogen Pollution Characteristics in Hangzhou Section of the Qiantang River', *Resources and Environment in the Yangtze Basin*, Vol. 12, No. 6, pp. 552–56.

Yang, Liankang and Yuntang Pan (1996) 'Regulation and Development of The Rivers and The Watercourses in Ancient China and Their Relationship with The Environmental Geology', abstracts of papers presented at the 30th International Geological Congress, Vol. 3, pp. 423.

Yang Zuosheng, K. O. Emery and Xui Yui (1989) 'Historical Developments and Use of Thousand-year-old-tide-prediction Tables', *Limnology and Oceanography*, Vol. 34, No. 5, pp. 953–57.

Zhang Huajuo, Huang Weigen (2005) *An Investigation of Coastal Changes in Hangzhou Bay Using Multi-temporal Remote Sensing Imagery*, Laboratory of Ocean Dynamic Processes and Satellite Oceanography, Second Institute of Oceanography and Ocean University of China.

Zhu, Chen, Zhou, Wang and Wu (2001) 'Distribution of Heavy Metals in the Sediments from The Grand Canal (Hangzhou section)', *China Environmental Science*, Vol. 21, No. 1, pp. 65–9.

Zhu, G., Y. Chen, G. Zhou and B. Qin (2002) 'Study on The P Release From Sediments of the Hangzhou Section of the Grand Canal, China', *Journal of Lake Sciences*, Vol. 14, No. 4, pp. 343–49.

Zhu, Guangwei (2002) 'Release of Oxygen-depletion Materials From Sediment of The Hangzhou Section of the Grand Canal, China', *Environmental Pollution and Control*, Vol. 24, No. 4, pp. 232–35.

Zhu L.Z., J. Cai, X.F. Wang (2005). 'PAHs in Aquatic Sediment in Hangzhou, China: Analytical Methods, Pollution Pattern, Risk Assessment and Sources', *Journal of Environmental Science*, Vol. 17, No. 5, pp. 748–55.

Zhou Rongbing, Lizhong Zhu, Kun Yang and Yuyun Chen (2006) 'Distribution of Organochlorine Pesticides in Surface Water and Sediments from Qiantang River, East China', *Journal of Hazardous Materials*, Vol. 137, No. 1, pp. 68–75.

8

Beginning a Conversation on Chinese Urbanization

PARTHA MUKHOPADHYAY[a]

INTRODUCTION

The scale and variety of Chinese urbanization can overwhelm attempts at analysis. This paper is an exploratory attempt to relate broader patterns of economic transformation in India and China. It addresses specific issues related to various aspects of urbanization, responding largely to issues raised by Zongyong Wen (chapter 5 in this volume). It then situates the specific model of urban transformation described by Zuojun Yang (chapter 6 in this volume) in an Indian comparative context before concluding with an agenda for future conversations, drawing on Brian McGrath (chapter 7 in this volume), which emphasizes the importance of the specificity of the Indian and Chinese urban experience.

INDIA AND CHINA

One of the greater misfortunes of history is the breakdown in familiarity between two large Asian civilizations, India and China.

Zongyong Wen (chapter 5 in this volume) describes the Indian character as follows:

It seems that India is self-contained, slow-paced, self-contented, mysterious, tolerant and contradictory, all at the same time... Most Indians seem to have a resigned and passive outlook towards life. They believe in karma and are usually at peace. From Agra to New Delhi to Mumbai, you would see smiling faces everywhere, including the slums. This is a testament to the optimistic attitude of the citizens of this nation. The peace-loving character of Indians was witnessed during the non-violent independence struggle led by Gandhi...Usually, Indians are active thinkers, who think more than they act, whereas the Chinese ... cross the river by feeling the stones. This difference in people's character is closely related with the cultural traditions of the two countries.

It is true that some Indians would be fatalistic and content with their fate, but the non-violent character of the Indian independence movement should not be conflated with mildness.

---

[a] Though it has been four years since I received the India China Fellowship from the New School University, I am still hesitant to write on Chinese urbanization. This paper is written on the premise that it is necessary to articulate ones views if one has to learn how mistaken they are. Its genesis is a series of responses motivated by discussions with my three good friends and partners in inquiry, Zongyong Wen, Zuojun Yang, and Brian McGrath, who are completely absolved of responsibility for my limited understanding of the Chinese situation. I am also indebted to the other Fellows of my cohort, Ashok Gurung and others then at ICI, specially Arjun Appadurai and Anita Patil-Deshmukh for their support.

FIGURE 1: INDIA'S EXPORTS AND IMPORTS AS A SHARE OF GDP

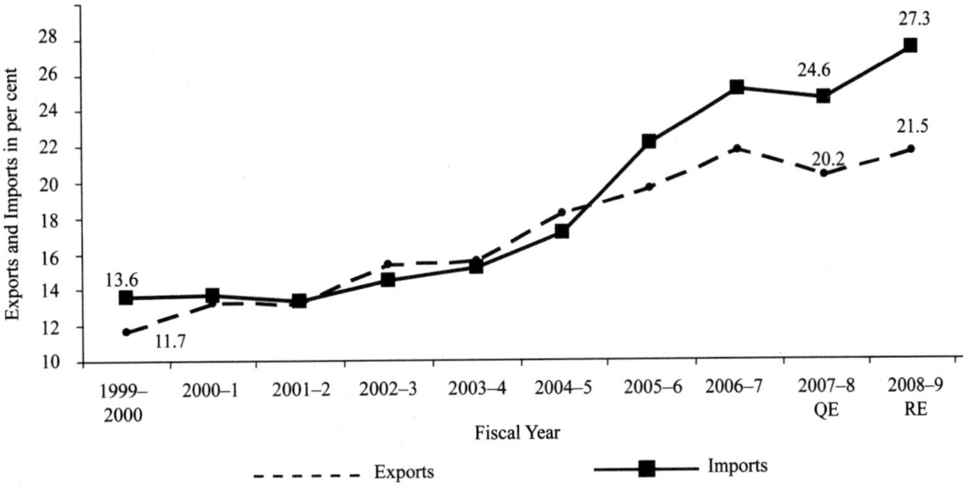

Source: Author's calculations from Government of India (2009)

Its strength was in the same levels of mass mobilization as seen in China and a determination that is evident today in the intense participation in our electoral processes. Indeed, for all its flaws, the Indian election process has created a degree of democratic plurality in the past sixty years that is truly more representative of the population. The question is how this change affects the progress of democracy. On this there are many views.

As for the 'smile' on the faces of the underprivileged, it is easy to romanticize. There is however a kernel of truth in that romance, which has much to do with, the heightened levels of agency that these people enjoy, as compared to their previous situation. The poor of the city have seen an expansion of opportunities as Indian cities have become the hub of growth. Migrants coming into the city experience greater degree of control over their lives, as compared to villagers, especially, in terms of social relationships such as caste (Prasad 2009).

Those who doubt that Indians experiment actively, only need to observe the extent of *jugaad*[1] that permeates the private and especially informal sectors in India. However, in the public sector, there is no incentive to experiment. The culture of process accountability implies heavy-handed oversight by bodies such as the Comptroller and Auditor General, the Central Vigilance Commission and the Central Bureau of Investigation. If innovations fail, the innovators are castigated. If they succeed, there are no significant benefits in a bureaucracy where out-of-turn promotions are not prevalent. The incentives for innovation in the public sector are therefore very limited. In China, by contrast, the re-engagement with the market economy since 1980s has been through scaling up of a series of experiments, beginning with the household responsibility system and the Special Economic Zones (SEZs) to the current attempt to evolve political liberalization without democratization (Zhao 2003).[2]

The remarks about the 'big elephant that is India' by Zongyong Wen (chapter 5 in this

---

[1] Jugaad is a colloquial Hindi word that can mean an innovative solution to a problem, either technical or institutional (e.g., solutions that bend rules). It is used in the context of street-smart mechanics and reflects locally devised solutions and lateral thinking.

[2] See also the work of Qin Hui, outlined by Cheng (2008) and the work of Yu Jianrong on social conflict, e.g., Yu (2007)

volume) are indeed spot-on, given that one of the common metaphors for India is often that of seven blindfolded persons trying to describe an elephant, each from experiencing only a part of the pachyderm, such as the trunk, the tail or the feet. It is no less or more mysterious than the Chinese are to the non-Chinese. India's diversity of languages, cultures, ethnicities and religions compels it to be tolerant—indeed, that is perhaps a core principle of its existence, regardless of the various intolerant tendencies that occasionally rise to the surface, a full discussion of which needs to be deferred. It is perhaps just as contradictory as China, which on the surface has the appearance, perhaps cultivated by the leadership, of a homogenous monolith, but is composed of heterogeneous tendencies that are now beginning to emerge, both economically, culturally and to some extent, even politically. This is seen in the different paces at which representation in village government was adopted in China, and the nascent efforts to take such experiments to other levels of government.

India may appear self-contained from the viewpoint of China today, which, especially in the coastal regions, appears deeply integrated with the outside world. One wonders whether the Chinese appreciate exactly how exceptional their experience of international (re)integration really is. While not as dramatic as China's, in relation to its recent past, India is remarkably more open. As Figure 1 shows, the trade ratio has doubled, with the share of exports and imports in total income rising from 11.7–21.5 per cent[3] from 13.6–27.3 per cent, respectively, in 2008–9. This is concomitant with a quantum increase in the engagement of the Indian elite (in terms of their personal international interactions in matters of travel and education) and the economy with the outside world.

In terms of pace, India's growth is second only to China and increasingly, consumer surveys in India show that the urban consumer is no longer contented but is instead voracious. The Indian 'world office', while common as a metaphor, is overplayed. Growth in the service sector in China may actually be faster than in India! By one estimate, over 1980–2000, China's share of value added from services rose by 12 percentage points, about the same as India's but China's share of employment in services rose by 18 percentage points, much more than India's, which rose by only 4 percentage points (Kochhar et al. 2006). Also, exports from both India and China focus more on manufacturing than services. Most of the Indian manufactured exports consists of engineering and chemicals, besides textiles and garments, gems and jewellery and leather. Services exports are however growing more rapidly than manufactured exports.

On savings, both Indian and Chinese households save almost similar proportions of their income, the Chinese about a quarter and the Indians slightly less, but more than one-fifth of their income. The key difference in investments arises from the extent of government saving, and private corporate saving, both of which are higher in China. The extent of government saving in China has a negative flip side, namely under-investment in social services such as health and education, though this has changed in recent times. As far as private corporate saving is concerned, some of it may be related to the differences in market structure, where Chinese firms may be able to maintain higher margins. This, however, comes at the cost of reduced competition and higher prices for consumers. Over time, there has been convergence in India and China on this score. India is saving more; up to 33.5 per cent of income from 22.8 per cent in 1999–2000 (GoI 2009). As Figure 2 shows, while household savings have risen, and corporate savings as a share of output have doubled, the really big news is the reduction of dis-saving by government. Government, which saved -5.1 per cent of output in 1999–2000, has stopped doing so completely. This rise in savings has been matched by a concomitant rise in investment. Gross fixed capital formation has risen to 32.2 per

---

[3] This is driven in part by oil refining for export, a recent entrant to the Indian export basket.

FIGURE 2: GROWING SAVINGS AND INVESTMENT IN INDIA

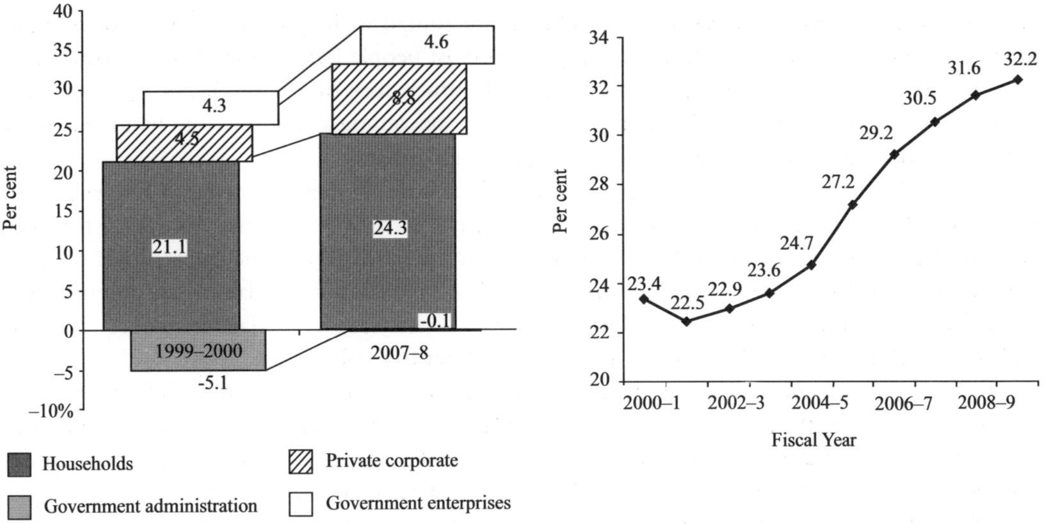

(a) Composition of Savings

(b) Gross Investment as a share of GDP

Source: Author's calculations from GoI (2009)

cent from 23.4 per cent of output ten years ago (GoI 2009). Over three-fourths of this increase is from the private corporate sector, half from machinery and equipment, and a quarter from construction. The share of investment by manufacturing has jumped from 31.7 to 39.5 per cent, with over two-thirds of the increase coming from the registered segment (GoI 2009).

The Indian growth rate has been achieved with proportionately lower investment than China's, that is, India uses its capital more efficiently. However, this may also be because it is still taking advantage of its excess capacity. In some areas, Chinese build capacity, especially infrastructure, ahead of their needs, whereas India barely manages to keep up with the pace of growth in demand for its infrastructure.

The other key difference between India and China is that of implementation capacity which may also be reducing. As the Indian system has numerous institutional and political checks and balances, the executive does not have unrestrained power to implement policies. Such constraints are also becoming evident in the waning power of the Chinese national government, especially its limited ability to influence governments at a subordinate level, in particular city governments.

URBAN GROWTH OF CHINA AND INDIA

If we look at the world today and focus on the countries that are growing rapidly but still have relatively low urban shares of populations and large overall populations, China and India stand out, being in the bottom third in terms of share of population in urban areas (World Bank 2009). They are the only two large economies that have a low level of urbanization and high growth (more than 7 per cent) in the recent past. At this pace, these countries will move fast from being rural societies to being urban countries. Indeed, the question appears to be whether they will become urban before they become richer or vice versa. China, already a middle income country with urbanization over 40 per cent, is succeeding in doing both simultaneously and trying to do so harmoniously! In India, not only is the growth in incomes a more recent phenomenon, there is also a much greater ambivalence about urbanization and until recently, there was almost a policy choice to restrict it to the extent possible. Even today, a number of policies including the flagship National Rural Employment Guarantee Scheme are touted as helping to restrict rural–urban migration and indeed it may help by altering the mix of people being pushed out of rural areas due to economic reasons and people being pulled into urban areas due to economic opportunities. However, historically, there is no example of a country becoming a high income nation without becoming urban, though many poor countries are largely urban.

Unlike the urban explosion in many regions of the world, especially in Latin America, and more recently in China, India's level of urbanization has increased gradually from 17.6 per cent in 1951 to 27.8 per cent in 2001. By comparison, over the same period, the urban share in Brazil grew from 36 to 81 per cent. Despite this low level of urbanization, India's urban population is more than the total population of the United States. The increase in the last decade, of about 70 million, is itself larger than the urban population of all but five countries.[4]

Figure 3 presents the standard projections of population for India and China. The projections assume that the growth rate of Indian urban population will rise only slightly from its historical levels of a little over 2 per cent per decade. If, however, it approaches anything like the Chinese experience of almost 5 per cent per decade or peak rates in the past decade of nearly 10 per cent, then the share of Indian urban population may change significantly. To the extent that the Indian GDP growth rate is now much higher than before and closer to China's, this is not an implausible scenario. However, some commentators like Kundu (2009) argue that the current pattern of urbanization is exclusivist and discourages people from moving to the cities. If so, the UN projections may well be overestimates. Zongyong Wen (chapter 5 in this volume) mentions that the share of urban population in China increased from 36.09 per cent in 2000 to 42.99 per cent in 2005, averaging 1.38 percentage points each year. While the Indian growth rate of

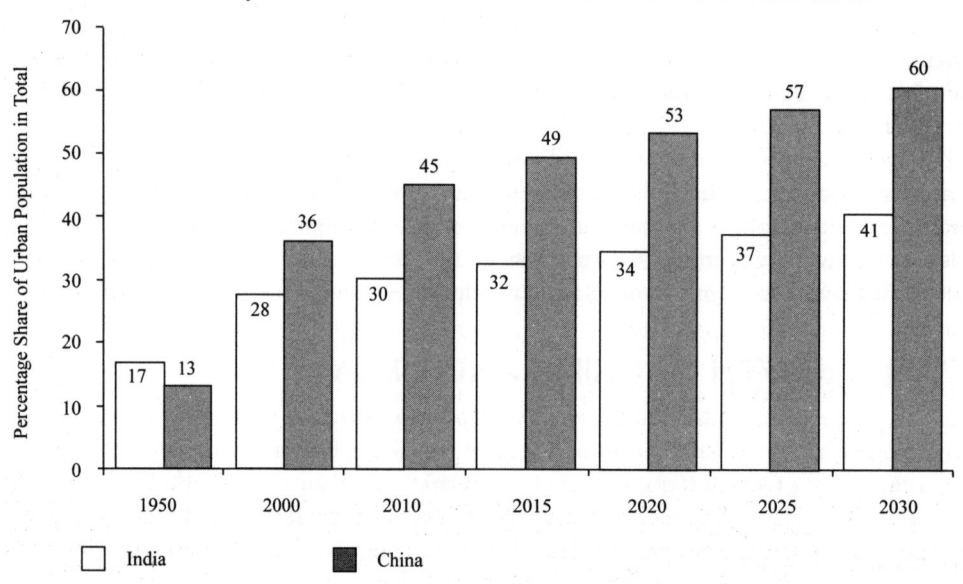

FIGURE 3: PROJECTIONS OF URBAN POPULATION SHARES IN CHINA AND INDIA

Year	India	China
1950	17	13
2000	28	36
2010	30	45
2015	32	49
2020	34	53
2025	37	57
2030	41	60

Source: United Nations (2008)

[4] These are Brazil, China, Indonesia, Russia, and the United States. See UN (2008)

urbanization under similar conditions of high income growth will be known only after the next Census that is due in 2011, it is unlikely to be anywhere close to that level.

A better understanding of this would need an examination of the three broad sources of urbanization, namely: growth due to (i) natural increase, (ii) migration and (iii) redefinition. India and China differ on all these three dimensions. While the natural increase in India is higher since the one child policy in China is relatively well-accepted and enforced in urban areas, migration is higher in China especially, when the floating population of unregistered migrants is accounted for and redefinition of China's urban areas usually includes a much larger area than in India.[5] Large sections of rural Chinese population are therefore becoming urban either through migration or by envelopment by nearby cities, as Zuojun Yang (chapter 6 in this volume) brings out.

THE EFFECT OF URBAN GROWTH ON NATURAL RESOURCES

The nature of urbanization in both India and China is leading to the growth of large existing agglomerations as well as a number of new urban areas. In China, there are now more than 100 million-plus agglomerations, while India has nearly 40 such cities, spread across the country. In that sense, the growth in urbanization is both deep and broad. This, of course, has implications for the kind of impact that urban centers have on natural resources.

At one level, the intensification of growth, that is, the increase in the size of existing large agglomerations that already strain the local natural resources may push the impact in some of these areas to a point where they become irreversible. On the other hand, these large cities are similar to gigantic point sources of environmental impact. If it were possible (and this is a BIG 'If') technologically and politically, to mitigate the impact in these areas, the benefits would be considerable. As such, they present significant opportunities as well as threats. Similarly, the spread of urbanization makes city-related impacts on resources much more dispersed and therefore requires attention to urban governance at a much wider scale than in other countries where the urban population is more geographically concentrated. To the extent that access to technical resources is limited in these newly urbanizing areas and the effects of urban growth on natural resources less evident because they have not yet passed a 'threshold of visibility', the broadening of urbanization poses significantly different challenges.

Zongyong Wen (chapter 5 in this volume) too laments the fact that the rapid Chinese urbanization is tapping natural resources without constraint, resulting in the deterioration of environment. Indeed, the environmental impacts of cities and industrialization, as exemplified by incidents such as the pollution of Lake Taihu in 2007 in Wuxi, Jiangsu and the Songhua River in 2005 in Harbin, Heilongjiang or more dramatically by the submergence of the Three Gorges are among the most discussed costs of rapid Chinese growth. This appears to seriously concern authorities.

In 2007, the State Environmental Protection Administration (SEPA), rated air and water pollution in the urban areas of 585 cities in China.[6] Only 37.6 per cent met the goal of air quality, down 7.3 percentage points from 2005. On limited aspects, there seemed to be some progress. Fewer cities—thirty-nine, which was four less than in 2005—had severe air pollution. Of these, seven each were in China's coal belt in Shanxi and its heavy industry belt in Liaoning. While water quality had deteriorated, more water was being treated. Compared with 22.9 per cent in 2005, 42.5 per cent

---

[5] Here it is important to distinguish between the core city and the total population of large municipalities like Chongqing, which have large rural populations within them.

[6] Reported in http://www.chinadaily.com.cn/china/2007-06/12/content_891904..htm

> **BOX 1: GUJARAT'S INDUSTRIAL POLLUTION CORRIDOR**
>
> The 400 km industrial corridor in Gujarat stretches from Vatwa (A), just outside the state capital of Ahmedabad, to Vapi (D), near the Maharashtra border on the highway to Mumbai, with large industrial estates in Nandesari (B) and Ankleshwar (C). These industrial estates contain a large number of dye factories, textile, rubber, pesticide and paint manufacturers, pulp and paper producers, pharmaceutical, engineering and chemical companies. This area has seen growth at Chinese levels, with similar consequences on natural resources, with particularly extensive pollution of groundwater (SCMC 2004).

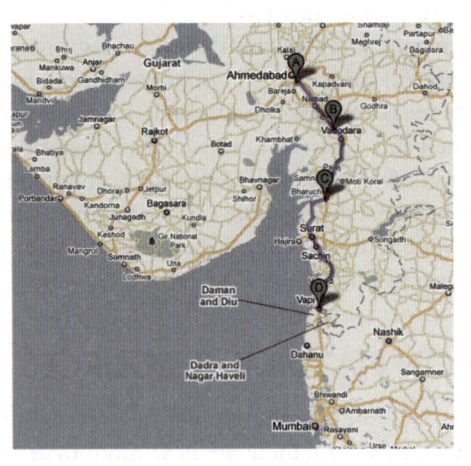

of urban sewage was being treated in these cities. Solid waste management had also improved. As against less than 20 per cent in 2005, in 2007, 59.5 per cent of household garbage was being handled properly. However, 200 cities still had no centralized sewage management system, and 187 cities had no garbage disposal plants.

There have been significant effects of urbanization on the environment in India also. Indeed, were Indian cities to grow at Chinese rates in terms of population and industrialization, its impact may be worse than China's (see Box 1). In this respect, it appears that the Indian democratic tradition has not been able to prevent an unsatisfactory inter-temporal trade-off and in Zongyong Wen's words, '…problems are being tackled temporarily within a myopic perspective at the expense of long-term objectives and overall interests…'. In this respect, China may be just an example of the problems that India is yet to face, as its industrial growth accelerates. The question is whether such forewarning will help India deal with these problems better.

Democratic mobilization has been somewhat more successful on inter-temporal trade-offs with respect to more visible natural and architectural heritage such as the Silent Valley Project in Kerala and the Taj Mahal in Agra. In the first, a dam project that would have submerged a pristine ecological area was halted in response to popular protests, while in the second, industrial and commercial development was not permitted to proceed in order to protect against possible damage to the Taj Mahal. Such reprieves may, however, be temporary. Recent attempts to build the Pathrakkadavu hydro-electric project in Kerala[7] signal a revival of efforts to exploit natural resources in the Silent Valley area.

URBAN GROWTH AND LOCAL GOVERNMENT

The trade-off between growth and the environment is one of the key points of tension between the national and local governments in China. Much of the striking growth in urban China is owed to action by a large number of local governments. A key difference between China and India lies in the extent of agency that the city administrations have. In China, cities compete with each other and there is a discernible element of city-specificity in economic strategies developed

---

[7] See http://beta.thehindu.com/news/states/kerala/article 13892.ece

by local governments in the larger municipalities. In India, however, this is lacking, as the city governments have limited agency. Little authority and financial capacity have been devolved to them, with significant differences in the treatment of land as a source of revenue, as elaborated later in the discussion of land redevelopment. Concomitantly, the capacity of the city to do damage is also limited. The locus of government action in India is at the level of the state (comparable to the province in China).

Along with the responsibility and authority for city officials in China comes accountability, not directly to the citizens as in an electoral democracy but vertically, through the administrative and party hierarchy, as in a large firm. Mayors of cities in China are assessed on a formal report card (Landry 2003) that includes a variety of factors, primarily focused on economic growth. Factors related to income levels, economic structure, trade orientation and urbanization account for 28 per cent of the score, while consumption and infrastructure-related indicators like electricity consumption and use of motor vehicles and availability of paved roads account for another 28 per cent. Public services like health, education and public security add up to another 32 per cent and the remaining 12 per cent is for waste treatment and air quality. Good performance in a particular position can be expected to lead to positions of higher responsibility in the administrative and party hierarchy though Landry (2003) does not find statistically significant evidence of this. This can have deleterious consequences, for example, the single-minded focus on growth is substantially responsible for the kind of environmental problems alluded to earlier.

In India, city politicians are accountable horizontally to the people, through local elections. However, in the absence of significant authority, the transfer of blame to other levels of government is a widely used route to mitigate accountability pressures. City politics in India has also not been a way of moving up the party ladder given the limited nature of inner party democracy in India across political parties. Consequently, the vertical accountability through the party hierarchy is also limited.

Two of the key challenges that China faces today in the context of urban growth are: (a) developing a model that reconciles economic growth with resource responsibility, and (b) ensuring the acceptance of such a model across various local governments, each with considerable independent agency.

Since a number of vested interests have developed around the existing growth-first model, not the least of which is its easy measurability discussed above, and consequent attraction for a meritocratic bureaucracy that the Chinese Communist Party (CCP) strives to be (see Li 1998), the momentum of the existing model is considerable. While there has been much discussion of environmental consequences, the incorporation of environmental factors in evaluating performance of party cadres remains an unfinished task and economic growth still dominates.

It remains to be seen whether, to evolve the new model, China adopts the same local experimental approach that served it so well in evolving the existing model of economic growth. A more experimental approach would permit different local governments to discover their own pace of acceptable growth and the extent of trade-off with competing goals. This discovery in developed countries is facilitated by democratic institutions that mediate between different interests. The limited extent of such mechanisms in China makes this task harder.

BUILDING THE CITY

A visible consequence of the growth-first model is the extensive physical redevelopment of Chinese cities. As Zongyong Wen (chapter 5 in this volume) notes:

It is almost certain that not much traditional architecture is left in Beijing. It is not that old houses are devoid of value, but that culture, when locked in competition with the economy, always tends to be the loser in the face of rapid growth of the latter.

But, there are limits to change in the urban fabric of even a place like Beijing that otherwise is relatively free from the constraints of civil society process. The pace and nature of change can be influenced by sensitive experts.

On 19 December 2007, 188 buildings built in Beijing within the past 160 years were given government protection.[8] The buildings are split into two categories based on antiquity, namely from 1840–1949 and 1950–76 and include public buildings like the 50-year-old Great Hall of the People and the city's first water works, which dates from 1908 as well as schools built by missionaries in the nineteenth century. Under the new ruling, the listed structures cannot be demolished, and any renovation work done on them must ensure their historical authenticity is preserved. The report quotes Zongyong Wen, in his capacity as Deputy Chief of Beijing's Planning Commission, as saying:

Beijing is home to many spectacular modern buildings, but their protection had not been on the government's agenda until very recently. [These] buildings reflect either the historical development of society or the evolution of the art of construction.

This is an instance of local governments discovering their own pace of acceptable growth and trade-offs with other goals.

For India, the question is, how much time does it have to evolve a more sensitive urbanization

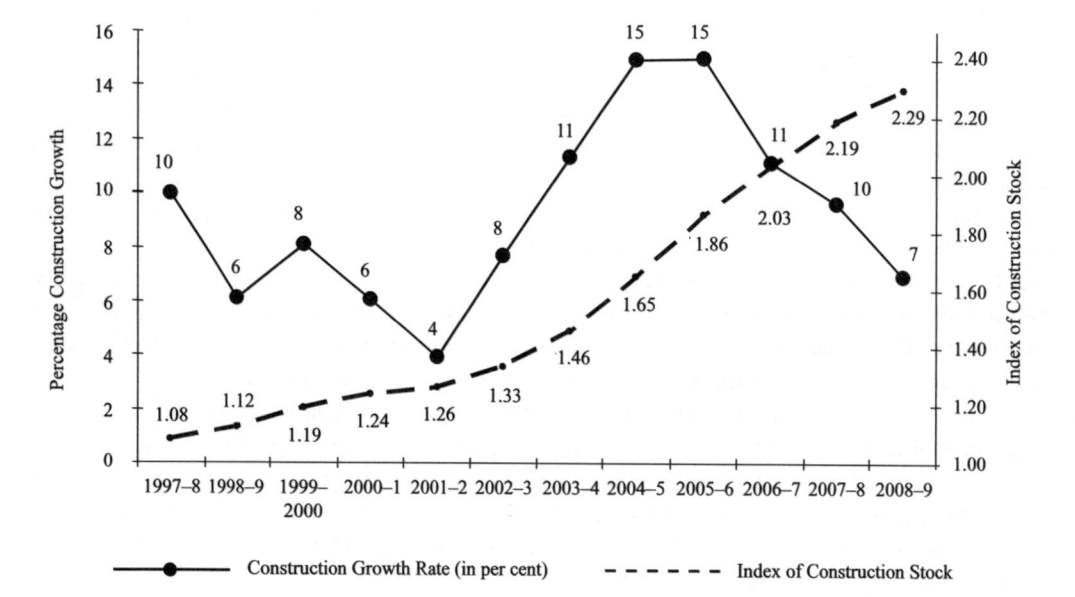

FIGURE 4: CONSTRUCTION GROWTH RATES IN INDIA 1997–8 TO 2008–9

Source: Author's calculations from GoI (2009)

[8] Reported in http://www.chinadaily.com.cn/olympics/2007-12/21/content_6339080.htm. The buildings referred to are modern relative to the older heritage buildings/areas such as the Summer Palace and Forbidden City, which are already protected.

process? Evolving consensus is often confused with an attempt to block progress. The significant private benefits from continuing with the existing urbanization model generate strong pressures to continue on the well-trodden path. It is in this context that the relentlessness of development in Beijing shows how quickly the urban fabric can change. Figure 4 shows construction growth in India. Even at this pace, much slower than China's, almost 60 per cent of the stock in 2008–09 is less than ten years old! The concern is that, once we, in India start down that path, we might travel too far before there is consensus that we are traveling in the wrong direction. Even after the consensus, it would take time and effort to build the politics to overcome the vested interests that would have been developed as a result of investments on the traditional path.

THE LAW AND THE CITY

The management of construction is often the subject of rule making by city authorities, usually by local governments, but in India, this is often superseded by the state or federal government, as in the case of the Mumbai mill lands (D'Monte 2007) and the Delhi Master Plan. China is now in the process of instituting 'rule by law', in order to increase the transparency of administration. Even though the process of lawmaking appears simple in a single-party system, there is often substantial prior negotiation before laws are brought to the annual session of the National People's Congress (全国人民代表大会). While the existence of laws, in and of themselves, need not assure redress when the court system is not independent, it does appear that the recourse available to the Chinese citizens from arbitrary action by authorities is increasing. In India, conversely, authorities are often unable to prevent self-serving action by citizens.

The Indian experience indicates that the existence of laws need not imply that they will be enforced. The implementation of the law and the protection of the laws depend to some extent, possibly, on the political positioning of specific groups. For example, in many areas of Delhi, zoning laws have been ignored and mixed-use neighborhoods have evolved that combine residential with industrial and commercial use. In some instances, this allows hazardous industrial activities to grow without safeguards, but in many areas there have been broader benefits from such mixed use. Subsequently, acceding to the popular pressure created by such organic growth, the federal urban ministry (note where the locus of planning authority lies) modified the zoning laws, ex-post facto, when the Supreme Court insisted on enforcing the by-laws.[9] Thus, laws themselves are a response to politics. India is in the process of passing a new law on land acquisition, rehabilitation and resettlement, the timing of which is partly in response to agitations over land acquisition for industrial purposes, specifically a large number of SEZs and the manner in which political parties have defined themselves as representative of particular interests, particularly that of the poor.

DEMOCRACY AND URBANIZATION

In this context of representation and the law, the relationship posited by Zongyong Wen (chapter 5 in this volume) between income and a quasi-Maslovian hierarchy of needs with respect to rights, is debatable. Taken literally, this characterization would mean that most countries would not be able to achieve 'harmony', since the USD 12,000 per capita is a very high bar to cross. Furthermore, if one uses purchasing power parity (PPP), then the numbers will be much closer, since the PPP

---

[9] See 'Response to immediate concerns' in http://www.pib.nic.in/release/rel_print_page.asp?relid=24726

factor for China is about 2.27 (India is about 2.88), which means that Beijing city is already far beyond even the USD 12,000 level indicated here.[10]

Protests in response to perceived violations of rights are dependent on (a) extent of rights violation, (b) awareness of the violation and (c) benefits vis-a-vis costs of protest. These differ among the various groups. Is the awareness of rights greater in urban areas or is it the case that urban citizens feel more secure, relative to isolated rural citizens, in demanding their rights because government reaction is necessarily more in the glare of domestic and international media? Furthermore, the greater density in urban areas makes it possible for a larger group to be assembled to seek redress of grievances. So, is it harder to ignore a larger number of people, even though they may be a smaller proportion of the populace? These are unresolved questions in our discussions.

Democratic privileges of protest often come with NIMBY (not in my back yard) phenomenon for undesirable public facilities; a fact which is well documented elsewhere. This is often the reason why certain facilities are located in less politically influential locations in a city, such as the contentious nature of opening of diesel bus depots in Harlem in New York City (while closing similar depots in West Village) which allegedly increase the incidence of asthma among children in the area; an issue that we were made aware of during our visits to New York (see also Sheppard 2005 and Northridge et al. 1999). The resolution of such issues in India is supposed to occur through the political process where these competing claims are delineated and hopefully mediated, though, often, as in New York, politically powerful private or small group interests may override broader but less powerful interests. The existing situation in China is that the urban officials are supposed to internalize this mediation through discussions with the local community, but the extent to which it actually occurs varies widely. In the case of Hangzhou, as detailed by Zuojun Yang (chapter 6 in this volume), such engagement with the local community appears to be extensive. In many other areas, this can be perfunctory. However, the tolerance of such local variation, especially on the liberal side, by the national authorities is a positive sign.

FIGURE 5: GROWTH IN CHINA'S REAL ESTATE SECTOR

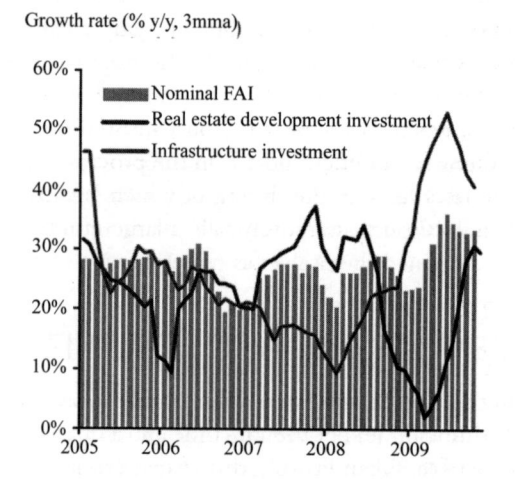

Source: NBS, CEIC and UBS estimates in Wang and Hu (2009).

---

[10] In 2009, Beijing's GDP was expected to exceed USD 10,000 per capita. It was more than USD 9,075 in 2008 and USD 7,370 US dollars in 2007. This is partly due to the appreciation of the RMB. See the report on 8 January 2010 in http://english.peopledaily.com.cn/90001/90778/90862/6862825.html

THE CITY AND THE MARKET

The recent downturn has also cast doubt on the existing growth-first model and brought out the effects of misallocation of investment, for example, in larger housing units, as mentioned by Wen (chapter 5 in this volume). The market system assumes that these decisions will be corrected over time as entrepreneurs who make mistakes will lose money and exit the business. However, behind this story lie the costs of adjustment and the loss of unwanted investments. In an economy populated by market driven banks and real estate firms, the slowdown in real estate should see the prices of the larger individual units adjust so that they become affordable, as exemplified by the fall in housing prices in the United States. However, in China, many of the banks are state owned and many of the real estate companies have ties to local governments and state owned enterprises, which delays this adjustment. Even in India, we see that the adjustment has yet to occur. Of course, some of this can be explained by the fact that growth in these two economies has remained quite robust, though not as high as before. Figure 5 shows the rapid increase in construction in China with new construction of property rising almost 200 per cent year on year. The government's hand is seen in the surge in infrastructure investment to compensate for the fall in real estate investment, helping to keep nominal fixed asset investment (FAI) stable. The extent to which this rise in government-sponsored construction affects the urban fabric will be only known later. However, as part of the stimulus, construction of residential units below 90 square meters is being encouraged to redress the lopsidedness of investment mentioned earlier.[11]

As Zongyong Wen (chapter 5 in this volume) underlines, a well functioning market economy needs effective competition regulation, sensible macroeconomic policies, transparency in reporting and accounting, and supportive public services including infrastructure. The common perception is that India has better regulatory environment and market transparency as compared to China, while Chinese infrastructure and macroeconomic policies (captured in an indicator such as their fiscal deficit) are in better shape. However, the truth may be somewhere in between. The new Indian competition regulator was hobbled since its inception in 2003, with a full commission being appointed only early in 2009. The recent accounting fraud in Satyam Computer Services, one of India's marquee software companies, has exposed the chinks in its market transparency. Though the response to the event was swift in terms of keeping the company alive, the prosecution of the management has lagged, compared to similar corporate frauds in the United States. Conversely, Chinese fiscal deficits have been kept low by inadequate investment in social services and unfunded mandates to local governments, leading to declining health and educational attainments in rural areas, lacunae that are only now being recognized and redressed partially (Wang 2008).

URBANIZATION AND SLUMS

The growth of the market economy has changed the urban landscape in India, along the peripheral ring road in Bangalore, in Gurgaon on the outskirts of Delhi, in Bandra-Kurla complex in the heart of Mumbai. One of the striking differences between India and China is the visible co-existence in India of these glittering glass and steel edifices with slums (some of which may be populated largely by specific communities, much like the province-specific *cuns* in Beijing). One reason for this is the difference that flows from a prior (though possibly eroding) culture of toleration and symbiotic

---

[11] By early 2009, sales of housing of less than 90 square meters a unit in Shenzhen were rising. By one estimate, it was 73.5 per cent of the total, compared to 50.56 per cent in 2007 and 68.13 per cent in 2008. See http://www.chinastakes.com/2009/3/house-market-in-shanghai-shenzhen-rebounding-for-now.html

relationship between the elite and providers of personal services, such as drivers, servants and cooks, coupled with a relatively disinterested government with strong pro-poor overtones.[12] One can also argue that electoral democracy in a poor country has automatic pro-poor mechanisms, due to political reluctance to act against the large number of people who live in slums. Both are no doubt true, but it is also true that until recently, there was no corresponding benefit to bearing the political cost of slum removal. With the rise of importance of real estate, the involvement of various political personages in the sector has also risen, for example in Hyderabad, Lagadapati Rajagopal, a member of national Parliament from the Congress Party is also a leading real estate developer. Similar instances abound elsewhere too across parties and cities. In China, such real estate benefits engendered by its high urban focused growth have provided a strong economic rationale for various relocation initiatives. Will this lead to lower tolerance for slums in India? It may very well be the case, as for example the relocation of the Yamuna Pushta slums in Delhi, documented by Menon-Sen and Bhan (2008). The residents of these slums were relocated to a remote location on the periphery of Delhi. We discuss this urban transformation below in more detail, in the context of the excellent granular account of the Che Cun Jian Ju (撤村建居) policy in Hangzhou by Zuojun Yang (chapter 6 in this volume).

However, the reasons why slums are invisible in China go beyond the nature of the government and the political tolerance of slums or the lack of it. These reasons are: (a) the existing extent of housing stock, (b) the gendered nature of migration and the associated provision of accommodation by employers and (c) limited extent of informality in manufacturing.

It is important to recognize that Chinese cities were strictly controlled areas in the past and that all residents who were in the city were provided housing by the work unit or danwei (单位). Thus, when the Deng reforms happened and the hukou (户口) restrictions were relaxed, the existing housing stock was substantial. Much of this housing stock of the old state owned enterprises (SOEs) was transferred to the employees as part of their severance package when large scale lay-offs began in the mid-1990s. As existing urban residents moved to newly built housing, these units became available for use by the incoming migrants (see Walker and Buck 2007). Their affordability was ensured by increasing density, that is, multiple tenants rented the spaces which were formerly used by a single family (Chan 2007). In Beijing, this is seen, for example, in the densification of the hutong (胡同) areas south of Tiananmen Square, as also in some of the older industrial work units.

In China many migrants also stay either at worksites (for example, male construction workers) or dormitories (for example, female factory workers). This has been the pattern for quite some time, as seen for example in Shanghai in the early 1990s (Roberts 2001), as also in other cities (Zhang 1995). Whether or not married women migrate with their husbands depends on the type of job available, else they may migrate independently, while their child is raised back home (Roberts et al. 2004). These workers work mostly in the formal sector. This pattern of migration has two implications, namely (a) housing needs can be met with much less space, for example, six construction workers may share a 12 square meters space and (b) residential locations are not required to function as workplaces. By contrast, slums in India are populated by family units that need places to stay together. Many of these slums are also thriving hubs of independent economic activity, like miniature urban versions of township and village enterprises (TVEs) in China.

The relative availability of infrastructure in rural China and the formal restrictions on migration to towns, through the hukou, made TVEs a rural phenomenon, albeit in proximity to larger towns.

---

[12] I do not use this in the sense defined by another of our partners in inquiry, Yang Yao (chapter 11 of this volume).

In India, on the other hand, supporting facilities for industrial activity are available only in the larger urban areas and there are no restrictions on migration. Consequently, low cost industrial enterprises in the informal sector tend to emerge in unregulated parts of the urban space, that is, the slums. Lately, however, the acceptance of slums has declined among the elite, seduced as they are by the glass and steel visions that emanate from the West and now China.[13] Slum removal, until recently largely a practice in Delhi, is now spreading to other cities, without a full appreciation of the role they play in the economic and social life of the city. Policies for slum redevelopment in India such as the recent *Rajiv Awas Yojana* (RAY) or Rajiv Housing Scheme, named after the former Prime Minister, Rajiv Gandhi, and the schemes under the Jawaharlal Nehru Urban Renewal Mission (JNNURM) treat the slum solely as the manifestation of a housing problem and therefore fail to provide for economic activity that is an integral part of informal settlements in urban India.

In China, though there is now a substantial informal service sector, especially since the lay-offs in the SOEs, most urban manufacturing is formal.[14] Thus the need for informal housing locations to also function as production spaces is limited. The creation of mixed informal spaces that combine informality, housing and workspaces, a role that the slum provides in India, is much less of a requirement in China—that is, the demand for slums is less. Where needed, this role is fulfilled at the periphery, as in Beijing; or in urban villages, as in Shenzhen (Du 2008).

URBAN TRANSFORMATION

Zuojun Yang (chapter 6 in this volume) provides a rich description of urban relocation in Hangzhou through the implementation of Che Cun Jian Ju. As he puts it, the 'process of urbanization mainly comprises two kind of changes: the first is that agricultural land is used for non-agricultural purposes; the other is that farmers become urban residents after losing most or all of their agricultural land'. This acceptance of transformation at two levels; that of the land and the people, is not so clear in India, where the need to prepare the 'farmers [to] become urban residents' is less recognized and agitation over compensation is often about providing alternate land for land acquired by authorities.

The process of expansion of Hangzhou is mirrored in many Indian cities. The limits of Hyderabad were expanded from 175 to 650 sq. kilometer, that of Bengaluru (Bangalore) from 226 to 696 sq. kilometer and now that of Chennai (Madras) from 174 to 426 sq. kilometer. It is instructive to compare the situation in Hangzhou with the canonical situation in India. First, urban villages in Zhejiang often include factories as in the Xintang village mentioned by Zuojun Yang (chapter 6 in this volume). Land in these villages is under the control of the local village government, unlike in India, where land is under the control of the state government. If secondary or tertiary industry activities bring more benefits than traditional agricultural activities, these agricultural collectives in China can establish factory buildings or commercial office buildings on their own land by attracting outside investment without any need to acquire land. In India, the development rules of the expanding city automatically extend to the new areas, though there are some exceptions. Just as in Hangzhou, in building Lutyen's imperial Delhi, only the agricultural

---

[13] For one such version in Mumbai see www.romf.org and http://www.ctbuh.org/

[14] Huang (2009) estimates that workers who have no security of employment, receive few or no benefits, and are often unprotected by labor laws currently account for 168 million of the 283 million urban employed in China. See also Solinger (2005). Many of the informal workers are however former SOE employees who received their danwei accommodation as part of their severance and thus do not need housing, while others, like restaurant workers, often stay at the worksite.

lands were acquired and the residential areas were delimited by a red line or *lal dora* (钉子户). Over time, the process of urbanization has engulfed these *lal dora* villages. Residents of these areas are exempted from obtaining sanction of building plan for their residential units but not from the purview of building by laws, that is, they are supposed to self-regulate. These areas have evolved in much the same manner as urban villages in Hangzhou. However, while 70 per cent of the urban villages in Hangzhou have been assimilated within a decade, there is no such effort in Delhi as yet, though the latest Master Plan for Delhi suggests permitting commercial development in these *lal dora* areas—regularizing what the de facto situation is on the ground.

Indeed, the development that can be expected to follow would largely be privately initiated, sporadic and patchy. This is in contrast to the orderly transformation of Xintang that one sees in Hangzhou. In part, this is possible because of the higher (in?)voluntary acceptability of high rises for relocation in Hangzhou, perhaps because the extent of non-residential activity is limited in the urban villages. Such an acceptance may be limited in Delhi, given the variety of activity in *lal dora* areas. A more apt comparison may be with the urban villages of Shenzhen, described by Du (2008), given that the organic process of growth in Shenzhen is more akin to that of Delhi. There are other factors too. The control over land use in Delhi vests in the federal government, not the local government, as in Hangzhou or even Beijing. Most of the land conversion happening within the city boundaries of India is the transformation of defunct manufacturing land into real estate and commercial developments. Here, the issue is not one of ownership, which lies with the defunct corporate, but with permissions needed for the development, in particular, the change of land-use, often outside the ambit of local government.

But, similarities between Hangzhou and Delhi are deeper. Both India and China are struggling with the pressures that rapid economic transformation entails. In both countries, acquisition has to be for 'public interest', a term that gains meaning only in a political context. The provincial High Courts and now even the Supreme Court in India are consistently reinforcing the validity of acquiring land for 'economic development'. On 5 September 2008, Justices C.K. Thakker and D.K. Jain of the Supreme Court, dismissed a complaint against the Andhra Pradesh government for acquiring land for Andhra Pradesh Infrastructure Investment Corporation saying that the Government as a 'sovereign power can acquire land for public purpose', which could include 'industrial and other infrastructural developmental needs for the common good of the citizens.' It also cites *Kelo v. City of New London*, 545 U.S. 469 (2005) of the US Supreme Court in support of its decision.[15] The second is the decision by Chief Justice S.S. Nijjar and Justice P.C. Ghosh of the Calcutta High Court in the well-reported Singur case in the state of West Bengal in India, where the land acquired for the private Tata Motors, to establish the factory to build the world's least expensive car, the Nano, was held to be in public interest. A vigorous local agitation against the acquisition of land ultimately led to the withdrawal of Tata Motors from Singur with significant political consequences in West Bengal, where the Communist Party of India (Marxist) had won six consecutive elections, ruling there since 1977. In acquiring land for economic development, the most striking difference between China and India is in the structure of the compensation package.

---

[15] In her dissent from the majority opinion in this case Justice Sandra Day O'Connor quotes Justice Chase in *Calder v. Bull*, 3 Dall. 386, 388 (1798) 'An act of the Legislature (for I cannot call it a law) contrary to the great first principles of the social compact, cannot be considered a rightful exercise of legislative authority… A few instances will suffice to explain what I mean… [A] law that takes property from A. and gives it to B: It is against all reason and justice, for a people to entrust a Legislature with such powers; and, therefore, it cannot be presumed that they have done it.'

Mukhopadhyay (2007) argues that compensation needs to fulfill three conditions, namely (a) provide financial security, (b) appear fair and (c) be future-ready. A first and basic level of compensation would allow the affected person to retain his current living standard for the foreseeable future. In India, implementing even this is a challenge, especially for farm laborers and sharecroppers, who ordinarily receive no compensation. Here, a severe problem is lack of information on farm laborers and sharecroppers, given that even the land records are flawed. This problem is much less significant in China. The second, fairness involves providing facilities to the affected persons to share in the gains. This would compensate for the psychological cost as well as the option value of the land, were the existing owner to retain it. This could contain the payback from successful projects, which could go into a community fund. Finally, future-readiness involves the provision of facilities to take advantage of the changes in economic structure; the transformation of the economy from agriculture to industry/services. It is about ensuring that the affected persons are given the full opportunity and resources to participate in the changing economy.

The components of compensation in the Hangzhou Che Cun Jian Ju model meet these three conditions to some extent. Hangzhou provides market compensation for the existing house, which Zuojun Yang (chapter 6 in this volume) says could reach one million RMB. It also provides 50 to 55 square meters per person, that is, about 200 square meters per nuclear family at 900 RMB per square meter. Not only does it enable each family to use one house for habitation and put the other one out on rent, it leaves a substantial portion of the compensation amount with the family. Recently, Hangzhou also permitted the sale of the allotted houses, enabling the family to raise more capital for investment in any enterprise that they may undertake. In contrast to the Indian compensation, which allows for 22 square meters per family, this is substantially more able to provide financial security.[16]

But, what about land transformed directly from agriculture for areas such as the Hangzhou Economic and Technological Development Zone?[17] Can a hardworking farmer accept the transformation to an indolent landlord? An official in the development zone told us that he knew that while he could compensate the acquisition of land from the farmer to build the zone, he could not provide that person with work, since he was unsuited for the occupations generated in the zone. But he could offer the promise that the children of the farmer would have the same opportunities as his own children and it was this hope of a better future for his children that enabled the farmer to rationalize the sacrifice of his land and vocation.

This is in contrast to the Indian situation, as presented in a segment of the documentary *Abad Bhumi* by Dayabati Roy and Parthasarathi Banerjee on the Singur agitation[18]. In this segment, a local leader of the ruling communist party in Singur is patiently explaining to the interviewer that the farmers of Singur could become factory guards, and the women, many of whom now travel to find work, could become maids in the houses of the people who will work in the factory. In the

---

[16] The Indian compensation is for slum dwellers and not necessarily urban villagers who own their land. However, similar schemes are also being proposed for places in Dharavi, like Koliwada, where residents do have title to the land.

[17] Hangzhou Economic and Technological Development Zone is a state-level development zone that was approved by the State Council of China in 1993. The zone covers an area 104.7 sq. km. of which 34 sq. km. is currently, developed, with a population of 200,000, as of 2009. It includes an export processing zone, the Xiasha Higher Education Park with fourteen higher education institutions with 120,000 students and firms such as Allergan, Eastcom, Foxconn, Mitsubishi, Motorola, Panasonic and Toshiba. See http://www.zhejiang.gov.cn/zjforeign/english/node577/node583/node585/userobject1ai5587.html

[18] http://video.google.com/videoplay?docid=3052261023426138538

next scene, a farmer expresses doubt that he could find work in a factory in his mid-forties and questions the value of the project. There is little mention of the children of the farmer.[19]

One of my enduring puzzles is this ability of an unelected communist bureaucrat to recognize that land acquisition affects not just wealth, but livelihood and self-image and understand what would motivate the farmer, contrasted with the inability of an elected popular local representative, albeit also from a communist party, to understand his electorate.

Hangzhou also returns 10 per cent of the arable land acquired to the farmers' collective to be jointly owned and exploited. In the case of Xintang, given the limited extent of continuing arable use, this was a 4000 square meters plot that could be used for commercial development, with the profits accruing to all the farmers. In part, this is possible because of the nature of land ownership in Chinese villages. While Chinese urban villages have a collective identity, dating back to their Maoist origins, thus facilitating a comprehensive approach, in cities like Delhi in India, they are simply agglomerations of individual landowners. But this is also because some Chinese local governments recognize the need to share the profits of redevelopment with the original users of the land. This eases the land transformation process and increases the perception of fairness.

Finally, by enabling the urban villagers to officially access the urban services, in particular, health and education for their children, by giving them urban hukou, the Hangzhou compensation is future-ready. As the official in the development zone said, there is a clear promise for a better future for the children as full participants in the higher echelons of China's booming economy. This promise is backed up by prompt delivery on the compensation schemes, while in India, it is often the case that even resettlement promises take many years to be actually delivered. The village of Xintang has already been transformed and its people moved to their new houses. Only time will tell whether or not they will benefit from their new life.

Hangzhou is not necessarily the norm. Indeed it may be the exception. A frail old woman in Chengdu, Sichuan in western China was incarcerated for nine months because she protested the acquisition of her land was finally released on the intervention of a high-ranking military official. As such, both her oppression and reprieve depended on the caprice of officials[20]. The Chinese state now appears to be engaged in transforming this caprice into rule by law, but at times, old habits die hard. This is especially so when the caprice itself is attributable to the presence of a single party system, without effective opposition. Zhang and Fang (2004) note that Beijing demolished 4.2 million square meters of housing over 1990 to 1998, while Shanghai demolished five times as much; 22.5 million square meters. By 1998, 1.5 million,[21] i.e., one-sixth of Shanghai's urban residents had been relocated (Zhang 2002). Neither is the generosity of the compensation even across China. Nail houses[22] in Chongqing and in many other cities are testimony to this. In most other localities, the families are allotted 15 square meters per person, rather than 50 square meters. In such cases, the family gets only one house instead of two and cannot enjoy rental income.

---

[19] Tata Motors undertook an initiative to train some local Singur youth in ITIs, but the number involved was limited (see http://www.tatamotors.com/our_world/press_releases.php?ID=341&action=Pull).

[20] Personal interview, 2 June 2007

[21] The number of residents was estimated as the product of the number of households and the average family size of the year. If the family size of those in low-quality shelters is larger than the city average, the number of those relocated may be even larger.

[22] A nail house or dingzihù (钉子户) is a term used for homes of people who resist relocation, mostly unsuccessfully. For a report on the Chongqing nail house, see Ewing (2007). The house in question was finally demolished on the night of 2 April 2007.

FIGURE 6: NAIL HOUSE IN CHONGQING

Source: China Photos/Getty Images

The value of the urban hukou also depends on the quality of the services in the city. This is not universally good, as the variation in the scores reported in Landry (2003) shows.

But, what happens to the low rental opportunities that were available in the urban villages? In Hangzhou's and Delhi's urban villages, many erstwhile farmers had become landlords who were the suppliers of affordable housing. With Che Cun Jian Ju, this supply will fall and affect those who rented these places. Where will they go? In focusing on the owners of these areas, we often tend to forget the users, and this may have effects on the economy of the city. Brian McGrath (chapter 7 in this volume) finds part of the answer in the migrant settlements on the outskirts of Hangzhou. More broadly, there is a strong impression that the working poor are being peripheralized across Asia (Kundu 2009), but in India, this may be less of an issue. The data on slums in Delhi from NSSO (2004) indicates that over three-fourth of the slums are located in residential areas and not on the fringes and along the canals and railway lines and river beds, but this is changing.

In Hangzhou, a rather old but dignified building, much like the bungalows in Bandra, a neighborhood in Mumbai, stands on a small patch of land between two glittering high rises on one of the main thoroughfares. It survived because it was too expensive to compensate the owner, since the extent of development that could be undertaken on that patch would not justify the compensation. Its survival is both an affirmation of the rule by law and acknowledgement that cities in China can be allowed to be a little untidy. In our rush to beautify our cities, as with Delhi for the Commonwealth Games to be held in 2010, we often forget that works in progress are rarely neat, and Indian and Chinese cities are nothing if not works in progress.

HANGZHOU AND THE NEXT STEP

Hangzhou is connected to India in a special and deep way. As Tan Chung (1998) writes:

In Chinese historical and semi-historical documents: there are places called 'Shang Tianzhu', 'Zhong Tianzhu', and 'Xia Tianzhu' which literally mean, 'Upper India', 'Middle India', and 'Lower India'. These three names actually indicate just a few square kilometres in Hangzhou City in Zhejiang Province in eastern China. How has such a mix-up come about? It is because of a legend that was the making of an ancient Indian Buddhist monk-scholar 'Huili' (whose real identity is lost). In 326 AD, this monk from western India came to Hangzhou. After seeing a hill in this area (in the vicinity of the scenic West Lake), he authoritatively proclaimed that the hill had been flown to China from Magadha (Bihar)! The Chinese believed him and, henceforth, called the hill 'Tianzhushan' (the 'Indian Hill') and 'Feilaifeng' (the 'Peak that has flown here from India'). It was this legend that has contributed to the existence of 'Upper', 'Middle' and 'Lower' India on the Chinese map.[23]

Tan Chung goes on to say that Rabindranath Tagore, who went to China in 1924, came to know of this legend when he visited Hangzhou and made a significant observation:

'[T]he real fact is that the hill which he [Huili] had known in his own country had a Sanskrit name meaning the Vulture Peak [grdhrakuta]. When he saw a hill here so like the one he had loved in India, he felt a great delight and gave it the same name'...'This man [Huili] ... not only discovered a resemblance between the hills here and those of his own land, but found his unity of heart with the people of this country' (Tagore (1925) quoted in Chung 1998).

Today, even as it is firmly anchored in China's remarkable development, its future aspiration, as Brian McGrath (chapter 7 in this volume) describes it, is to become 'Silicon Valley in Paradise'[24]—a civic imagination that corresponds more closely with the United States and California, even as a number of significant Indian and American software firms are now locating in Hangzhou. In Hangzhou's past, present and its conception of its future, it straddles India, China, and the United States.

As this conversation is carried forward, urbanists will need to explore how Indian and Chinese cities can address the use of scarce resources through the lens of cities such as Hangzhou and the manner in which such cities address issues relating to water, land and cultural heritage. The city matters for sustainability and Chinese and Indian cities will matter even more.[25]

The first two elements, water and land, characterize the two critical resiliencies, environmental and political, essential to the sustainable development of cities. The issue of water is paramount in many studies of cities and there is considerable physical evidence of the centrality of water management in the design of cities in China, as evidenced by the analysis by Brian McGrath (chapter 7 in this volume), where he shows how in Hangzhou, they managed to kill and then resurrect the West Lake. Similarly, in India, it can be stated, with just a little exaggeration, that 'every large city has killed at least one river'. Indeed, India seems to have learnt little from history. According to Agrawal (2002), the Harappans of the Indus Valley civilization were forced to move eastward due to water shortages, first to present day Rajasthan by the end of the third millennium; and then, as increasing aridity succeeded the mid-Holocene warmth and turned the region's lakes

---

[23] According to Tan Chung, the archival source of the legend is *Fozu tongji* (History of Buddhist system compiled by monk Zhipan of the 13th century), *juan* 36. Huili is said to have founded the Lingyin Temple.

[24] See also http://tradeinservices.mofcom.gov.cn/en/i/2008-08-19/53759.shtml

[25] Urban areas consume about two-thirds (estimated at 7,900 Mtoe) of the world's energy in 2006, which the IEA projects, will increase to three-fourths (about 12,400 Mtoe) by 2030. About 80 per cent of this projected increase is expected to come from non-OECD countries. Already, Chinese cities consume 1424 Mtoe, i.e., 75 per cent of Chinese energy consumption (IEA 2008, Chapter 8)

saline, further east to the Gangetic *doab*, where they died out. Reurbanization of the doab region had to wait till the first millennium BC.

Along with water, land is as much of an issue. Here, the immediate effects on resource sustainability may be less visible (in terms of lower food production, destruction of green cover, etc.) and many of the effects may manifest themselves through the impact on other resources such as water (lower levels of recharge from built up areas, etc.). However, its effect on social and political sustainability is much more visible and direct. The transformation of land from existing use to urban use is an issue of major socio-political contention in both India and China and the manner in which this transformation is mediated has major consequences for the path of urbanization that these countries will take.

Even if China and India did manage to achieve a certain political coherence with respect to their cities, which direction would they take? The average urban American consumes more than twice as much energy as an urban European and even within the United States, it varies by a factor of three across cities (Brown et al. 2008). Cities like Hong Kong, Tokyo, Singapore and Amsterdam require less than a seventh of the energy of Houston, Phoenix, Detroit and Denver to meet their transportation needs (Newman and Kenworthy 1999). Already, in China, energy use varies by a factor of seven from Chongqing to Hohhot, depending on income, climate and energy intensity of industries (Dhakal 2009). Cities in China and India cannot travel the American or even the European way[26] if the planet is to survive.

Cultural heritage is, as Brian once put it, the locus of the human in the environment. But it is also important from two key instrumental perspectives. First, the manner in which these cities address their cultural heritage, whether or not they address it and if they do, whether they address only its manifestations or its deeper contexts, provides indicators as to the relative importance the city accords to inter-temporal trade-offs and current trade-offs—the key distinction between sustainable and unsustainable consumption. Second, both India and China face the choice between following the traditional path to urbanization or developing a *sui generis* approach essential for the planet's survival. Jiang (2009) posits two philosophies of building design and use, viz.: 天人合一 (Tiān rén hé yi), that is, the oneness of man and nature vis-à-vis the 'high modernist' straw 人定胜天 (Rén dìng sheng tian) i.e., the triumph of man over nature. But, will China and India think and build differently?[27] This decision, will be based in substantial measure on the self-image and self-confidence they have in their own traditions of urbanization and the heritage associated with it.

It is often remarked that if one set someone down blindfolded in a Chinese city and then opened the blindfold, it would be difficult to tell which city one was in since they all look the same. A mistaken conception about China is about its homogeneity, brought about by the external markers of a common language and ethnicity. In practice, however, different Chinese regions take pride in defining themselves distinctively in relation to other regions. As Chinese self-confidence grows, many cities, especially those with a long historical tradition, are likely to seek to project and protect their particular distinctive identity—like Hangzhou's privileging of the West Lake.

It is possible that the salvation of the planet may depend on this distinctiveness of China and India to counteract the consumptiveness that one has seen so far from the United States. It is in our collective interest to nurture it, even if and especially if such individuality is at risk of being

---

[26] See Nivola (1999) for a lucid account of the difference.

[27] At the Shanghai World Expo (whose theme is 'Better City, Better Life'), scheduled for May 2010, the centerpiece of the Indian pavilion is a 35 meter wide bamboo dome, powered by solar panels and windmills. See http://www.hindu.com/2010/02/28/stories/2010022862341800.htm.

rejected. It is towards this conversation, of three nations, one young and two ancient, and three elements—that of water, land and culture—that we need to take our next step.

REFERENCES

Agrawal, D.P. (2002) 'Urban Origins in India', in Paul J.J. Sinclar (ed.) *The Development of Urbanism from a Global Perspective,* Uppsala University, Uppsala, Retrieved from http://www.arkeologi.uu.se/afr/projects/BOOK/agrawal.pdf.

Brown, Marilyn A., Frank Southworth, and Andrea Sarzynski (2008) *Shrinking the Carbon Footprint of Metropolitan America,* Brookings Institution, Washington DC.

Chan, Deland (2007) 'How Migrant Workers Find Housing in Beijing: The Role of Individual Agency in Differential Housing Access and Outcomes', Honors thesis, Program in Urban Studies, Stanford University

Cheng, Edmund W (2008) 'Slums as a Recognition of Migrants' Rights: A Proposal from Qin Hui', *China Perspectives,* No. 2008/4, pp: 84–9.

Chung, Tan (1998) 'Across The Himalayan Gap: A Sino-Indian Perspective For India-China Understanding' in Tan Chung (ed.) *An Indian Quest for Understanding China,* New Delhi, IGNCA and Gyan Publishing House, New Delhi, http://ignca.nic.in/ks_41019.htm

Dhakal, Shobhakar (2009) 'Urban Energy Use and Carbon Emissions from Cities in China and Policy Implications', *Energy Policy* 2009, Vol. 37, No. 11, pp. 4208–19.

D'Monte, Darryl, [ed.](2007) *Mills For Sale: The Way Ahead,* Marg Publications, Mumbai.

Du, Juan (2008) 'Don't Underestimate the Rice Fields', in Ilka Ruby and Andreas Ruby (ed.) *Urban Transformation,* Ruby Press, Berlin.

Ewing, Kent (2007) 'The Coolest Nail House in History', *Asia Times Online,* 31 March 2007, retrieved from http://www.atimes.com/atimes/China_Business/IC31Cb01.html

Government of India [GoI] (2009) *National Accounts Statistics 2009,* Central Statistical Organisation, Ministry of Statistics and Programme Implementation, New Delhi, retrieved from http://mospi.nic.in/rept%20_%20pubn/ftest.asp?rept_id=nad01_2009&type=NSSO

Huang, Philip (2009) 'China's Neglected Informal Economy: Reality and Theory', *Modern China,* Vol. 35, pp. 405–38.

International Energy Agency [IEA] (2008) *World Energy Outlook 2008,* International Energy Agency, Paris.

Jiang, Yi (2009), 'Harmonious with Nature: The Chinese Approach to Building Energy Reduction' in Mark Kelly (ed.) *Public No. 5: A Human Thing,* retrieved from http://www.woodsbagot.com/en/Documents/Public_5_papers/Harmonious_with_nature.pdf

Kochhar, Kalpana, Utsav Kumar, Raghuram Rajan, Arvind Subramanian, and Ioannis Tokatlidis (2006) 'India's Pattern of Development: What Happened, What Follows?', *Journal of Monetary Economics,* Vol. 53, No. 5, pp. 981–1019.

Kundu, Amitabh (2009) 'Urbanisation and Migration: An Analysis of Trend, Pattern and Policies in Asia', UNDP Human Development Research Paper 2009/16, April.

Landry Pierre F. (2003) ' The Political Management of Mayors in Post-Deng China', *The Copenhagen Journal of Asian Studies,* Vol.17, pp. 31–58.

Li, David D. (1998) 'Changing Incentives of the Chinese Bureaucracy', *The American Economic Review,* Vol. 88, No. 2, Papers and Proceedings of the Hundred and Tenth Annual Meeting of the American Economic Association (May, 1998), pp. 393–97.

Menon-Sen, Kalyani and Gautam Bhan (2008) *Swept off the Map,* Yoda Press, Delhi.

Mukhopadhyay, Partha (2007) 'How Can Land Acquisition be Made Humane?', *Economic Times,* New Delhi January 16, retrieved from http://economictimes.indiatimes.com/articleshow/msid-1208046,prtpage-1.cms

National Sample Survey Organisation (NSSO) (2004), *Housing Condition in India, 2002: Housing Stock and Constructions*, NSS Report No. 488, Ministry of Statistics and Programme Implementation, Government of India, March.

Newman, Peter and Jeffrey Kenworthy (1999) *Sustainability and Cities: Overcoming Automobile Dependence*, Island Press, Washington DC.

Nivola, Pietro S. (1999) *Laws of the Landscape: How Policies Shape Cities in Europe and America*, Brookings Institution Press Washington DC.

Northridge, Mary E., Joanne Yankura, Patrick L. Kinney, Regina M. Santella, Peggy Shepard, Ynolde Riojas, Maneesha Aggarwal, Paul Strickland and the Earth Crew (1999) 'Diesel Exhaust Exposure Among Adolescents in Harlem: A Community-Driven Study', *American Journal of Public Health*, Vol. 89, No. 7, pp. 998–1002.

Prasad, Chandra Bhan (2009) 'For a New Dalit Social Contract', *The Mint*, March 16, retrieved from http://www.livemint.com/articles/2009/03/15212222/For-a-new-Dalit-social-contrac.html.

Roberts, Kenneth (2001) 'The Determinants of Occupational Choice of Labor Migrants to Shanghai', *China Economic Review*, Vol.12, No.1.

Roberts, Kenneth, Rachel Connelly, Zhenming Xie and Zhenzhen Zheng (2004) 'Patterns of Temporary Labor Migration of Rural Women from Anhui and Sichuan', *The China Journal*, No. 52 (July), pp. 49–70.

SCMC (Supreme Court Monitoring Committee on Hazardous Wastes) (2004), *Report on Water Contamination of Madhya Pradesh and Gujarat Villages*, April retrieved from http://www.toxicslink.org/docs/SCMC_Report_Water_Contamination_MP_Gujarat.doc

Sheppard, Peggy (2005) 'Breathe At Your Own Risk: Transit Justice in West Harlem', *Race, Poverty & the Environment* Winter 2005/2006.

Solinger, Dorothy (2005) 'The Creation of a New Underclass in China and its Implications', University of California, Irvine: Center for the Study of Democracy, retrieved from: http://www.escholarship.org/uc/item/7bc0p0gb.

Tagore, Rabindranath (1925) *Talks in China*, Visva-Bharati, Santiniketan.

United Nations (2008) *World Urbanization Prospects: The 2007 Revision Population Division*, Department of Economic and Social Affairs United Nations, New York.

Walker, Richard and Daniel Buck (2007) 'The Chinese Road: Cities in the Transition to Capitalism', *New Left Review*, 46 July–Aug

Wang, Shaoguang (2008) 'The Great Transformation: The Double Movement in China', *Boundary*, Vol. 35, pp.15–47.

Wang, Tao and Harrison Hu (2009) 'China Question of the Week: How Hot Can Property Get?', China Economic Comment, UBS Investment Research, 10 December.

World Bank (2009) *World Development Report 2009: Reshaping Economic Geography*, The World Bank, Washington, DC.

Yao, Yang (2009) 'The Disinterested Government: An Interpretation of China's Economic Success in the Reform Era', UNU-WIDER Research Paper No. 2009/33.

Yu Jianrong (2007) 'Social Conflict in Rural China', *China Security*, Vol. 3 No. 2, pp: 2 – 17.

Zhao Suisheng (2003) 'Political Liberalization without Democratization: Pan Wei's Proposal for Political Reform', *Journal of Contemporary China*, Vol. 12, No. 35.

Zhang, Q. (1995) 'A Survey of Floating Population in 50 Townships in China', *Chinese Journal of Population Science*, Vol. 7, No. 3, pp. 229–40.

Zhang, Tingwei (2002) 'Urban Development and a Socialist Pro-Growth Coalition In Shanghai' *Urban Affairs Review*, Vol. 37 No. 4, pp: 475–99 .

Zhang, Yan and Ke Fang (2004) 'Is History Repeating Itself?: From Urban Renewal in the United States to Inner-City Redevelopment in China', *Journal of Planning Education and Research*, Vol. 23, pp: 286–98.

PART THREE

**Dispatches from the Field:
Intellectuals, Fat Cats, and Democracy**

9
Social Transition in India and China[a]

CHAKRAPANI GHANTA

China Moving Ahead! Where is India?[b]

Popular opinion in India generally creates a poor image of both China as well as Chinese goods. However, contrary to the common perception that China Bazaar is a place where cheap plastic goods are sold, China is the world's biggest manufacturing destination today.

Almost all the major countries of the world depend on China for their production. Two decades ago, Chinese goods were sub-standard but now China is producing goods on par with US, Europe, and Japan and has carved its own place in the international market.

Whether it is London, Tokyo, or Delhi, nearly every product, from shoes, apparel, and toys to electronic goods, carries the 'Made in China' mark. China has become synonymous with quality goods today, with Walmart significantly dependent on China and companies such as Nike and Adidas setting up manufacturing units there.

The question that comes to mind is: how did China, with its larger population, higher poverty rate, and fewer resources overtake us, and where do we stand?

IS THIS DEVELOPMENT?

Globalization has changed the yardstick of development. The prevalence of market economy has introduced new goods, measures, and languages and has made foreign direct investment the only indicator of development, irrespective of the countries' social security or development programs.

The volume of foreign direct investment inflow into China is ten times that coming into India; while in terms of GDP, China has grown beyond India's reach. Taking the previous year's figures, FDI in China including Hong Kong, was USD 106 billion, while in India it was just USD 3.6 billion. However, the majority of FDI into China comes from its diaspora—Chinese living abroad contributed nearly USD 70 billion in terms of FDI while NRIs' contribution in terms of foreign investment into India is yet to reach a million. Fifty per cent of Chinese GDP is from the manufacturing sector while in India it did not exceed even 25 per cent. Not just production, even in exports, India is lagging far behind China. In 2005–6, China was about 1000 per cent ahead of India in exports. Excluding Hong Kong, mainland China's exports stand at 700 per cent more than those of India.

---

[a] All contributions except 'SEZs: A Dangerous Imitation' have been translated by the author from original articles published in Telegu newspapers and periodicals. Since they are essentially journalistic pieces, they do not always carry detailed bibliographical references.

[b] First published in Telegu in *Ee Bhoomi*, 15 August 2007.

China produces 103 million tonnes of steel while we produce 19 million tonnes. China manufactures 650 million tonnes while we are at 95 million tonnes, coal mined in China is 1300 metric tonnes while in India it is 300 metric tonnes annually.

China's success story is not just confined to trade and market economy, but extends to successful tapping of human resources as well. Hemmed as it was, between floods and drought, China could yet reap a good harvest from agriculture, producing 415 tonnes of foodgrains—more than double the yield of India —with half the irrigation resources available in India. On the human development front, China has managed to curtail its infant mortality rate to 25 per thousand, while in India it continues at 61 per thousand infants.

How was all this made possible? The vision of Communist leadership could be one of the reasons, which, while giving equal importance to agriculture and industry, did not ignore development in the areas of education and medical facilities either.

The stringent implementation of minimum education up to ninth standard has bolstered the literacy rate from 19 per cent in 1949 to 99.1 per cent now. Health insurance and other social security schemes have reached the common man. In the past 40 years, China has successfully shaped a healthy social system. The reforms of 1970 had shaken the country's economy. Confining SEZs and FDI to particular zones, China opened up to the global market and secured a place for itself in the world economy. However, the boom in China is not the harbinger of unmitigated jubilation. It has given rise to inequalities which have affected the country's social and political spheres. It is now trying to mend fences by bridging the gaps created by the market economy between the people, and major gaps between cities and villages through strategic and comprehensive decentralization.

Billed as the world's largest democracy with patriotic leaders and parties, why could India not achieve even half of China's success? Where do we stand after sixty years after independence? Why are we unable to achieve the smallest thing without struggle? Where does the fault lie? Is it in our forgotten socialism or is it in China's newly acquired democracy? Answers to these questions remain to be found even today.

China Cat and Big Cat[c]

Whether a cat is black or white makes no difference. As long as it catches mice, it is a good cat.

— **Deng Xiaoping**

This was Deng Xiaoping's reply to critics' comments on his economic reforms in Communist China. Ascending to power in 1978, Deng was derisive of the Cultural Revolution slogan that it was 'better to be poor under socialism than rich under capitalism.' The blunt, practical Deng sternly believed that 'we need not bother from where the money comes as long as it helps the country prosper.' He encouraged the creation of a market economy and capitalist-like enterprises, and by the early 1990s, his reforms had helped lift an estimated 170 million Chinese peasants out

---

[c] First published in Telegu in *Andhrajyothy*, 19 December 2007.

FIGURE 1: NEW DRIVING FORCE

The major emerging markets have become the main engines of world growth. For the first time China and India are making the largest country-level contributions to global growth.
(Based on PPP weights, per cent of world growth)

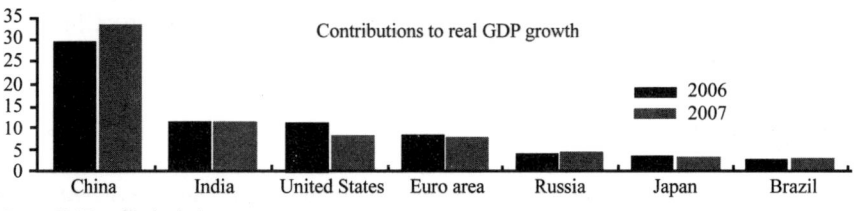

Contributions to real GDP growth — 2006, 2007
China, India, United States, Euro area, Russia, Japan, Brazil

Source: IMF staff calculations.

FIGURE 2: PULLING ITS WEIGHT

China is also making the largest contribution to world growth at market prices.
(Based on market GDP weights, per cent of world growth)

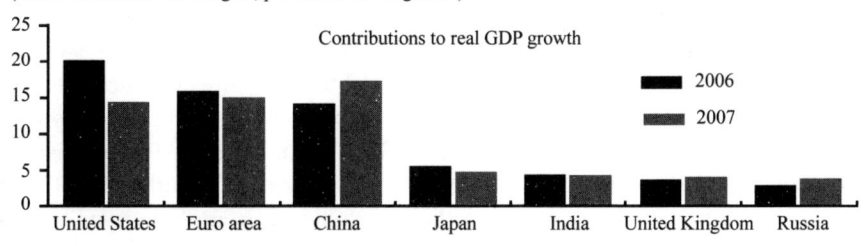

Contributions to real GDP growth — 2006, 2007
United States, Euro area, China, Japan, India, United Kingdom, Russia

Source: IMF staff calculations.

of extreme poverty.[1] His belief has been vindicated over time and his dreams have come true. China has taken its place among the leading and most prosperous nations of the world. Deng's slogan is working like a charm in modern China as the country's speed of attracting foreign direct investment (FDI) scales unprecedented heights, making the entire world sit up and take notice of China's success story on the world map.

According to the World Investment Report issued by the United Nations Conference on Trade and Development in September 2004, China emerged as the foremost destination for foreign investment in 2003. The country has since then retained its top rank among attractive destinations for foreign capital investment in the world. Foreign direct investment flows into China in 2006 topped USD 63 billion: a five per cent growth over the previous year's levels[2] according to official sources. However, according to reports, although China is the largest recipient of foreign investment among all developing nations in the past 15 years, much remains to be done to improve both its quality and quantity in terms of global growth.

According to the latest survey report of the International Monetary Fund (IMF), released in October 2007 (see Figures 1 and 2), 'China is now the single most important contributor to world growth, both in terms of market and purchasing-power-parity (PPP) exchange rates. China's economy gained further momentum in 2007, growing at 11.5 per cent, and was expected to grow by 10 per cent in 2008. The report further predicts that China's economy would continue to grow at breakneck speed, turning it into a major driving force in the global economy, even as other emerging markets are also growing strongly.[3]

[1] http://www.chinadaily.com.cn/bizchina/2007-01/15/content_78351.htm
[2] http://www.chinadaily.com.cn/bizchina/2007-01/15/content_78351.htm
[3] Tim Callen, IMF Research Department, Emerging Markets: Main Engine of Growth, IMF Survey Magazine.

Deng's slogan 'to get rich is glorious' is working in China. 'Work, save, and live with dignity through prosperity' is the ideology that drives modern day China. However, in view of the sheer magnitude of burgeoning FDIs, reserves, and high rate of saving prevalent in the country, economists in China are perplexed about how to regulate this wealth, narrow down inequalities, and place the country on a socialist path—an issue that is bothering both the Chinese leadership as well as the economists.

THE ROAD MAP

According to supporters of China's Open Door Policy, the enormous inflow of foreign direct investment has single-handedly brought about substantial economic upswing in the country. Being the world's largest FDI recipient among developing countries since the early 1990s, China has accounted for a quarter to one-third of the world's total FDI inflow to developing countries in recent years and FDI has become an important source of China's investment in fixed assets, accounting for 12 per cent of the country's annual investment in fixed assets in 1996, as against 3.8 per cent in 1981. This share fell to nine per cent and seven per cent respectively in 1998 and 1999 in the wake of the Asian financial crisis of 1997 and the consequent reduction in FDI inflow. However, recent figures released by the government show an average 10 per cent growth rate in the past four years, with total FDI touching USD 720 billion. China's FDI receipts amounted to USD 69.5 billion in 2006 and USD 67.8 billion in the first ten months of 2007. Apart from solving the capital shortage problem, foreign direct investment is also perceived to bring other benefits such as better access to technology, indirect productivity gains through spillovers, programs related to world class labor training and management strategies, etc. China's success story started way back in late 1970, when it gradually started opening its economy for foreign businesses and attracted large amounts of direct foreign investment. The Government of China carefully evaluated its policies in each phase of economic development and incorporated appropriate changes in policy priorities based on its experiences. In the first stage, during the late 1970s and early 1980s, government policies were characterized by new regulations to permit joint ventures with foreign capital and Special Economic Zones (SEZs) and Open Cities[4] which opened their doors to FDI. The State Council also awarded autonomy rights in foreign trade to provinces of Guangdong and Fujian and in 1980, set up four SEZs in Shenzhen, Zhuhai, Shantou, and Xiamen. Later on, in December 1982, the decision to open up China to the world economy was formally included in the 1982 State Constitution adopted by the Sixth National People's Congress.

In late 1983, Regulations for the Implementation of the Law of the People's Republic of China on Joint Ventures using Chinese and Foreign Investment was formulated to further liberalize the domestic market and prepare the business environment for overseas joint ventures. Since 1984, China has opened its economy even further to foreign direct investment. In the same year, the concept of SEZs was extended to fourteen more coastal cities and Hainan Island.[5] Twelve of the fourteen cities were designated Technology Promotion Zones in 1985 to expedite transfer of technology. The development triangles—the Yangtze River Delta, the Pearl River Delta in Guangdong, the Min Nan region in Fujian, Liaodong, and Shandong Peninsulas; and the Bohai Sea Coastal Region—were also opened to foreign investors in this year. Later, in 1990, the Pudong district of Shanghai was designated as a new development zone to lead development along the Yangtze River.

[4] The second session of the Fifth National People's Congress held in July 1979 was adapted into the Law on Joint-Ventures using Chinese and Foreign Investment.

[5] Hainan Island became a province and the fifth, the largest SEZ in 1988.

Article 226 for Encouragement of Foreign Investment (1986) adopted more favorable regulations and provisions that helped in attracting direct foreign investment inflow, especially export-oriented joint ventures and joint ventures using advanced technologies. This amendment allowed setting up of wholly foreign-owned enterprises and gave foreign joint ventures preferential tax treatment, freedom to import input material and equipment, right to retain and swap foreign exchange with each other, and simpler licensing procedures. Additional tax benefits were offered to export-oriented joint ventures and those employing advanced technology. The government further attempted to guarantee the autonomy of joint ventures from external bureaucratic interference, to eliminate many 'unfair' local costs, and to provide alternate ways for joint ventures to balance foreign exchange. Privileged access was provided to supplies of water, electricity, and transportation on par with other state-owned companies and these were further facilitated to provide interest-free RMB (Ren Min Bi) loans.

To strengthen Article 22, another regulation known as Article 37 was introduced, which explicitly linked (Article 3) the establishment of wholly foreign-owned enterprises to the development of China's national economy, and required such enterprises either to be export-oriented or to use advanced technology and equipment. The amendment of the '1979 Joint Venture Law' (1990) further relaxed the rules by allowing non-Chinese individuals to act as Chairmen of the Board of Directors, extensions to the terms of operation of joint ventures, and removal of the upper limit to the proportion of registered capital that could be contributed by the foreign partner, all of which resulted in increasing inflow of foreign capital in the late 1980s and early 1990s. From the mid-1990s, while maintaining a favorable environment for foreign businesses, government policies began to focus more on linking foreign direct investment promotion to the objectives of domestic industry.

Generally speaking, China's policies towards foreign direct investment can be viewed in roughly three stages: gradual and limited opening, active promotion through preferential treatment, and promotion of foreign direct investment in accordance with domestic industrial objectives. These changes in policy priorities inevitably affected the pattern of FDI inflow in China. Between 1978 and 1982, about 920 companies invested just USD 1.8 billion. In the following decade, although the number of companies went up to 48,764, the FDI did not cross USD 4.5 billion. Thereupon, stepping up the economic reforms, China started SEZs, which were autonomous business zones along the coastal region. This resulted in a ten-fold growth of FDI in the next ten years. Currently, Hong Kong, Macau, Taiwan, Japan, America, and the European nations are investing millions of dollars in the country, resulting in an increase in average per capita income from USD 200 in 1979 to USD 1269 in 2004. By the end of 2005, about 552,960 projects had been funded and the country had realized USD 6.9 billion in overseas direct investment, excluding the financial sector (up 25.8 per cent over 2004); USD 21.8 billion in overseas contract projects (up 24.6 per cent over 2004); and USD 4.8 billion worth of business volume from cooperative labor services involving other countries (up 27.5 per cent over 2004).[6]

Apart from domestic capital formation, foreign direct investment has also had several direct impacts on the people and their lives in China. The most significant effect is the unusual expansion of the job market. Both total employment and urban employment in FDI firms in China have increased rapidly. While foreign firms employed 4.80 million (total) and 1.65 million (urban) workers in 1991, thus accounting for 0.74 per cent of China's total and 0.97 per cent of its urban employment in that year, they employed four times as many people in 1998 (18.39 million and 5.87

---

[6] *China Business Guide*, 2006, China Council for the Promotion of International Trade, published by China Chamber of International Trade.

FIGURE 3: GROWTH IN GDP, MERCHANDISE TRADE AND FDI INFLOWS 2000–05

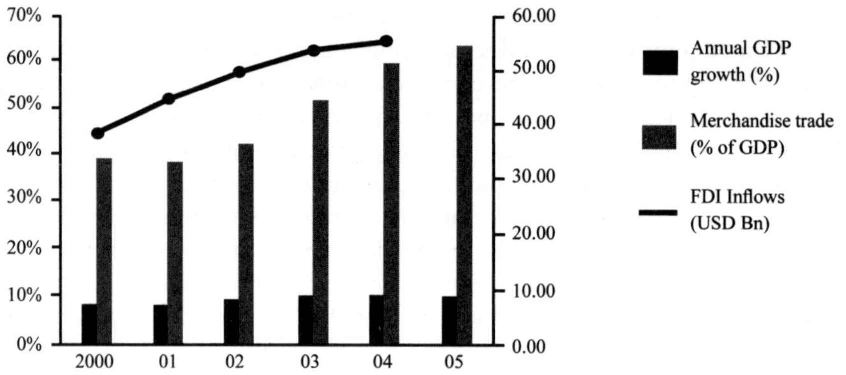

Source: World Development Report, The World Bank, various years.

million workers respectively) or 2.63 per cent of China's total employment and 2.84 per cent of its urban employment. At the end of 1998, urban employment was primarily concentrated around the selected provinces where FDI- funded industries and investment congregated, thus contributing to widening the income gap between the eastern and western regions of the country. However, FDI firms not only created jobs but also facilitated skill enhancement for Chinese workers. Of course, this led to a new division of labor and hierarchy, and income differences among the workers. Moreover, FDI firms attracted higher quality of labor in their employment composition than domestic firms. These firms tend to hire more employees with university degrees and higher education than domestic firms, particularly in capital-intensive and technology-intensive industries.

Because FDI firms pay higher wages and employ higher standards of labor than domestic firms, there is a real risk that more and more quality labor will be drawn into foreign firms, away from domestic firms. Another divide fostered by these firms is that of income differences within the labor force, since they pay higher rates of employee compensation (wages, salaries, bonuses, and monetary and non-monetary fringe benefits) than domestic and state-owned firms. The most crucial impact of these firms is technology transfer. A study conducted by the Organization for Economic Co-operation and Development (OECD) finds that 'there is clear evidence that technology and managerial skills have been transferred to China by these firms. Such evidence was found *inter alia* in the size, physical and capital intensities of the FDI firms, and their factor intensity. The size of a firm can be measured by its total assets. On an average, the size of FDI firms is nearly 100 per cent larger than that of China's domestic firms. As a category they are 170 per cent larger in labor-intensive industry, 124 per cent larger in technology-intensive industry, and 40 per cent larger in capital-intensive industry than that of China's domestic firms respectively.[7] This implies that FDI firms are more technically efficient in their methods of production, and thus benefit more from economies of scale than China's domestic firms. Because of their ownership advantages, FDI firms, as a general rule, also have a higher capital to labor ratio than domestic firms in the same industry. On an average, the capital to labor ratio of FDI firms is 141 per cent higher than that of China's domestic firms. The difference in physical capital intensity of FDI and domestic firms is the largest in technology-intensive industry (17.67 per cent), followed by capital-intensive sector (9.83 per cent). Thus, capital in the form of FDI has radically changed the structure of Chinese industry.

[7] *China Business Guide*, China Council for the Promotion of International Trade published by China Chamber of International Trade.

THE GLORY OF PROSPERITY

Before making China the world's foremost destination for industry and prosperity, Deng discontinued several 'old' practices and reformed China from the grass roots. He reversed Mao's slogans and trained the Chinese to live with money. One of Deng's first reforms was to abolish Mao's rural agricultural communes and allow peasants to cultivate family plots. Grain harvests quickly increased, and other reforms followed. City dwellers were allowed to start small-scale businesses, ordinary Chinese allowed to buy consumer goods; Deng actively courted international investors.

Today, the average Chinese city dweller firmly believes what Deng had said long back: 'Poverty is not Socialism. To be rich is glorious'.

The flowing in of FDIs and other investments completely changed the social and economic structure of China. This has also changed the lifestyle of people living in or migrating to cities. Seventy per cent of the people living in Chinese cities have an annual income between USD 2000 and USD 8000 while in Indian cities, people earn not more than USD 2000 annually. Calculations by Asian Demographics showed that average urban household incomes in the two countries in 2002 were roughly similar. However, China has greater number of urban households. Because of the one-child policy, the average household size is smaller—usually three people rather than five, as in India—and therefore these households have more money to spend.

In 2002, around 70 per cent of urban Chinese households earned between USD 2000 and USD 7500 a year. In India, a higher proportion earned more than USD 7500 (6.4 per cent compared with China's 1.2 per cent), but 73.5 per cent earned less than USD 2000. China has a fairly broad-based middle class. India has a narrow affluent elite.[8]

More than six lakh foreign companies are operating in China and employment generation benefiting over 15 crore people. China has attracted more FDI than any other country in the world including the US. The country achieved 15 per cent industrial growth since 1980 and diverted the profits towards developing infrastructure. It has built 30,000 km of express highways while India could not build one-tenth of that stretch. Chinese investment in these projects is very nominal. The 1.3 billion strong country has turned its manpower into a major factor in the development process. People above 16 years are estimated to be about one billion and 76 per cent of this populace participates in the country's development process.

At least 60 per cent of the Chinese population has primary or secondary education as well as some technical knowledge on account of vocational training. This is how China's workforce of 78 to 80 crore is working to its advantage. There are no legal hurdles for those who want to invest in China, which provides the workforce. There is no minimum wage norm. Earnings vary according to the nature of work, place of work, and the industry one works for. This method is always beneficial to the company, leaving the workers with hardly any bargaining power or chance of trade union activity or workers' organization. This is a major attraction for companies to set up shop in China and the primary reason for the substantial foreign investment pouring into the country. Though there are people in India willing to work at nominal wages, trade unions, minimum wages, long working hours, and labor courts are standing in the way of investors who find an easier, if less fair, alternative in China.

With its new found wealth, China has embarked upon twin plans of massive urbanization and infrastructure development, phenomena which are percolating to rural areas as well. Beijing is trying to reduce the dependency of its populace on agriculture. The swelling of investments

---

[8] *The Economist*, 'Survey: India and China, The Insidious Charms of Foreign Investment', 3 March 2005.

is creating heartburn among the people. There are warnings that the Socialist philosophy of the country would be harmed unless the untrammeled growth in wealth, facilities, and assets in cities are regularized. Burgeoning incomes have changed the lifestyle in cities. The Chinese are buying more luxury goods now than ever before. From jewelry and fashionable clothing to expensive cars and beauty care, products are flooding the markets. The number of US-dollar-millionaire households in China was 250,000 in 2005, the sixth highest in the world, according to a study by the Boston Consulting Group.[9] It has reported that the Chinese luxury goods market is expanding at an annual rate of 10 to 20 per cent. Forecasts suggest that by the year 2015, China will become the second largest luxury goods consumer market in the world, next to the US.

According to economists, the soaring property markets, as a result of the boom in real estate in China, make up one-third of the country's gross domestic product. Property values have risen 300 per cent in three years, pricing many out of the market on the one hand, and resulting in China's neo-rich class in the industrialized areas going in for luxury cars and jazzy lifestyles.

This had become a cause for concern, because, as TIME magazine observed: 'Decades after Mao realized his vision of a classless, property-less society by destroying wealth and all of its manifestations, China's monied elite is making a boisterous comeback. With the unleashing of private enterprise and the rapid development of coastal cities, China now boasts nearly 10,000 entrepreneurs, each worth USD 10 million or more, according to researchers at the Chinese Academy of Social Sciences in Beijing. The country's affluent ranks are among the fastest growing in the world. Their commercial successes aren't necessarily glamorous—one of the richest men in China, billionaire Liu Yongxing, built his empire supplying pig feed. Nor are they superlatively well-off by the standards of America's Bill Gates or Saudi Arabia's Prince Alwaleed bin Talal. But the economic clout of China's nouveaux riches has become hard to ignore. Last year, the Communist Party finally admitted these once shunned capitalists into its fold'.[10] There is mounting concern that this rapid accumulation of wealth might be getting out of hand.

The gulf between the super rich and the poor has expanded to its widest extent in little more than half a century. The Wall Street Journal[11] observes that 'the US may be home to the largest number of millionaires and billionaires in the world, but China is quickly moving up the wealth ladder'. Most rich Chinese are young, self-made entrepreneurs who made their money in real estate; only 50 of the top 500 are women. Further, some things do not seem to have changed: 'A political connection is still extremely helpful. Years ago, being listed on China's top 50 meant a visit from the tax police, legal actions from communist officials, and public resentment. There was a lot of hostility towards people on the list,' says Hooge Werf. 'If you were a rich man, you had to be corrupt.' Now, with rising stock markets in China, wealth is out in the open, and is viewed as more legitimate.

THE OTHER SIDE OF THE COIN

Foreign direct investment may have fostered capital formation and development in Communist China, in the teeth of opposition from popular sentiment, but in spite of eulogies from optimists such as leading economist Professor Lin Yifu, advisor to the Chinese State Council (citing China's

---

[9] Boston Consulting Group, White Paper, *China Report: Studies in Operations and Strategy*, September 2005.

[10] Hannah Beech, 'Wretched Excess', the *Time* magazine Monday, 16 September 2002.

[11] 30 May 2007, China's New Rich, http://blogs.wsj.com/wealth/2007/05/30/chinas-new-billionaires/

position in the global economy: fourth in GDP, third in Trade, second in Foreign Direct Investment, and first in Foreign Exchange Holdings),[12] the obvious and growing social divide and dissent in China cannot be ignored. Perceiving this as a possible hindrance to growth, the Chinese government has initiated the exercise of narrowing regional inequalities through development of remote as well as rural areas. It has further plans to ban FDI in some core areas. The country which preached development through FDI is now trying to wriggle out of the web of FDI-created wealth in recognition of the looming crisis, and is trying to construct a framework for a *harmonious society*. The bleak picture in China was highlighted in a report by the Asian Development Bank (ADB) released in August 2007, which said that China now trails behind only Nepal as the Asian country with the worst rich-poor divide. Moreover, Chinese official statistics[13] released in September supported the ADB's findings, showing that China's rural–urban income gap has widened from 3.21 times in 2004 to 3.23 times in 2005, to 3.28 times last year.

When Deng Xiaoping launched his program to implement economic reforms, the Chinese could not have anticipated that their drastic policies would transform Socialist China into the kind of 'decadent society that they have always identified with capitalism. Chinese economists also pointed out that while farmers' annual incomes have increased by an average of six per cent since the mid-1980s, they are still far behind urban salaries that have increased by eight or nine per cent. The economic experts noted this as a major factor in triggering urban–rural tension in the country.

Such an obvious disparity in wealth distribution may well turn out to be the final straw that breaks the camel's back, and with 1.3 billion people, if the volcano of China does indeed erupt, the results could devastate its society. The ideals of an egalitarian society that are trumpeted so loudly by CCP leaders appear to be no more than an illusion. The economic divide in China has become a nightmare that will haunt its leaders for many years to come.

Whatever might be its colour, the cat has caught the mice, but will it survive the onslaught of the big cat?

China's Agriculture, Reaping A Rich Harvest[d]

India and China are both traditionally agricultural economies. However, while the agricultural scenario in India continues to be pathetic, China has managed to galvanize its agricultural sector to the level of an industry and to give to its rural areas a near urban look.

Recently, a Chinese developmental research organization provided an in-depth analysis on farmers' suicides in China between 1997 and 2005, along with the causes of their distress and the economic reforms that were in full play. Simultaneously, a report based on a study by Prof. K. Nagaraj of the Madras Institute of Development Studies (MIDS), published by The Hindu on 12 November

---

[12] Lin Yifu, addressed a seminar on the theme 'Made in China 2007: The Truth'; seminar held on 3 November 2007 in the London office of the China Council for the Promotion of International Trade (CCPIT).

[13] Report by the National Development and Reform Commission, PRC, 2006.

[d] First published in Telegu in *Vaartha*, 28 December 2007.

2007, claimed that about 150,000 farmers in India committed suicides during these seven years and that the number is on the increase. The report revealed that while the number of suicides in 1997 was recorded at 14,000, it crossed 17,000 in 2005. The number of Indians committing suicide each year rose from around 96,000 in 1997 to roughly 1.14 lakh in 2005. While the rise in farmers' suicides has been observed for over a decade, there have been sharp spurts in some years such as 1998 and 2004. These suicides, taken on the basis of a proportion of total suicides, rose from 14.2 per cent in 1997 to 15 per cent in 2005.

Professor Nagaraj also pointed to the Annual Compound Growth Rate (ACGR) 'for suicides nationally, for suicides amongst farmers, and those committed using pesticides.' The ACGR for all suicides in India over a nine-year period is 2.18 per cent. This is not higher than the population growth rate. However, for farmers' suicides, this rate is much higher, at 2.91 per cent while that for suicides committed by consuming pesticide is 2.5 per cent. Such suicides are often linked to farming crises, with pesticides being easily available to the farmer. 'There are clear disturbing patterns and trends in both farmers' suicides and pesticide-related suicides.'

Alarming though this is, it still does not capture the full picture. The data on suicides are complex, and sometimes misleading. Farmers' suicide rate as a percentage of total farmers is hard to calculate on a yearly basis. A clear national 'farmers' suicide rate' can be derived only for 2001 because we have the Census to tell us how many farmers there were in the country that year. Surprisingly, the suicides are more in the developed states.

The situation in China is totally different. There farmers, farmers' unions, and local industries have, through concerted effort, painted a rosy rural landscape. A week before the report on suicides in India came out, the report published in 'People's Daily Online' on 5 November 2007 based on the survey of the Chinese rural–urban developmental federation was prepared by the Chinese Association for promoting townships and village development.

This report stated that Chinese villages and the rural economy are prospering substantially with every passing day. This year, as per the statistics from the Chinese Association for Promoting Township and Village Development, the value of production in about 8000 villages amounted to more than 100 million yuans (USD 13.3 billion). Further, each of these villages on the Chinese mainland has generated wealth to the extent of 100 million yuan or more since the first of its kind emerged in 1987. According to a recent survey, the villages including 11 whose gross domestic product surpasses 10 billion yuan (USD 1.3 billion) each, create a total of 1.6 trillion yuan of wealth.

The survey shows that more than 60 per cent of the 100-million-yuan villages are located in the eastern developed regions such as Beijing, Shanghai, Tianjin, Jiangsu, Guangdong, and Zhejiang. The development of the villages is mainly driven by special farming and animal raising industries, heavy industries, tourism, and trade and commerce. Daqiu village in the suburbs of Tianjin became the first 100-million-yuan village in 1987 on the Chinese mainland, driven by industries such as steel and printing since the country started on its economic reforms and opening-up policy in 1978. In 2003, Huaxi village in east China's Jiangsu province, became the first village to generate 10 billion yuan of gross domestic product.

China now has 600,000 villages. 'The rich villages will play an active role in driving the underdeveloped rural areas in China through economic strength and experience,' said Yang Yongzhe, a consultant to the Association.

With focus on irrigation, village industries and other progressive plans could help China to earn USD 1.6 trillion. Of the six lakh villages, about 10,000 villages prospered to a position which could be envied by cities with increased production. This does not mean that there is no poverty in China. More than 100,000 villages are reeling under poverty. It is the villages in coastal areas which have seen massive industrialization and market economy in play that are prosperous.

Development of rural China is progressing in a planned manner. After the revolution, Peoples' China has laid the necessary foundation for rural development through proper reforms. China had instituted major rural reforms in 1978, keeping in view nationalization of land and commune farming experiences. As part of the reforms, China registered families in rural areas and introduced 'hukou' which provides data pertaining to manpower, families, and natural resources, and how these might be utilized.

Land reforms had ensured even distribution as well as proper protection of fertile land. The reforms have developed 84,000 new reservoirs besides regulating rain water and provided water to 20 million hectares of land. The radical measures taken up by the Chinese government have increased water availability in 16 million hectares at the time of the revolution to 50 million hectares as of now.

In the second phase, the country modernized its agricultural sector and created a new record in increasing productivity. The number of tractors increased from 1300 in 1950 to seven lakh in 1999 and the figure is estimated to be about 12 lakh in 2007. China brought down the prices of agricultural implements and popularized their use among farmers. Agriculture was given 20 per cent of the budgetary allocation and steps taken to ensure that the agricultural sector accounted for 10 to 15 per cent lending of banks.

All these measures enabled China to revolutionize its agricultural sector. Further, with the advent of the World Trade Organization (WTO), China initiated steps to increase its exports and cut down imports. Thus, because of proper planning, the balance of payments situation in China is remarkably healthy.

The rural economy also got a boost with decentralization of power to local bodies, providing unrestricted trade to farmers, encouraging agro-based industries, and investments in rural areas. As the benefits of research percolated down to the farming community in the form of new breeds for their main crops such as paddy, cotton, and soybean, the budget for agro-based research increased three-fold and was taken care of by the government, along with the budget allocation for rural development, encompassing development of infrastructure such as roads and irrigation. During 2006, around USD 20 billion was pumped in and 325,000 rural roads laid as part of infrastructural development.

Agencies such as the United Nations (UN) 'recognize that the boom in rural economy aids the process of poverty alleviation in China. There are at least 80 to 100 million migrant laborers in China as a result of poverty in rural areas. Estimates of the extent of poverty vary depending on which indicators one chooses. Using the government poverty line, the number of China's rural poor fell dramatically from 250 million in 1978 (30 per cent of the rural population) to 42 million in 1998 (4.6 per cent of the rural population). Using a standard international poverty line of USD 1 per day would result in a substantially greater number of absolute poor, but the trend in poverty reduction remains to be confirmed'.

Relatively speaking, India's progress on these fronts, despite its vast and rich resources, has been proceeding at a snail's pace. While on the one hand China, the second largest country in the world, has much more land than India, the cultivable land in India (about 161 million hectares) is much more than that of China at 130 million hectares. In China, land under irrigation is pegged at 54.5 million hectares while in India it is 55.5 million hectares. The average landholding size in our country at 1.4 hectares is much larger than in China, where land reforms reduced the average holding to 0.4 hectares.

In the past 15 years, China has achieved a growth rate between four and five per cent, resulting in prosperity for farmers. Differences in approach to agriculture between India and China, which become obvious with comparative studies of crop patterns, have resulted in much higher yields in China than in India. In 2003–5, the average yield of foodgrains in India was 3034 kg per hectare for paddy and 2688 kg per hectare for wheat, while the corresponding yields in China were 6233 kg and 4155 kg per hectare for both crops respectively.

In 1980, the horticulture ratio between the two countries was 55:60 million tonnes in favor of China. By 2003, China had reached 450 million tonnes while India came up to only 135 tonnes. Further, the reforms in agriculture were not just confined to yield in paddy, wheat, cotton, soya, vegetables and fruits, but also encompassed modernization of medicines, livestock, and aqua culture.

With the growing rural–urban divide in China, the government identified new rural areas for development and launched various schemes to take care of insurance, medical, and education needs of the populace in the most backward areas. Orders were issued to cut down fees in educational institutions in backward regions. Subsidy on agricultural implements was increased to 50 per cent in these areas by pumping in huge sums in terms of investment.

China recently released its first major document of the year, which calls for the construction of a 'new socialist countryside' as the foremost task facing China in the five-year (2006–10) period. The document embraces a set of ideas set forth by the CCP, Central Committee, and the State Council. It is the third consecutive time since 2004 that agriculture, farmers, and countryside development have been the subject of the first document from the central authorities, showing the government's determination to solve the problems existing in rural areas.

The document said that the next five years will be the key to laying a solid foundation for the new socialist countryside. Its aim is to boost modern agriculture, develop new relationships between industry and agriculture, cities and countryside, and increase rural affluence.

The ideas set forth by the central authorities listed eight policy priorities to promote reconstruction of the countryside:

- Plan economic, social development in urban, rural areas as a whole, and firmly promote construction of the new countryside;
- Boost modern agriculture to consolidate industrial support to the new countryside construction;
- Ensure sustained increases of farmers' income to lay a solid rural economic foundation;
- Increase infrastructure construction in rural areas to improve rural material conditions;
- Accelerate development of pubic services in the countryside and encourage new farmers;
- Deepen comprehensive rural reforms to guarantee systematic protection for rural people;
- Improve democracy in rural areas and perfect rural management; and
- Enhance leadership and motivate all party members and the entire society to care, support, and participate in the construction of a new countryside.

As mentioned in the document, constructing a new socialist countryside is an important historic task in the process of China's modernization because the document clearly says that 'with more than 800 million people living in the countryside, the only way to ensure sustainable development of the national economy and continuous expansion of domestic demand is to develop the rural economy and help farmers to become more affluent'.

Today, in China, agriculture and villages are listed as 'top priority' and money is being pumped into rural areas to develop villages. The Government of India, on the other hand, is continuously deprioritizing agriculture.

China, Is the Model in Rehabilitation?[e]

The recent verdict of the National Environmental Assessment Authority (NEAA) has raised questions about the future of Polavaram project initiated by the Andhra Pradesh government. Although the state government did not bother about the people's opinion and started work on a war footing, having obtained permission from the various central government departments, it has been forced to reconsider construction of that project in line with the NEAA verdict, which in case of the Polavaram project, is not confined to environment and protection of forests alone, highlighting as it did, the problem of rehabilitation of the tribals who survive on the forests. Polavaram is a problem that concerns three states and their tribal population. Orissa and Chhattisgarh are contending that their forest areas and people are threatened by the Polavaram project, which had been initiated by the Andhra Pradesh government unilaterally, without any consultation with them. People's organizations as well as political parties have been agitating over Polavaram for the past two years.

Thousands of major projects are being undertaken in developing countries for basic facilities such as irrigation and electricity (with the blind belief that major projects are the only way forward). However, it is also being proved that the costs of these projects in terms of degradation of living standards of the people displaced often outweigh their benefits. With 4000 major projects, India occupies the third place in the world with regard to major projects, next only to China (22,000) and US (6390). Our projects have been undertaken primarily for agricultural needs and provide irrigation to 38 per cent of the agricultural land in our country. However, according to an estimate, almost eight crore people have been displaced by these projects by the year 2000. Between 1986 and 1993, when project construction was on the rise, almost four crore people became homeless (as their habitations, fields, and villages were submerged).

The projects under construction in our country are becoming more controversial than the ones in China and US. Hasty decisions of the governments, lack of clarity on the location and dimensions of proposed dams, inaccurate estimates of not just the benefits but also the threats to the people and the environment, and neglect of these aspects are becoming major reasons for these controversies. Also, till recently, there were no proper laws or plans for project-rehabilitation in the country. The World Bank has formulated some guidelines for projects under construction in developing countries and has complimented China on the efficacy of its rehabilitation measures for the displaced population in the Three Gorges Dam project, recommending it as a model for other developing countries. Several other international organizations have also complimented China in this regard.

China had only 40 small projects and some major reservoirs in 1949. It built 70,000 dams and 80,000 reservoirs by 1985, while displacing only one crore people as per the statistics of the World Commission on Dams. Further, rehabilitation is being provided in other places for people who have lost land, shelter, and work because of these projects. Although the figures have been greeted with skepticism by non-governmental organizations (NGOs), experts and media world-wide, especially with regard to the Three Gorges Dam, China is moving ahead with its major project.

The Three Gorges Dam is a sensation of contemporary times. Its construction expenditure is USD 11 billion (Rs 20,000 crore). Because of this project, almost 13 lakh people from nine districts of two provinces, Sandouping and Hubei, have been evacuated. 355 villages and towns have been submerged either partially or completely. The area of this project reservoir is 632 sq kilometer and its full capacity is 39.3 billion cubic meter. The construction work that began in

[e] First published in Telegu in the *Andhrajyothy*, 2 January 2008.

1992 was completed in September 2009, except for six additional generators which are going to be installed by 2011.

Environmental, social, and economic experts across the world have questioned China's motivation behind such a major experiment, involving such a mass scale evacuation. There are those who say, 'Three Gorges is the magnified manifestation of China's destructive nature.' The Government of China, however, maintains that the project is crucial for their development and that many historical problems of China will be solved by this project. The primary objective of Three Gorges is to check the Yangtze river, which has been called the 'Sorrow of China' since ancient times, as also increasing the country's electricity production substantially.

Compared to other countries, China faces fewer hurdles in formulating and implementing projects due to its extensive land availability and the limited voice of the people in matters related to wealth and property. The rehabilitation measures implemented by the Chinese government in the wake of its major projects are also more effective on ground.

Agricultural land in China is completely under the local government. Before commencing construction of the projects, matters such as how much land is available in which village and under how many farmers are discussed and decided upon. The extent of displacement, the requirements for rehabilitation, and the modalities as well as logistics of the rehabilitation process are subsequently discussed and related decisions taken. Depending on the availability of land, the displaced people are evacuated to different villages in the same area. The local government is responsible for conducting this process within the proposal stage of the project. In the second stage, people's (family) property is calculated, and accordingly, the value of immovable property such as houses and others are determined to calculate the suitable compensation. In the third stage, taking into consideration the other kind of losses of the family members (professions, jobs, and other works), action is taken to rehabilitate them or pay them appropriate compensation. Also, based on the number of family members, some money is allotted for these families to migrate and settle in the rehabilitation areas and for the farmers to make their allotted land fit for agriculture.

Apart from government representatives, experts, educationists, and people's representatives are assigned the task of these calculations. How many people are shifted to which villages is also identified so that land can be allotted to them for their residential requirements in the respective villages. This land has to be bought at the rate fixed by the government with the money that they receive as compensation from the government.

Anticipating criticisms with regard to Three Gorges, China has taken several precautionary measures and designed a very liberal rehabilitation package. While it, has a number of drawbacks in actual practice, in principle, China's rehabilitation package is being appreciated by many, including the World Bank. In its report published in 1998, the World Bank expressed complete satisfaction saying, 'this should become a model for all developing countries and this plan is helpful not only for rehabilitation but also for complete economic and social self-reliance for the evacuated people.' Almost one and a half million lakh hectares of land for fruit groves and 20 lakh hectares of land for agriculture were allotted in the upper hill regions to ensure rehabilitation for almost half of the displaced people.

Although there was not enough land to replicate that of the displaced population, land was, nevertheless allotted to every family to suit its requirements. Attempts are being made to provide employment to approximately four lakh people in towns and cities. China is involved in developing Chang Ching city, located near the dam, into an industrial center. Almost a thousand factories that existed in the now submerged villages and towns are being constructed in this city. The remaining people are being sent to far away villages and industrial centers.

To its detractors, who oppose in principle the destruction of human habitations and evacuating them to new places, the Government of China says, 'We want development. Our people should become partners in development. We will not hesitate as far as expenditure is concerned.' China is far ahead when compared to rehabilitation schemes in our country. Our governments, unable to formulate proper rehabilitation packages for projects such as Polavaram, end up being scolded by the Courts.

Special Economic Zones: A Dangerous Imitation[f]

The American poet, Ralph Waldo Emerson wrote in his classic work 'Self-Reliance', that 'imitation is suicide'. As per popular Indian perception, China is infamous for its imitations. China Bazaar, in the Indian sense, is a place where cheap goods are sold. However, India's signal failure to emulate China in the matter of Special Economic Zones (SEZs) raises several issues related to the social and political economy of the two systems.

Although the concept of SEZs originated in western capitalist economies, China, by virtue of being a Communist nation, was able to use it as a successful tool to attract huge amounts of capital into the country, while India, being a democratic nation, failed to emulate this feat. Indian SEZs came up twenty five years after those of China and attracted more criticism than investments from the global community, even as China emerged as the world's most favorable destination for FDI.

Special Economic Zones are particular areas located in distinct or 'different' economic and geographical areas within a nation. In contemporary economic terms, the SEZs can primarily be defined as duty-free zones. Complete exemption from excise duty, custom duty, sales tax, *octroi*, *mandi* tax, turnover tax, as well as income tax holiday for ten years are some of the inducements. Also spelt out are provisions for 100 per cent FDI, exemption on income tax on infrastructure capital fund and individual investment, and an assurance of round-the-clock power and water supply. The SEZ promoters have also been given a waiver on Environment Impact Assessment (EIA). In a way, these zones are unique, special, and almost insulated from rest of the country's regular rules and regulations.

The government's intention in creating SEZs is to attract FDI to expand the economy and to generate employment. Voices in political opposition, however, are pointing to the negative aspects of SEZs, that is, damage and destruction in terms of their impact on the social fabric of Indian villages and agriculture, as well as to other negative implications of the policy. An attempt has been made here to understand the policies, practical issues, and experiences of SEZs in India and China. It also examines the aspects related to the success of Chinese SEZs and the practical implications and public concerns with regard to the Indian situation. In a way, it is an articulation of the story of two nations which are racing in the global market.

The idea of SEZs is not originally a Chinese one. As the Government of India officially claims,

[f] Paper presented in the National Seminar on Special Economic Zones: Engines of Growth and Social Development for India, organized by Department of Sociology, Osmania University, Hyderabad, India, 16–17 October 2008.

it is an innovative Indian economic model. India was one of the first nations in Asia to recognize the effectiveness of the Export Processing Zone (EPZ) model in promoting exports, with Asia's first EPZ being set up in Kandla in 1965.[14] With a view to overcome the shortcomings experienced on account of the multiplicity of controls and clearances; absence of world-class infrastructure, and an unstable fiscal regime, and with a view to attracting larger foreign investments in India, the Special Economic Zones (SEZs) Policy was announced in April, 2000. After extensive debate and protests, the SEZ Act, 2005, supported by SEZ Rules, came into effect on 10 February 2006, providing for drastic simplification of procedures and for single window clearance on matters relating to central as well as state governments.

As specified by the Ministry of Commerce and Industry, Government of India, the main objectives of the SEZ Act are:[15]

- Generation of additional economic activity;
- Promotion of exports of goods and services;
- Promotion of investment from domestic and foreign sources;
- Creation of employment opportunities; and
- Development of infrastructure facilities.

As per the policy document prepared by the Ministry, this is expected to trigger a large flow of foreign and domestic investment in SEZs, in infrastructure and productive capacity, leading to generation of additional economic activity and creation of employment opportunities.

The SEZ Act, 2005 envisages a key role for state governments in export promotion and creation of related infrastructure. A single window SEZ approval mechanism has been provided through a 19-member inter-ministerial SEZ Board of Approval (BoA). The applications duly recommended by the respective state governments/UT administration are considered by the Board periodically. All decisions of the Board are consensual. The SEZ Rules provide for different minimum land requirement for different classes of special economic zones. Every SEZ is divided into a processing area where the SEZ units would come up and the non-processing area where the supporting infrastructure is to be created.

The SEZ Rules provide for:
- Simplified procedures for development, operation, and maintenance of the special economic zones and for setting up units and conducting business in these zones;
- Single window clearance for setting up of an SEZ;
- Single window clearance for setting up a unit in an SEZ;
- Single window clearance on matters relating to central as well as state governments; and
- Simplified compliance procedures and documentation with an emphasis on self certification.

STRUCTURE OF SEZS

The developer submits the proposal for the establishment of SEZs to the concerned state government. The state government has to forward the proposal with its recommendation within 45 days from the date of receipt of such a proposal to the BoA. The applicant also has the option of submitting the proposal directly to the Board.which has been constituted by the Central Government in exercise of the powers conferred upon it under the SEZ Act. The functioning of the SEZs is governed by a three-tier administrative set-up. The BoA is the apex body and is headed

[14] Special Economic Zones in India, Ministry of Commerce and Industry, GoI, http://sezindia.nic.in/

[15] http://sezindia.nic.in/

by the Secretary, Department of Commerce. The Approval Committee at the zone level deals with approval of units in the SEZs and other related issues. Each zone is headed by a Development Commissioner, who is the ex-officio chairperson of the Approval Committee. Once an SEZ has been approved by the BoA and the central government has notified the area of the SEZ, units are allowed to be set up in the SEZ. All the proposals for setting up of units in the SEZ are approved at the zone level by the Approval Committee consisting of Development Commissioner, Customs Authorities, and representatives of the state government. All post-approval clearances including grant of importer-exporter code number, change in the name of the company or implementing agency, broadbanding diversification, and so on are given at the zone level by the Development Commissioner. The performance of the SEZ units is periodically monitored by the Approval Committee and units are liable for penal action under the provision of Foreign Trade (Development and Regulation) Act, in case of violation of the conditions of the Approval Committee.

The incentives and facilities offered to the units in SEZs for attracting investments into the SEZs including foreign investment are:

- Duty-free import/domestic procurement of goods for development, operation, and maintenance of SEZ units, 100 per cent income tax exemption on export income for SEZ units under Section 10AA of the Income Tax Act for first five years, 50 per cent for the next five years thereafter and 50 per cent of the ploughed back export profit for a further five years;
- Exemption from minimum alternate tax under section 115JB of the Income Tax Act. External commercial borrowing by SEZ units up to USD 500 million in a year without any maturity restriction through recognized banking channels;
- Exemptions from Central Sales Tax and Service Tax. Incentives also include single window clearance for central and state-level approvals; and
- Exemption from state sales tax and other levies as extended by the respective state governments.

The major incentives and facilities available to SEZ developers include:

- Exemption from customs/excise duties for development of SEZs for authorized operations approved by the BoA;
- Income tax exemption on export income for a block of 10 years in 15 years under Section 80-IAB of the Income Tax Act;
- Exemption from minimum alternate tax under Section 115 JB of the Income Tax Act;
- Exemption from dividend distribution tax under Section 115O of the Income Tax Act;
- Exemption from Central Sales Tax (CST); and
- Exemption from Service Tax (Section 7, 26 and Second Schedule of the SEZ Act).

Based on the size and nature of the business, the SEZs of India are of three types: (a) multi-product SEZs occupying minimum 1000 hectares of land which may produce garments to automobiles; (b) sector-specific SEZs occupying minimum 100 hectares of land, mostly for garment, leather, electronics, industrial products, gems and jewelery, IT-ITeS-BPO, and biotech; and (c) service sector SEZs occupying minimum 10 hectares of land. In some cases, the size of the land may be reduced to four hectares: for instance, backward states have the option of relaxation of minimum criteria of land.

The country is divided into two territories—SEZs and Domestic Tariff Areas (DTAs). The areas outside the SEZs are DTAs where the laws of the country are applicable. On the other hand, in the SEZs, the laws and courts of the country may be applicable only partially. In fact, the SEZs enjoy special laws. Private developers are allowed to build SEZs and are even offered fabulous incentives to do so. 'Processing units' set up in the SEZs also enjoy several incentives/concessions. A minimum of 35 per cent of SEZs must be the 'processing area' while the remaining 65 per cent is meant for developing housing complexes, hotels, restaurants, hospitals, shopping malls, entertainment centers, multiplexes, playgrounds, golf courses, and so on. Each SEZ is a 'township', as can be seen in Greater Bombay, Navi Mumbai or Gurgaon in Haryana.

The present SEZs in India are the result of reforms carried out in four different phases.[16] The **first phase** was an experimental phase between 1965 and 1985. The first zone was set up in Kandla in a highly backward region of Kutchh in Gujarat as early as 1965. It was followed by the Santacruz Export Processing Zone (EPZ) in Mumbai which came into operation in 1973. There was no single window facility within the zone. Entrepreneurs had to acquire individual clearances from various state and central government departments. Day-to-day operations were subject to rigorous controls. Custom procedures for bonding, bank guarantees, and movement of goods were rigid. The FDI policy was also highly restrictive. Various committees were appointed by the Government of India during this period to review the working of these zones. The committees pointed out that the growth of EPZs in this phase was hampered by the absence of comprehensive policy, absence of an implementation authority to centrally co-ordinate and control the zones, procedural constraints, infrastructural deficiencies, limited concessions, and limited powers of the zone authorities to take action on the spot, subsequently resulting in inordinate delays.

These committees made several concrete recommendations to improve the functioning of these zones. The policy regime, however, remained virtually static. In 1980, the government introduced the Export-Oriented Units (EOU) Scheme. This scheme facilitated the setting up of these units beyond the boundaries of EPZs. The responsibility of administering these units was also entrusted to the zone-level administration.

The **second phase,** between 1985 and 1991, was expansionary in nature. Towards the end of the 1970s, India's failure to step up significantly the volume of her manufactured exports in the background of the Second Oil Price Shock began to worry the policy makers. To provide a fillip to exports, the government decided to establish four more zones in 1984. These were at Noida (Uttar Pradesh), Falta (West Bengal), Cochin (Kerala), and Chennai (Tamil Nadu). Thereafter, the Visakhapatnam EPZ in Andhra Pradesh was established in 1989, though it could not become operational before 1994. All these zones, with the exception of Chennai, were set up in industrially backward regions. The primary objectives of the zones were still not specified and there were no significant changes in other laws and procedures pertaining to the EPZs.

The **third phase** was a consolidating phase during 1991 to 2000, when a massive dose of liberalization was administered to the Indian economy. In this context, wide-ranging measures were initiated by the government for revamping and restructuring EPZs as well. This phase was thus marked by progressive liberalization of policy provisions, relaxation in the severity of controls, and simplification of procedures. The focus had been on delegating powers to the zone authorities, providing additional fiscal incentives, simplifying policy provisions, and providing greater facilities. The scope and coverage of the EPZ/EOU scheme was enlarged in 1992 by permitting the agriculture, horticulture, and aqua culture sector units as well. In 1994, trading, re-engineering, and reconditioning units were also permitted to be set up.

The **final and significant 'emergence phase'** began from 2000 onwards, which has shifted the direction, thrust, and approach of the reforms. The EXIM Policy (1997–2002) introduced a new scheme from 1 April 2000 for the establishment of the SEZs in different parts of the country.

[16] Aradhna Aggarwal (2005), 'Impact of Special Economic Zones on Employment, Poverty and Human Development', Indian Council for Research on International Economic Relations, New Delhi, February.

The Government of India too launched the second-generation reforms a few years ago, with SEZs as a vital initiative. While eight of the existing EPZs were converted into SEZs, the new initiative also called for setting up of new SEZs in the public, private, joint sector or by state governments. As a result, approval has been given for setting up of over 117 SEZs in various parts of the country. The present shape of the SEZs is no doubt an imitation of the Chinese model. After success of the Chinese SEZ-led economic growth, the Indian government attempted to further liberalize its policies in the form of the EXIM Policy. According to annual report of the Ministry of Commerce and Industry, Government of India (2006–7), there are 234 valid formal approvals and 162 in-principle approvals for setting up SEZs in India. Against this background, it may be desirable to examine how far the key policy parameters that contributed to the success of SEZs in China have been incorporated in the Indian policy framework.

Almost 45 to 50 per cent of exports in the major economies of the world (and not in China alone) are channelized through SEZs. There are about 750 SEZs the world over, with China as the leader, with over USD 300 billion worth of exports out of its SEZs. The total world trade through SEZs was worth USD 950 billion in 2004.

CHINA: A SUCCESS STORY

Since the late 1970s, in line with the People's Republic of China (PRC) government's bid to reform the national economic set-up, the basic state policy has focused on the formulation and implementation of overall reform and opening the Chinese economy to the outside world. During the 1980s, the PRC passed several stages, ranging from the establishment of special economic zones and opening up coastal cities and areas, to designating open inland and coastal economic and technology development zones. Since the 1980, the PRC has established special economic zones in Shenzhen, Zhuhai and Shantou in Guangdong Province, and Xiamen in Fujian Province, and designated the entire province of Hainan a special economic zone. In August 1980, the National People's Congress (NPC) passed 'Regulations for The Special Economy Zone of Guangdong Province and officially designated a portion of Shenzhen as the Shenzhen Special Economy Zone (SSEZ). In 1984, the PRC further opened 14 coastal cities to overseas investment. After their success since 1988,[17] mainland China's opening up to the outside world has been extended to its border areas, areas along the Yangtze River, and inland areas. First, the state decided to turn Hainan Island into mainland China's biggest SEZ and to enlarge the other four SEZs. Shortly afterwards, the State Council expanded the open coastal areas, extending into an open coastal belt the open economic zones of the Yangtze River Delta, Pearl River Delta, the Xiamen-Zhangzhou-Quanzhou Triangle in south Fujian, Shandong Peninsula, Liaodong Peninsula (Liaoning Province), Hebei, and Guangxi. In June 1990, the PRC government opened the Pudong New Area in Shanghai to overseas investment, and additional cities along the Yangtze River valley, with Shanghai's Pudong New Area as its 'dragon head'. Since 1992, the State Council has opened a number of border cities, and in addition, opened all the capital cities of inland provinces and autonomous regions.

Further, 15 free trade zones, 32 state-level economic and technological development zones, and 53 new- and high-tech industrial development zones have been established in large and medium-sized cities. As these open areas adopt different preferential policies, they play the dual roles of 'windows' in developing the foreign-oriented economy, generating foreign exchanges through exporting products and importing advanced technologies and of 'radiators' in accelerating inland economic development. Primarily geared to exporting processed goods, the five SEZs are

---

[17] Approved by the 1st session of the 7th NPC in 1988.

foreign-oriented areas which integrate science and industry with trade, and benefit from preferential policies and special managerial systems. In 1999, Shenzhen's new and high-tech industry became the one with the best prospects, and the output value of new and high-tech products reached 81.98 billion yuan, making up 40.5 per cent of the city's total industrial output value.[18] Since it was founded in 1992, the Shanghai Pudong New Zone has made great progress in both absorbing foreign capital and accelerating the economic development of the Yangtze River valley. The state has extended special preferential policies to the Pudong New Zone, not yet enjoyed by the SEZs. For instance, in addition to the preferential policies of reducing or eliminating customs duties and income tax common to the economic and technological development zones, the State also permits the zone to allow foreign business people to open financial institutions and run tertiary industries. The SEZs in China are truly export-driven, capital-intensive and limited in number, as also very large in size. For instance, the famous Shenzhen SEZ is around 32,700 hectares. Ultimately, all the SEZs in China are controlled and closely monitored by the government.

CHINA INDIA COMPARISON

Though the Indian SEZ policy is not a true copy of the Chinese SEZ model, it is nevertheless obviously inspired by China's success. The key to inspiration is foreign capital. Over the last ten years, aggregate inflows of FDI to India averaged roughly USD 45 billion against over USD 150 billion to China in new agreements. India firmly believes that the model will lead the country into the world capital market. The Indian Commerce and Industry Ministry strongly feels that 'they are engines of growth that lead to job creation'[19] and 'it is high time we did something about it', further adding that 'until we provide a single window clearance for FDI, we will not be able to keep pace with the investments taking place in Asia, more so in China. That is why we are laying added emphasis on the special economic zones (SEZs).'[20] Even the Prime Minister of India has said that 'the Government of India firmly believes that the SEZs are vehicles to deliver the results of the economic growth of the country.'

However, what is true for China may not necessarily be true for India, given the different historical, political, and sociological backdrops of the two nations. In economic terms, China, along with countries such as South Korea and Taiwan, was well behind India in 1947 when India gained its independence. Thereafter, the 'export-led' growth initiated in the late 1970s had a remarkable success in China, albeit at enormous costs to the people of China over three decades in terms of leveling the post-liberalization social inequalities.

China initiated basic land reforms in a revolutionary way, which enabled it to overtake India. Further, the Chinese SEZ initiative is government-driven while the Indian SEZs are driven by the private sector. It is primarily the non-resident Chinese of Hong Kong who invested massive amounts (almost 60 per cent) of FDI in these zones.

The primary motivation of these FDIs coming from Hong Kong and Taiwanese firms was to sub-contract the products in Chinese SEZs with the goal of re-export,[21] and also to sell the products in the fast developing Chinese markets. Hence, the geographic locations of the Chinese SEZs acted as a booster for their 'development.' Chinese SEZs are not open for sale as is the

[18] B.P. Nansi, 'China's amazing SEZs', *Project Monitor*, 19 June 2006.

[19] Kamalnath, Minister for Industry and Commerce, The *Hindu Business Line*, 4 November, 2007.

[20] Manmohan Singh, the Prime Minister of India.

[21] *The Hindu Business Line*, 7 May 2001, New Delhi.

case with Indian SEZs. They have gradually opened to attract FDI; most of them were in joint sectors, later opening up wholly-owned foreign private units, even as some units remained under the provincial government's autonomous governance; and the local governments were given the freedom to attract foreign investments.

In China most of the SEZs were established near the coastline near Hong Kong and Taiwan, enabling them easy access to capital, information, technology, modern communication, and transport facilities. Contrary to this, Indian SEZs are mostly concentrated near major cities and more than half are being developed by real estate companies in order to make a quick buck by grabbing land at cheap prices under the SEZ Land Acquisition Act, which is a scam in itself.

Another secret of the success of Chinese SEZs is their size. These zones are spread over thousands of hectares at a stretch. For instance, Shenzhen is the largest SEZ in China, spread over 493 sq mms.(49,300 hectares). While the largest SEZ in India, Reliance in Navi Mumbai and Greater Mumbai SEZ, is a mere 14,000 hectares. Exports from Shenzhen SEZ reached USD 100 billion in 2005. Total Chinese exports for 2005 were around USD 700 billion, which implies that Shenzen contributed 15 per cent of Chinese exports.

The main reason for growth in Chinese FDI is the flexibility in its tax and labor laws. Though China appears never to have lost control over SEZs' functioning and management, it has provided more freedom to companies as far as labor regulations and environmental laws are concerned. In Chinese SEZs, exemptions from export and import duties and from after-tax profit remittance were made. Other tax rates were pegged at 15 per cent, which were withdrawn totally in later phases. The main attraction in China is cheap labor. Chinese labor is paid very low wages in the absence of labor laws. The wages of SEZ workers were 75 per cent to 80 per cent lower than in Hong Kong. Free large scale movement of labor from other regions was allowed. Strikes were prohibited in 1982 in mainland China, which was extended to SEZs as well. Labor laws concerning minimum wages and eight hour day work schedules are frequently violated and temporary contracts are made with individual laborers for particular orders of exports.

TABLE 1: SEZs IN CHINA AND INDIA

	China	India
Number	7	Ultimately 400–500
When started	1980	Mostly after 1991
Democratic decision?	A lot of discussion and debate preceded the setting up of SEZs	No discussion. Parliament passed the Law easily
Size	Very large (Shenzhen: 32,700 hectares)	Small (3000–14,000 hectares)
Ownership	State	Private corporations
On what kind of land	Mostly coastal wasteland	Mostly fertile cultivated land
Exports	Very good (Shenzhen: Net exports in 2006, USD 35 billion)	Poor so far (in 1998 a waiver of USD 1.67 billion on customs duties was given to earn USD 1.04 billion in foreign exchange)
Employment	Substantial number of low-paid jobs	Very limited so far: 100,650 in all SEZs till March 2005
Tax revenue collections	Only selective tax incentives provided	Across-the-board tax holiday given to companies
Overall success	Mostly very successful	Largely unsuccessful so far
Ease of land acquisition	Land battles in some areas	Bloody, bitter resistance

Although India is offering more freedom and more flexibility to SEZ management, the labor aspect is where they fall behind. The Indian labor force has emerged as an organized, and sometimes militant lot over six decades of democratic political process. The multinational corporations (MNCs) and foreign companies are apprehensive about Indian trade unions after the Hero Honda episode in Gurgaon.[22]

Moreover, Chinese foreign investments are not really foreign. The primarily investments come from non-resident Chinese of Hong Kong, Taiwan, and Macao. From the mid-1990s, large amounts of FDI were being poured in from Japan, USA, and European countries. Between 1979 and 2005, total FDI of USD 633 billion came into China. The leading investors were Japan, USA, Taiwan, and South Korea investing USD 53.3 billion, USD 51.1 billion, USD 41.8 billion, and USD 31.8 billion respectively.[23] Interestingly, the share of non-resident Indians (NRIs) in foreign investment in India is minimal, standing at USD 2.6 billion in 2005.[24] In 1979, primary products were the main component of exports from China. By 1990, manufactured goods comprised 80 per cent of Chinese exports. By 2005, this had grown further to 93 per cent. On the other hand, the share of manufacturing in the total merchandised exports of India reduced from 74.7 per cent in 1995–6 to 70 per cent in 2005–6.[25]

In the meantime, drastic changes occurred in the composition of manufacturing exports of China. In 1990, the country's manufacturing exports were composed of low-tech toys, shoes, garments, leather products, and so on. By the end of the 1990s, these manufacturing exports became overwhelmingly high-tech including electronic goods and chips, computer parts, automobiles and spares, and so on.[26] On the other hand, India's manufacturing exports are predominantly low-tech gems and jewelry, apparels, and so on. Therefore, China is not only far ahead of India in manufacturing, exports, foreign direct investment but has also successfully transformed its industrial products from low-tech to high-tech ones.

COST AND BENEFIT ANALYSIS

While the gross benefits of SEZs are still open to debate, there is already much concern about the aggregate social and economic costs of this strategy, making the net benefits even more uncertain. So far, strong concern has emerged on three major areas: land transfer and displacement, employment generation and workers rights, and the fiscal costs and benefits. Estimates from a report prepared by the Citizens' Research Collective[27] in March 2007 show that close to 114,000 farming households (each household on an average comprising five members) and an additional 82,000 families of

---

[21] *The Hindu Business Line*, 7 May 2001, New Delhi.

[22] Around 4000 casual workers of Hero Honda were on strike from 10 April 2006 against the anti-worker stance of the management that had ignored the demands of the workers for a long time. The main demands placed were wage hike, job regularization, extra casual leave and medical benefits at par with the permanent workers.

[23] W.M. Morrison, 'China's Economic Conditions', *Foreign Affairs*, 12 July 2006, Defense and Trade Division, USA.

[24] *Business Line*, Thursday, 21 December 2006.

[25] *Economic Times*, 16 October 2006, New Delhi.

[26] *Business Week Online*, 22 August 2005.

[27] SEZs and Land Acquisition (2008), *Factsheet for an Unconstitutional Economic Policy,* Citizens' Research Collective, New Delhi.

farmworkers that are dependent on these farms for their livelihoods will be displaced. In other words, at least 10 lakh (1,000,000) people who primarily depend on agriculture for their survival will face eviction. Experts calculate that the total loss of income to farming and these families is estimated to be Rs 212 crore (Rs 2120 million) a year. This does not include other income lost (for instance, of artisans) due to the demise of local rural economies.

The government promises 'humane' displacement followed by relief and rehabilitation. However, historical records do not offer much hope on this count: an estimated 40 million people (of whom nearly 40 per cent are *adivasis* and 25 per cent *dalits*) have lost their land since 1950 on account of displacement due to large development projects. At least 75 per cent of them still await rehabilitation. Almost 80 per cent of the agricultural population owns only about 17 per cent of the total agricultural land, making them near-landless farmers. Far more families and communities depend on a piece of land (for work and grazing) than those who simply own it.

However, compensation is being paid only for those who hold titles to land. No compensation has been planned for those who do not hold land titles.

The growth of employment in the entire organized sector since the inception of the reforms in 1991 has been negligible. Total employment in the organized sector is still less than 30 million. Even in IT and ITES, the boom areas of the economy, employment is less than 1.5 million (60 per cent of SEZs are for IT). The Indian labor force is estimated to be 450 to 550 million. Thanks to growing automation, modern manufacturing grows joblessly around the world (in India, automobile production has grown rapidly while employing less labor than before). With more automation, organized services also require limited supplies of labor. SEZs attract modern industry and services in order to succeed. To that extent, they are unlikely to generate too many jobs. Moreover, the few jobs that are generated will be for highly skilled labor, usually not available in the countryside, from where people are being displaced to make room for SEZs. The Government of India's claim that SEZs will create lakhs of jobs[28] within a few years is a fantasy, says the Citizen's Report.

Further, if the experience of existing SEZs in places like Noida in India (or Shenzhen, China) is anything to go by, the working conditions—poor wages, non-existent benefits, long working hours, occupational hazards, and discrimination—under which people will be employed will inevitably violate human rights, apart from keeping the benefits of growth away from the poor.

Many SEZs, such as the Greater Mumbai SEZ (to be built by Reliance Industries), will be like mid-sized cities, over 100 sq. km in area (the size of Chandigarh). There will be no elected local government. A government-appointed Development Commissioner will govern the SEZ with the main aim of facilitating economic growth. SEZs have been declared 'public utilities' under the Industrial Disputes Act, making collective bargaining and strikes illegal. Infrastructure such as power, roads, and water supply will be guaranteed to investors and developers, but not to the people of the region. Several lakh people may be living/working inside the SEZ. In some cases, the developer may have the right to tax the population in order to provide essential services. The constitutional tenability of private monopolies running local governments (for a sizeable cluster of the urban population) without being elected is questionable. All the non-economic laws of the land under the Indian Penal Code and the Criminal Procedural Code would be applicable to SEZs. However, internal security will be the responsibility of the developer. The worry of people concerned is: 'Will SEZs turn ultimately into sovereign states and treasure islands of prosperity in a sea of poverty and misery—unaccountable to the vast majority of citizens in the neighborhood?'

Thanks to exemptions from customs duties, income tax, sales tax, excise duties and service tax, and even tax on luxury hotel facilities, shopping malls, health clubs, and recreation centers given

---

[28] *The Indian Express,* on NDTV 24X7's *Walk The Talk* programme, Monday, 25 September 2006.

to SEZs, the Finance Ministry estimates a loss of Rs 160,000 crore in revenue by 2010. The then Finance Minister P. Chidambaram wrote to his Cabinet colleagues saying: 'SEZs *per se* will distort land, capital and labor costs, which will encourage relocation or shifting of industries in clever ways that cannot be stopped. This will be further aggravated by the proliferation of a large number of SEZs in and around metros'.[29] Another important issue is that of what SEZs are likely to become in a few years' time. According to a clause in the SEZ Act (Section 5(2)), as much as 75 per cent of the area under large SEZs (above 1000 hectares) can be used for non-industrial purposes. This lacuna in the law is likely to become a loophole for the accumulation of land banks by private developers and property dealers for the purpose of real estate speculation (this explains why so many of them have been buying areas for SEZs). In fact, it may well be the case that the rationale for the above clause in the SEZ Act is the uncertainty surrounding the economic attractiveness (and ultimate viability) of SEZs. If adequate productive investment is not forthcoming, the SEZ developer can at least cash in on the land value. Conglomerates such as Reliance already own above 100,000 acres of land in the countryside.

Apart from several losses to the nation as well as the people striving for their livelihoods, the SEZ Act, 2005 poses serious challenges to constitutionally framed laws as well as a threat of legal violations. To sum up briefly, the SEZ Act violates the letter and spirit of the Indian Constitution by infringing upon the fundamental rights of citizens guaranteed in Part III of the Constitution. It encourages violation of workers' rights by making a number of labor laws, including those under the Industrial Disputes Act, Contract Labour Act, Factories Act, Minimum Wages Act, and Trade Union Act inapplicable in the special zones. The most serious violation will be the Environment (Protection) Act which is also inapplicable to SEZs. It violates the Panchayati Raj Act (1996) which gave power to the people on local self-government. The Act also violates laws granting rights and control to adivasi communities over their land, thus violating many international conventions on basic human rights regarding land, work, life, living and patterns of livelihood.

CONCLUSION

The SEZ policy clearly exposes the market interests of the government. Though time and again people say it is an imitation of Chinese model, there is a clear contrast between the two nations on several fronts such as size, location, nature of ownership, and management of the SEZs. The policy, which had been announced in view of the need to boost the export sector and attract foreign direct investment, has ironically been revealed as a failure by the performance of SEZs in the area of exports. When the government liberalized its overall policy, it decided to focus on one or two areas. The first being the social implications of changing land usage and impact on agriculture and other related sectors, more particularly on the people and their livelihoods. The second aspect is the issue of losses and benefits. The Indian experience predicts more losses than gains. To compete with China, a package of fiscal and non-fiscal incentives are being given but it has been overlooked that tax benefits in China's SEZs were available only to foreign investments, not exports. All exemptions and fiscal incentives should be deployed in the process of overall tax and labor reforms. Giving preferential treatment to any particular area in the name of exports cannot be justified in the democratic set-up. Democracy is, after all, the matter of 'general will' and collective choice and, in fact, it should be so.

---

[29] 'SEZ legislations will define all concessions', *Times of India*, 10 March 2005.

Optic Fiber Vs Iron Chimney[g]

Different Models of Development in India and China

An optic fiber wire gets snagged somewhere 5000 km away in the Mediterranean, near Alexandria, off the coast of Egypt, and the Indian economy gets a jolt. The back-up line saved the day, but mercantile activity was affected. Information Technology Enabled Services and other software units had a horrific experience, with internet connectivity working at half the pace.

This lone incident speaks of the weakness of the country's 'optic fiber' economy. It reflects the heavy dependence of software and its allied industries, which form about 50 per cent of India's service sector, on optic fiber lines. Today, the entire economic growth in India is linked to the wires of the internet, with the help of which the Indian service sector recorded a share of 55.1 per cent of national GDP in 2006–7, while the share of industry was 26.4 per cent and that of agriculture was a mere 18.5 per cent. Ever since the economic reforms came into play in the 1990s, the service sector has grown by leaps and bounds, while the industrial and agricultural sectors have witnessed a slide.

According to data released by NASSCOM, Business Process Outsourcing (BPO) cornered the lion's share in India's service sector. About seven lakh people are employed in the BPO sector use internet services and work for business houses of developed countries such as the US.

About 25 countries, mostly from the West, are employing Indians to work for their companies, banks, and hospitals to handle their clients. BPOs are netting somewhere around USD 11 crore per year. India holds 40 per cent of the world's share in BPO markets. In this scenario, what if the second optic fiber too were to snap, some other country were to provide cheap labor? How secure is the rapidly growing service sector? These are questions that remain unanswered.

In the meanwhile, the agricultural and industrial sectors are being ignored because of the undue focus on the service sector as the driver of the Indian market economy. Setting up a Ministry for Disinvestment shows the non-seriousness of our government towards industry. Rather than focusing on core strengths, we are training our youth to be fluent in English and software usage to form an army of workers for the BPO sector. Our neighbor, China, in contrast, has planned its economy meticulously and laid a strong foundation for long-term development by drafting its populace into the development fold and has become a global force to reckon with in both the service and manufacturing sectors.

China started its industrial reforms program in the 1980s. Till that time, the country's economy had been centered round coal and its ancillary units, power, and other agro-based production in the post-revolution era under Mao. After the founding of New China in 1949, the Chinese government initiated planned construction on a massive scale. As a result, the country's industrial foundation was strengthened and production levels rose rapidly. The metallurgical, mining and energy industries, airplane and automobile industries, and new industries including petrochemicals, computers, telecommunication equipment, instruments and meters, and aeronautics have been built up from scratch in China. All industries were owned by the government, and, as in India, there were situations when some of the industries had to be shut down due to power cuts and power shortage.

The focus of China's development activities shifted to rural areas in the late 1950s, with the establishment of the people's commune system, which attempted to promote rural industrialization.

---

[g] First published in Telegu in *Andhrajyothy*, 6 February 2008.

The vast majority of commune enterprises were backyard iron and steel furnaces, with the rest providing products to meet local agricultural needs.

The Second Five Year Plan or the 'Great Leap Forward', announced for the period 1958 to 1963, proved disastrous for China's economy. The number of commune enterprises came down from 2.6 million in 1958 to 45,000 in 1961. By the end of the 1960s, the government prioritized agricultural mechanization and modernization by sponsoring programs to develop the five small industries—iron and steel, chemical fertilizers, cement, energy (coal mines and hydropower), and farm machinery. Consequently, during 1961–5, rural enterprises and all other non-agricultural activities were essentially banned as rural industrialization came to a halt.

In addition, commune and brigade enterprises (CBEs) were revived. In 1976, the State Council established a special agency to administer CBEs and promote rural small-scale industries. Thus, the main objective of rural industrial polices was to support national agriculture and the needs of the rural population. However, because CBEs and the five small industries' support programs were decentralized, all these efforts were undermined by conflicts of interests between the central planners and local authorities.

Deng Xiaoping, who took over the reins after the death of Mao in 1976, initiated reforms by means of a new economic policy in 1978, giving top priority to the modernization of the four core sectors, namely. agriculture, industries, education, and science and technology. Tapping of natural resources went hand-in-hand with strengthening of the industrial sector and impetus to rural and allied industries of agriculture. Instead of closing down each and every loss-making unit, as was done in India, China converted them into joint stock companies, encouraging investments by roping in the workers as partners.

In 1984, the name Commune and Brigade Enterprise was replaced with 'Township and Village Enterprises' (TVEs). These were set up in two phases as industrialization was redefined in China. Rural folk were given industrial training by the government and TVEs were converted into a vibrant income-generating machinery which helped China to head towards self-sufficiency. TVEs effectively became an instrument of the government to achieve agricultural modernization, absorb surplus labor from agriculture, and alleviate poverty. Over the past two decades in China, TVEs have made a significant contribution to the strengthening of social structures in that they have created jobs and a second (industrial) pillar in the rural areas of the Chinese economy.

In the following decade (1988–99), TVEs achieved an annual growth rate of 19 per cent and contributed 61 per cent of the industrial production, while turning about 25 per cent of the population, that is, 120 million agricultural labor into industrial workers and producing USD 927 billion worth of goods.

In 1990, the contribution of the industrial sector to China's GDP was 61.2 per cent, that of agriculture was 24.4 per cent, and the service sector contributed just 14 per cent. In the following decade, China encouraged private–public enterprise along with substantial private–foreign collaborations.

The economy was strengthened by setting up SEZs, hi-tech cities, and export-oriented townships, which gave a fillip to industrialization. Since 1980, seven SEZs, 14 ports, 15 free trade zones, 32 provincial level techno-economic zones, and 53 modern industrial development areas were set up. These steps had a two-fold impact on the rural populace: that of providing exposure to industries, thereby increasing the output, which in turn brought foreign revenue, investments, and innovative technology, research, and development. By now industrialization and urbanization had explored new dimensions. Urbanization increased to 31 per cent in 1999 from 17 per cent in 1978. Annually about 10 million people were observed to move into industrial areas. While

TVEs employed 32 million people in 1983, the figure rose to 140 million by 1996. The economy bloomed 7.4 times with an annual growth rate of 9.6 per cent.

By the year 2000, the industrial landscape changed with the inflow of FDI. Between 1995 and 2005, China has seen phenomenal growth of industries in the private sector. The number of industries in the private sector went up from six lakh to 43 lakh in this decade and the share of private industries in GDP was 65 per cent. It can be seen that, between 1978 and 2006, the share of agriculture in total employment decreased by almost 30 percentage points, from 71 per cent to 43 per cent. In the meantime, the share of the secondary sector (that is, industry plus construction) in employment increased from 17 per cent to 25 per cent, and that of the tertiary sector (that is, services) increased from 12 per cent to 32 per cent. This substantial change in the sector composition of labor employment occurred in the context of a massive increase of the total, from 402 million workers in 1978 to 764 million in 2006.

However, China did not ignore the ITES and service sectors either. The latest figures show that these two contribute 35 per cent of the GDP. Instead of window dressing, China went into the heart of the problem and increased its capacity in core sectors in terms of assets, FDI, employment, and technology.

The Indian approach thus seems to be in total contrast to that of China. No concrete plans are to be seen on the developmental front at any level. The agricultural sector is totally ignored, industrial development is abandoned, and the country is running after the services sector. China, on the other hand, first made its rural populace a partner in the development process and is now trying to strike a balance between other sectors. An insight into the two models of development would give a clear view of where we (specifically India) stand.

From the Frying Pan to the Fire[h]

The Chinese Woman's 'Long March'

I won't lose any opportunity of living on my own with my head raised. Even if I feel it is difficult now, my dream is to live without any worry in future.

— Yang Shouling

Yang Shouling is working as a waitress in Hangzhou city (located on the lower reaches of the Qiantang river in south-east China) at the recently opened outlet of the Hooters chain of restaurants, which is rapidly consolidating its presence in China. Founded in the US in 1983, Hooters initially started a stag joint, where only beautiful young girls were employed as waitresses and it was part of their job description to use their feminine charms to attract male customers and to humor them. The chain, which is now successfully operating 435 restaurants in 23 countries, had previously openly declared that women were their investment and tacitly admitted to the objectification of

[h] First published in Telegu in the *Bhumika*, March 2008.

women, as much through their titillating 'uniforms' as through the terms of employment of the 'Hooters Girls.' However, after weathering several discrimination lawsuits brought against the chain by men wishing to be employed as servers, the group has changed its focus over the past decade, striving to cultivate the image of a 'neighborhood, family-friendly restaurant'. Hooter Girls are now trying to erase the stereotype of putting women down and demeaning them as sex objects.

Yang, who hails from a village near Shanghai, came to Hangzhou after completing college education, and after doing random small jobs, joined Hooters as a waitress. She had not informed her parents about the nature of her job, fearing that they would be upset. When asked why she is doing this particular job with so many other better jobs available, she said that this is one of the best paid options. Further, she explains, many English-speaking foreigners visit the restaurant and she sees this job as a means to improve her language skills, paving the way to her ultimate ambition to become an interpreter or an English language tutor.

In the wake of economic reforms, there has been a vast influx into China's major cities of people from different countries working in several foreign and multinational companies. This, in turn, has spawned hundreds of shopping malls, hotels, and restaurants to meet their requirements. Thousands of young women like Yang are moving from villages and remote tribal areas to these cities to take advantage of the myriad job opportunities that have opened up as a result of this phenomenon, but without any kind of employment security or guarantees about the future.

REVOLUTION FROM THE FEET

A glance at Chinese history reveals a tradition of oppression of women in the name of customs enforced by a patriarchal society, just as in India. Dowry system existed in traditional Chinese society, as did a form of *Sati* and widow remarriage as taboo. One oppressive custom, which was peculiar to traditional Chinese society, was the superstitious custom of binding up girls' feet, because of the belief that women with small feet brought prosperity. It was with a blow at this practice that the efforts towards the emancipation of Chinese women took off.

Crowds of women participated in the revolutionary movement and undertook the long march under the leadership of Mao Tse Tung. The Communist government under the leadership of Mao Tse Tung introduced several laws that facilitated equal participation of women in the political and economic fields after the revolution. It formulated several policies for equal political, economic, social and cultural rights for women, as well as equal wages for equal work alongside men and equal opportunities in work and education. The government also introduced marriage and family laws for social reforms and by the 1950s, made laws prohibiting dowry, creating equal rights, right to property, equal share in the inherited property, and the land cultivated by family, thus paving the way for women's freedom. Mao strongly believed that women's emancipation is possible only when they become partners in production and politics.

Mao's Cultural Revolution had a tremendous impact on the women's liberation movement in China, transforming the Chinese society completely by making women stronger physically as well as psychologically. The movement abolished gender differences in work, habits, practices, and lifestyles in order to enforce equal status of women and men. The traditional dress code of women gave way to mandatory pants and dark colored shirts. Feminine adjuncts such as long hair, ornaments, cosmetics, and so on were stigmatized as symbols of a bourgeois culture and completely banned. Women were exhorted to be just like men, not just in food, but also in physical strength, habits, walk and various dimensions of behavior.

However, although the Cultural Revolution laid a strong foundation for wiping out old traditions and for transforming China into a modern society, this did not last long. This can be clearly seen in China as it is now. Gender differences are clearly visible in modern China. Gender consciousness is silently expressed in dress and language among educated and upper class people.

The cultural values that had been enforced by Maoism are gradually becoming weaker, as the erstwhile Communists exchange the work ethics for pursuit of wealth. In this emerging scenario, women, stepping down from the Maoist pedestal of militant equality, are playing a pivotal role without de-gendering themselves in the name of equal rights.

However, the new profile of the modern Chinese women comes with its own intrinsic problems. The economic reforms that started a decade after the Cultural Revolution have completely changed the profile of China, not just in the economic sense, but also in the sense of social and family relationships. In the economic sphere, new cities and new industries led to the collapse of villages and the rural economic system as China became the world's factory. However, these industries and jobs are found in selected regions such as coastal areas and ports, where foreign investments are mainly concentrated. This has resulted in mass migration of labor, with its inevitable repercussions for social and family structures, the brunt of which is largely borne by women.

As the market economy has made its presence felt in rural areas, per capita land has fallen and agricultural incomes have dwindled. With farmers migrating to cities and towns in the quest for more remunerative industrial employment, the burden of agricultural development as well as of running the family has fallen largely on women. According to details provided by the Internal Fund for Agricultural Development, the contribution of women in agriculture grew from 20 per cent in the 1940s to 40 per cent in the 1990s, and stands at over 70 per cent today. Further, as per economic statistics, at the last count, there were 130 million Chinese living away from their families for years.

Women in villages have no information of their husbands' whereabouts unless the husbands call them from cities. Juggling responsibilities between parents-in-law, children, and agricultural work and debts, these women often take up small jobs as well to augment their meager incomes from the reduced per capita land. Frustration due to inadequate earnings among non-migrant agricultural labourers, on the other hand, is spawning increasing domestic violence in villages. A recent survey conducted by a women's organization in China says that almost 50 per cent women have confessed that they are victims of domestic violence, with their husbands are beating and torturing them.

In summation, it can be said that although reforms and development are creating employment opportunities for women, they are also exploiting female labor, in both urban and rural contexts. Where on the one hand rural women are bearing multiple burdens of housework, family, agricultural labor, and side-jobs (and more often than not, being physically abused in the bargain), a number of factors—family conditions, a longing to earn, desire to access new opportunities, and a wish to live independently—is driving a multitude of women into the migrant labor force category, along with its attendant hardships and insecurities in the cities.

THE CITY—HELL IN THE LITERAL SENSE

Economic reforms, development, and the consequent industrial revolution in China might be helping the country prosper, but certain outcomes of the process have been detrimental to women. Since women are paid less and are largely non-confrontational, industries prefer women rather than men in their labor force. Many multinational companies, foreign companies, and SEZs which don't abide by stable wages, labor laws, and restrictions, appoint only women. These companies are paying USD 50–75 (two to three thousand rupees in Indian currency) salary a month and making them work for eight to ten hours a day. Almost 40 million women are working in government industries and 55 million women in rural industries. Almost 300 million women are working in

SEZs and special industrial areas. The rules related to women laborers made by foreign companies and SEZs in China are extremely unjust and inhuman.

Two-third of the workforce in industries, SEZs, and new industrial areas in China comprises of women. Multinational companies, especially those manufacturing clothes and electronic goods, select mostly rural women for jobs. They are provided accommodation on the premises or in surrounding areas in the form of dormitories in large apartments to accommodate four to eight people in each room. Sleeping arrangements resemble berths in trains and no other facilities are provided in these rooms. Further, the female workforce has to sign a company agreement that the workers will not marry or have children for four years. They are paid a salary of USD 20–80 per month for working eight to ten hours per day, with no holidays except Sundays and no sick leave. American retail firms such as Wal-Mart draw up employment contracts for 11 working hours a day. Almost 30 million young women are working under these conditions in cities and industrial areas.

Recent surveys[29] reveal that such working conditions are adversely affecting the physical and psychological health of women. A recent survey by the All China Women's Federation affiliated to the Communist (Ruling) Party revealed shocking lacunae. Only 20 per cent of the workers are getting adequate wages, 40 per cent are contract laborers, and the remaining 60 per cent have no contracts. Only 23 per cent have health insurance and only 19 per cent have work-related injury insurance. Only 15 per cent have pension insurance and six per cent have maternity insurance. These industries do not even follow the limit of working hours. Sometimes, these women are made to work 48 hours at a stretch. Labor organizations in China have no liberty and there is no provision to establish labor organizations except the official Communist labor organization. A study by the Sociology Department of the Chinese Academy of Social Sciences reveals that these reasons are leading to a number of issues such as problems related to reproductive health and chronically suboptimal body weight among many women.

According to statistics, about 120 million migrants in major metropolises in China currently contribute to the development of industries such as construction, commerce, food, services, and sanitation. Almost 90 per cent of these laborers are not in social security (education, medicine, and other rationing) schemes. At least one-third of the migrants is female, and most of them are between 17 and 25 years of age. A research-action project, aiming to address urban poverty among young, and especially women migrants, was launched last year in seven pilot sites—Beijing, Shanghai, Chifeng of north China's Inner Mongolia Autonomous Region, Dalian of north China's Liaoning Province, Chengdu of south-west China's Sichuan Province, Kunming, and Diqing of south-west China's Yunnan Province.

A survey of their needs was carried out at the initial stage and as per a UNESCO project team leader Geneviève Domenach-Chich, besides material poverty, many migrant workers, especially women, suffer from 'psychological poverty' as they feel lonely and isolated in urban areas. Research showed that the migrant workers are marginalized and have the potential to become an increasingly isolated social group. All these are only some of the problems tormenting women laborers in China.[30]

The Government of China, however, declares that it has provided equal representation for women. Government estimates show that women have a 40 per cent participation, not only in industries, but also in parties, positions, and crucial administrative issues. China that is rapidly

---

[29] http://www.chinabusinessreview.com/public/0205/ye.htm

[30] Related Link 1 - URL m http://www1.chinadaily.com.cn/en/doc/2003-11/28/content_285440.htm

progressing in production, trade, exports, and foreign investments in the global arena is using the workforce of women as its fuel. Women may, indeed, be occupying half the share in its opportunities as well as its wealth, but they are shouldering almost the full burden of the attendant problems and repercussions!

THE ENTIRE BURDEN IS ON 'HER'

With the implementation of the 'one child policy' (whether it is a son or a daughter, not more than one child per couple is allowed), the burden on women has increased even further. With the prospect of responsibility of a husband, children, and parents-in-law looming before them after marriage, they are eager to do their bit for their own parents by saving money for them before marriage. Thus, young girls migrate to cities, to take up odd jobs and happily do whatever work is available.

In a number of instances, young girls keep postponing their marriage on the dual counts of having to leave their ageing parents without support, and the fear of losing their jobs as a result of getting married. Unofficial live-in relationships between co-workers are on the rise, with no children because of the employment conditions, which is further resulting in increasing issues related to late pregnancies and infertility. In fact, all things considered, it would not be too much to say that women in China are on a 'long march' to an unknown destination!

10
How Intellectuals Misinterpret Each Other
Globalization, Market Economy, and Chinese Peasants

Yukuan Guo

AM I SOMEONE WITH NO CONSCIENCE?

In China, I am often regarded as a right-winger, and some people even call me a 'radical rightist'. Generally, anyone who cares about the interests of peasants losing land is labeled a leftist. However, in China, such people are termed 'rightists', as people who are concerned about human rights, particularly freedom of speech, or the cultural autonomy of ethnic minorities. In the Chinese division of left and right, the boundary line lies in the loyalty to the Chinese Communist Party (CCP). People who have a clear stand in support of the party's absolute leadership are known as left-wing; all others are right-wing, including me, naturally. Although I feel uncomfortable with the 'Chinese New Leftists', I share a common language with international left intellectuals, such as Chomsky and Said and understand and respect the assessment of their respective countries.

I find that any discussion on the issue of globalization inevitably leads to fierce disputes. The majority of left-wing intellectuals in the West harshly criticize globalization, and the market economy, in some cases, for its exploitation and deprivation of peasants, ethnic minorities, and developing countries. However, I do not agree with this assessment. It is my belief that globalization has opened up new frontiers and created more opportunities for the majority of Chinese farmers. Due to this conflict in opinions, I am perhaps considered to be an intellectual without a conscience. Leftist intellectuals in the West are appreciative of representatives of the Chinese New Left who talk about the miseries faced by Chinese peasants because of globalization and the market economy. They are regarded as 'the conscience' of Chinese intellectuals.

In a trip to development zones in Sichuan province in China, I had the opportunity to meet the peasants and discuss their problems. Their land had been requisitioned by a state-owned arsenal at a very low price, and their representatives were imprisoned by the local government when they appealed to the central authorities for help. It is a sad truth that even if they reached the central government, their case would normally be kicked back to the local level, since such incidents occur in China every day. Such people are arrested for fear of public demonstrations, as it could damage the image of socialism.

Such an arrest of protesters is clearly a legal issue, and concerns the existing political system; however, global intellectuals find it convenient to blame globalization and the open-door policy.

The international intellectual community has a number of members who subscribe to this view.

An article in the *Guardian*, by Pankaj Mishra (who is in agreement with Wang Hui of the Chinese New Left on certain issues), discusses slave labor with reference to an incident in China where a Chinese village party secretary and his son forced abducted workers into slave labor in brick kilns The article passionately denounces globalization and neo-liberalism. The denunciation itself is not a problem, but it *is* a stretch to argue that this isolated action of two individuals has anything to do with globalization and neo-liberalism. The article is reminiscent of the reform-through-labor farms (Lao Gai Nong Chang) during Mao's rule. During this period, peasants were the leading class in name, while intellectuals were attacked by Mao. However, the reality was quite different. Peasants were deprived of private property rights in the name of the collective: even raising hens privately was treated as 'taking the capitalist road'. In the name of cooperation, they were deprived of the right to decide how to farm. More radically, because of Mao's policy, they were deprived of the right to flee from famine and to beg. There is no big difference between Chinese peasants at that time and slave workers in the recent brick kiln scandal. But that was a time when China was least globalized and open.

An interesting phenomenon is seen in China today. People criticize corrupt officials, the government and the CCP in private. Not many, except the Chinese New Left, would however attribute the injustices and suffering to globalization or the policy of opening up of the economy.

WHY IS GLOBALIZATION HATED?

The hatred of globalization stems from cognitive differences on the basis of different country experiences. Take India, for example. Its market reforms and opening up of the economy commenced in the 1990s. Prior to that, India was largely a socialist country, especially in its policy approach to rural areas and agriculture. Peasants were even subsidized for the fertilizer they bought. However, under the influence of globalization represented by the World Trade Organization (WTO), subsidies and benefits have been reduced in the name of fair play. Imports of more competitive products have slowly and gradually, exerted a great impact on the domestic price system, and of course, inflicted damage on some vulnerable groups whose livelihood are entirely linked to traditional agriculture and handicrafts. Their status evokes sympathy, and that is why, it is easy to understand the indignation of Indian scholars at the mention of globalization. The essential logic also holds for the well-protected French farmers who resist globalization. In the case of China's neighbours, South Korea and Japan, for example, agricultural products like rice, beef and apples here are ten times more expensive than in China due to government protection and subsidies. Once external shocks are allowed into the domestic market, it will be too much for their farmers to bear. Therefore, the opposition of farmers and intellectuals in these countries to globalization can be appreciated.

In the view of some left-wing intellectuals, globalization magnifies capitalist hegemony and oppression. However, it is hard for these thinkers to even imagine the unconscionable hegemony and oppression faced by Chinese peasants during Mao's era—at a time when there was no capitalist hegemony in the country. Of all the cases of contemporary capitalism in the world, it is hard to pick one that subjugates peasants with the same degree of deprivation as Mao's regime did. Most international left-wing intellectuals are not willing to believe that the Chinese people suffered during that period. They list the achievements in Mao's era, such as the number of roads built and dams erected, and reduction in illiteracy. In addition, they suspect that the abnormal death toll of 30 million people during 1960–2 in China was not as high as is claimed.

Chinese Peasants had Nothing to Lose...

Thinkers across the world are puzzled with the absence of any form of protest by Chinese peasants during the negotiations on China's entry into the WTO. This could very well be attributed to the lack of transparency and closed nature of China's politics. First, Chinese peasants have no right to know what the government is deciding for them. Even if they do learn about the same, there is no channel for their political participation. Anyone who dares to lead a protest would be immediately imprisoned. However, a comparison of Chinese agriculture with that in India, Europe, Japan and other countries, shows that this conclusion is probably one-sided.

It is not that Chinese peasants did not/do not oppose globalization or the open-door policy, because of their ignorance or because globalization favors them; it is because they had nothing to lose before globalization and the reforms. Since Mao's era, even in the absence of globalization, agricultural prices were depressed in the 'system of unified procurement and sale' (Tong Gou Tong Xiao), in the name of the 'War to Resist US Aggression and Aid Korea', or for building socialism. The system was to buy and sell by coercion and deprive the rural village peasants, in the form of 'price scissors', in order to facilitate industrialization and build atomic bombs. (Liang Shuming, the intellectual who spoke for peasants and proposed a rise in agricultural procurement prices, was labeled 'the rightist'.) Since 1949, the institution, forced upon Chinese villagers, particularly, the peasants had been exploiting them, but it was characterized by Mao as the 'policy of greater benevolence'.

The 'socialist subsidies' that Indian peasants miss, were never enjoyed by Chinese peasants who lived under the sunshine of socialism. The agricultural tax, designed especially for them, was not abolished until 2006. That's why they would feel baffled if they were asked to oppose globalization. While farmers in France, India and South Korea can protest against globalization because of the loss of subsidies and benefits, Chinese peasants would again have no reason to protest. Globalization cannot take away something they never had. In fact, thanks to globalization, the spring onions of Shandong and the dried mushrooms of Fujian are sold overseas at much more favorable prices than during the period of unified procurement and sale.

It is understandable when an Indian scholar says that he opposes globalization on behalf of Indian peasants. But when a Chinese scholar says the same thing in China, the only explanation is that Chinese peasants are too easily represented. Chinese people—including Chinese peasants—have been represented by the Party without elections or voting, and the same trick was quickly learnt by the Party's favorite scholars, while most peasants in China are accustomed to remaining in the 'silent majority'. Farmers in Europe or India may panic on hearing about globalization, whereas, Chinese peasants—who did not starve to death under Mao's rule—are tough enough to endure globalization.

Another difference, which possibly requires further study, lies in the cultural memory of the nation. When the word 'open' is used, Chinese people think back to the Tang dynasty, when China enjoyed an international status comparable to that of the contemporary US. Even ordinary Chinese people associate openness in history with Zhang Qian who opened up the 'Silk-Road' to western regions (164-114BC), or Zheng setting off on trade expeditions to west Asia and east Africa (fifteenth century AD); these were followed by foreign countries unanimously paying tribute to China. Disregarding the exact causal direction, Chinese peoples' memory of national strength is usually linked to the 'opening'. However, India is different in this respect. A strong unified empire was a rare experience in Indian history. Even Ashoka's era is not comparable with the Chinese Han and Tang dynasties. When 'opening' is mentioned, Indians usually think of the British colonial rule. In fact, India's national Independence Movement started with the revival of hand-powered spinning wheels and boycott of international trade.

As a result of these cognitive differences, apart from the Chinese New Left, it is extremely difficult for a Chinese and an Indian intellectual to speak a common language when ambitious propositions like globalization are discussed. Even those who have the same concept in mind, simply speak of different things.

CURRENT PRICE OF CHINA'S AGRICULTURAL LABOR FORCE DEMONSTRATES WORLDWIDE COMPETITIVENESS

In the event of more intensified globalization, China's peasants could turn into the biggest winners. China is not rich in farm lands when compared with countries like USA and Canada, however, it boasts of the most centralized and most industrious agricultural labor force in the world, which justifies its world-leading competitive edge in labor-intensive agriculture. Few countries in the world can offer a lower-priced agricultural labor force than China, except perhaps Burma or North Korea, where it is cheaper due to the oppression of the rulers. If China has less of an advantage in producing wheat and corn than the US, it maintains an unchallengeable position in the world in growing vegetables and rice—which require a heavy labor force investment.

If certain intellectuals in China are today identifying themselves as advocates of justice and peasants' rights, they are not doing the right thing by talking in alarmist tones to the Chinese peasants about the perils of globalization and market economy. In fact they are turning a blind eye to the fact that through means of a planned economy and monopoly, Mao and his party had deliberately lowered the prices of agricultural products and oppressed free trade since 1949. That was a period of complete exploitation of Chinese peasants, and it was the development of the market that helped to unshackle them.

What Chinese peasants should complain about is not globalization and the market economy but their halfway development. Assuming that Korea, Japan and Europe were to open their agricultural markets and free the flow of agricultural products, the low-price Chinese farm products would flood their domestic markets. In the end, farmers in these countries would be justified in protesting against the situation while Chinese peasants would receive doubled or tripled incomes. If the Chinese government were to relax price controls over agricultural products and make a greater endeavour to integrate with the global market, rather than manipulating the price; and if the Chinese government did not corner the land market and deny peasants their claims to property rights in land in the name of the hypocritical 'collective ownership', the price of rice in China would not be so low. And the commercial house price would not be so high. Consequently, China would benefit from a more sound and more reasonable economic structure. Taiwan's experience proves exactly that. Unlike their mainland counterpart, Taiwanese peasants enjoy private ownership over land and the associated economic freedom. As a result, the urban and rural income gap is much smaller in Taiwan, while Taiwan peasants are entitled to more social welfare.

Despite these self-evident facts, the Chinese New Left is still doggedly protesting globalization on the international stage in the name of Chinese peasants.

TRANSLATION OBSTACLES AND LANGUAGE INADEQUACY: CONFUSION OF CHINESE NEW LEFT AND NEO NAZIS

Influenced by antipathy for the Chinese New Left, I became biased against the trend of leftism in the world. Now I feel that I was making a mistake. In fact, the Chinese New Left has something uniquely Chinese, and probably has no counterparts worldwide. The extreme rightist Frenchman Le Pen, with his various positions including the election programs, 'farm products priority' agricultural policy, neo-protectionism, proposition for military rebuilding, the rejection of the Americans' 'New World Order', and retaining France's dominion over its overseas territories, would surely be regarded as a person of the Chinese New Left in China (if we exclude the issue of suppressing illegal immigration which is not applicable). However, when those belonging to the Chinese New Left advocate the retention of the household registration system that separates the rural from the urban, and neglect to propose 'farm products priority' in China, they appear to have a lesser sense of responsibility than Le Pen.

This explains why 'Left' is a very confusing concept. There seem to exist at least two types of leftists in the world: the Chinese New Left and all the other 'leftists'. However, no matter how the difference is elaborated, few people can understand the distinction. This can probably be ascribed to the differences between languages and experiences.

For a long time in the past, I could not figure out why western leftists would denounce liberalism, whilst enjoying the blessings of freedom of speech and thought. Neither Kim Jong-II nor Saddam would give them a title or a research fund. They needed to be exiled to North Korea or China during the days of the Cultural Revolution, so that they could witness the times when people had to 'beg for instructions in the morning, and report for work at night' under the leadership of Mao. They had to be extremely cautious about each word they said because friends and relatives were watching closely, ready to report them to the authorities. Or else, the leftists should be made to experience Pi-Dou meetings, so that they see the harshness of being censured and humiliated in public. It is only then that they would realize the real value of freedom.

The word 'neo-liberalism' bothers the leftists terribly. However bad neo-liberalism was, it could not be worse than absolutism. The neo authoritarians born from Russia's privatization policy—'secretaries' in old days—have turned to capitalists. If anyone blames this situation as being unfair, they should hold the autocracy of the CCP accountable rather than neo-liberalism.

After hearing stories about neo-liberalism repeatedly, I realized that it was essential to explore the relationship between 'neo-liberalism' and 'new liberalism'. My study of the literature explained that two different concepts were mixed up when the topic of liberalism was discussed in China—one is liberalism that is 'new' and the other is Neo-Liberalism (that is, a new kind of liberalism), which were all translated into 'xin zi you zhuyi ('new' and 'neo-' in Chinese are represented by the same character).

After having distinguished the logic of the two different concepts, I understood the fact that in a country where there is no constitutional democracy, it can be really harmful to unilaterally advocate neo-liberalism. Promoting neo-liberalism in US wouldn't stir up an upheaval because people enjoy freedom of speech and there exists an independent and efficient judiciary. If you dare to snatch other people's land, they will sue you; if you push them into a corner, they will shoot you; and if you irritate the masses, they will drive off the men in power. Also, the foundation of a good social welfare system has been laid in constitutional democracies, making it somehow reasonable when those who favor neo-liberalism in Europe and North America blame their social welfare systems. Social welfare systems in these countries remain strongly superior to that of China no matter how severe the voices of criticism. (In terms of social welfare, China cannot compete with these countries even in the proportion to gross domestic product [GDP], let alone the absolute figures.)

In countries that lack sound legal systems, where civil societies are not mature, where common people are denied basic social welfare, the practice of 'laissez faire' can easily go astray. Neo-liberalism is likely to align itself with autocratic powers, which explains why neo-liberalism achieved notoriety in South America and east Europe. The autocratic power cultivated under the circumstances of a centralized system, plays the role of hired roughnecks, and then neo-liberalism is responsible to legalize them in the name of laissez-faire. Both 'liberalisms' are against centralized control, but they are heading in totally different directions: one lets peasants' businesses go free by using a policy such as 'production contracted to each household', while the other indulges those who use violence to grab land under the umbrella of state machinery. In a country where there is no democracy and no constitutional system, the transformation from public to private and private to public are basically the same.

Unfortunately, most of the liberals in China have not distinguished between the two types of liberalism clearly. They do not have any doubts about advocating neo-liberalism, because no matter what type the liberalism is, it is still *liberal*ism; and no matter how bad neo-liberalism was it couldn't be worse than Mao's autocracy.

However, the Chinese cannot be blamed for harboring these ideas. They have experienced life under the reign of Mao Zedong and have never had a real taste of freedom of speech and thought. It would be an extravagant hope for them to learn about the nuances of liberalisms. Consider a French farmer who started tasting wine in his childhood; he would have learnt to distinguish across 100 wines. Similarly, a Chinese farmer who has been drinking *Er Guo Tou* (a local alcoholic drink) for his whole life is keenly aware of the different kinds of Er Guo Tou. But if you ask him to appreciate and differentiate French wine from *Tonghua wine* (a local cheap wine with inferior quality), it would be a 'mission impossible' for him.

Similarly, a western left intellectual may naturally find the word 'socialism' attractive whenever he hears it, but his personal experiences prevent him from distinguishing welfare socialism in north Europe from 'socialism with Chinese characteristics' or Hitler's state socialism.

Habermas was invited to China by the Chinese New Left. He felt that though the Chinese New Left spoke of popular academic concepts, they were in fact more like fascists. I believe that his perception probably had something to do with his experiences in Hitler's Germany. It enabled him to discern fascism under all sorts of banners, just like a wine expert who can tell the quality of the wine without being fooled by the package. Unfortunately, many young Western intellectuals, who grow up in a democratic atmosphere, can easily be tricked by the Chinese New Left. They may be enchanted by the Chinese New Leftists who proclaim their passion for socialism and their hatred for globalization.

POLITICIZED LOGIC—MY ENEMY'S ENEMY IS MY FRIEND

My argument in the paper so far explains why certain leftists from the West and Chinese New Left recognize each other as comrades even though they do not share the same views or beliefs, but simply the same signboard of 'Left'.

But it is often the shared enemy, rather than a shared vision, that brings people together. Those of the western left do have something in common with the Chinese New Left. Even though the latter does not share their social ideals, yet both groups have a common enemy. The western leftists, irrespective of whether they are Marxists or those belonging to the Frankfurt School, follow the tradition of taking a stand against [certain] institutions. They criticize the defects of the western system while examining it from inside. But the Chinese New Leftists, posing as unyielding heroes, also point their fingers at the western system, without looking at their own country.

The common meeting ground for leftists across the world including the Chinese New Left is attacking the dual standards pursued by American imperialism. These intellectuals are not really concerned about 'morality and justice', but 'foe-or-friend relations'. I find it surprising that in

US and in India, local people have barely heard of Chinese intellectuals such as Qin Hui and Wu Jinglian, who are influential figures in China. However, everyone seems to know about Wang Hui since he is regarded by the western leftists as the representative of China's Left Wing. Many people know about him because he has been written about by Pankaj Mishra in *The New York Times* . Mishra is dedicated to criticizing globalization and the market economy in the US, while Wang Hui is doing the same thing in China, giving them a common platform for convergence.

A renowned professor of international relations, accused the US of blunt imperialism for attempting to sustain the current Taiwan Straits situation by deterring China from using arms to unite the nation, but he also claimed that the Chinese government was correct in agreeing to maintain the separation between North and South Korea since that conforms to Chinese's interests.

Another professor of economics, citing Amartya Sen's views, criticized the developed countries, represented by the US for protecting the acquired fortune of their own nation by controlling the influx of new immigrants. However, to support his views, he also justified the strict household policies in big cities in China, such as Beijing and Shanghai.

A Chinese New Leftist professor's criticism of the invasion of American culture into China was immediately followed by accusation that the Tibetans' call for religious independence, and protecting Tibetan culture and traditions was 'separatist' in nature.

This mode of thinking about friends and foes was used to great perfection by Mao Zedong. By adopting certain 'foe-friend' criteria, he managed to unite farmers, intellectuals and entrepreneurs to overthrow Chiang Kai-shek. With another set of 'foe-friend' criteria, he called on farmers and intellectuals to dump the entrepreneurs. Next he summoned farmers to knock down the intellectuals, and even later aroused the poorer farmers to strike at the richer farmers. In any case, Mao himself stood firm on 'invincible land', and was always worshiped as the 'People's Saviour'. The opening chapter of *Selected Works of Mao Zedong* begins with the following lines: 'Who is our enemy and who is our friend?' That is a paramount question to be answered in regard to revolution. The core of Mao Zedong's philosophy was to: fight against whatever is supported by our enemy, and to support whatever our enemy fights against. Following the same logic, it can be safe to assume that our enemy's enemy is our friend. The enemy that Mao intended to destroy kept changing all the time, and naturally so did his logic. However, nobody dared to denounce him or even question him. As an individual Mao was successful. His way of thinking was very effective and pragmatic for a 'proletarian revolutionist'. However, if an intellectual thinks along the same lines, it is sad and disturbing. The Chinese New Left is not the only group addicted to this vice. Even some liberals share these ideas.

A cultural professional from India who I prefer not to name, was clearly anti-American and anti-globalization. He believed that American culture as represented by 'Hollywood' and 'McDonalds' was destroying the cultural diversity and traditions in India. He hero-worshipped Mao because he had the courage to fight against Americans and reject western culture. He took it for granted that Mao was the protector of cultural diversity. I showed him photographic evidence of Mao's 'Break Four Olds' movement when Buddha statues were burnt down, temples destroyed, monks forced to get married and folk traditions ruined, and he finally realized that Mao was worse than American imperialists in terms of destroying cultural diversity. In my opinion, such an individual who is willing to change his beliefs when confronted with a contrast reality can be regarded as a genuine intellectual.

I firmly believe that if intellectuals have a good reason to exist, they should adopt the truth-seeking 'mentality of logical coherence', rather than the power-seeking 'foe-friend logic'. Equipped with their insights, they should involve themselves in questioning the fundamental adversities of human beings, always seek answers, be aware of tyranny or enslavement in any form, instead of forming a gang and labeling themselves as 'the most conscientious intellectuals'. Alliances formed on vague and ambiguous political terms, such as 'anti-globalization' and 'anti-hegemonism', cannot work in the long run.

INTERPRETING THE 'JUNGLE OF ISMS' WITH THE CONCEPT OF 'FAMILY RESEMBLANCE'

I studied the literature to be able to find a clear and simple clue for generalizing those 'isms' that are flagged with left or right. But in the end I arrived at the conclusion that these entangled 'isms' are a jumbled mass, which I named the 'Jungle of Isms'. This experience pushed me to think about the limitations of one single cognitive approach.

The most comprehensive study on this type of question is Wittgenstein's pioneering analysis in the realm of philosophy, which produced the concept of 'family resemblances'. In his *Philosophical Investigations*[1], he explained why people are often confused with concepts. He explained that when a word is employed to demonstrate an entity, the word itself is inherently ambiguous. He writes

Think of the tools in a tool-box: there is a hammer, plier, a saw, a screw-driver, a rule, a glue-pot, glue, nails and screws. The functions of words are as diverse as the functions of these objects. (And in both cases there are similarities.) ... Of course, what confuses us is the uniform appearance of words when we hear them spoken or meet them in script and print. For their application is not presented to us so clearly. Especially [...] in] philosophy.

Wittgenstein's 'family resemblances' concept provides us a brand new perspective to understand human beings' thoughts that used to be tagged with different labels. Why do we always have to anxiously classify these thoughts briefly by their nature, as if we could really find the clear skeleton form of all human thoughts after we manage to categorize them and put them into different boxes with different labels of property?

My dissatisfaction with the above mentioned approach is most precisely expressed by Wittgenstein

If someone were to draw a sharp boundary I could not acknowledge it as the one that I too always wanted to draw, or had drawn in my mind, for I did not want to draw one at all. His concept can then be said to be not the same as mine, but akin to it. The kinship is that of two pictures, one of which consists of colour patches with vague contours, and the other of patches similarly shaped and distributed, but with clear contours. The kinship is just as undeniable as the difference.

In this sense, an intellectual can feel reasonably at ease if he can neither stir up troubles in the Left camp, nor becomes a general favorite in the Right camp, because every mind that is deeply concerned with seeking the truth is a member of the 'family' in certain aspects.

Speaking of being alert to the alienation among human beings imposed by industrialization, capitalism and competition, I can be taken as a Marxist or a Marxist with a prefix—a humane Marxist. In terms of my antagonism to violence and power politics, I am inclined to agree with

---

[1] *Philosophical Investigations* (*Philosophische Untersuchungen*) is, along with the *Tractatus Logico-Philosophicus*, one of the two most influential works by the 20th-century philosopher Ludwig Wittgenstein. In it, Wittgenstein discusses numerous problems and puzzles in the fields of semantics, logic, philosophy of mathematics, and the philosophy of mind. First translated in 1953, its third edition is now in publication, published by Blackwell Publishers, 2001 (ISBN 0-631-23127-7). This edition includes the original German text in addition to the English translation.

Gandhi's philosophy. When the abhorrence to totalitarianism is discussed, I respect the ideas of classical liberalism. In putting across the case that China requires greater public welfare and basic security, I identify with new liberalism. And if some day in the future, China actually succeeds in providing public welfare in as comprehensive a manner as in Europe, I will probably be inclined towards neo-liberalism. I am firmly against the general extreme black-or-white way of thinking, no matter which camp it comes from. I know that I will never be an aficionado of any 'ism'.

People who can stick to one simple belief are lucky, because a naïve belief can bring them euphoria throughout their life. I am unlike such individuals. I have been able to fight the inclination to be short-sighted by simple mindedness that would prevent me from perceiving and understanding the broader picture, make me kneel down before idols or 'isms' and prevent me from seeing what truly deserves reverence and pursuit, and to what I must remain alert—the quest for true knowledge.

11

A Future for Disinterested Governance?[a]

YANG YAO

Between 1978 and 2008, the Chinese economy grew at an average rate of 9.7 per cent per annum.[1] This record allowed the recent World Bank *Growth Report* to identify China as one of the thirteen successful economies that have managed to grow at a rate of 7 per cent or higher for 25 years or more since the Second World War (The Growth Commission 2008). As a consequence, per-capita GDP has grown by a factor of 12 in real terms to reach USD 3400 in 2008.[2] It is over this period that China moved from a planning economy to a 'mixed economy' with its private sector now accounting for two thirds of its national GDP. How has China managed this incredible feat?

A CASE FOR THE WASHINGTON CONSENSUS

To many, the explanation for China's economic success lies in its unconventional approach to economic policies and organizations. Joshua Ramo even gave it a name 'Beijing Consensus' (Ramo 2004). To be sure, China is unique in many ways. The Chinese leadership is unusually pragmatic, enabling it to succeed in a complex and constantly changing world. The Chinese transition has followed a gradual trajectory, allowing China to avoid the institutional and organizational disruptions that have plagued most other transition economies. Equally, China's economic organizations lack the clear-cut features of a standard market economy, yet they have been adaptive in the evolutionary settings of the recent past. The list could go on. However, a serious examination will raise the question whether these features constitute a new model of economic growth or are they intermediate yet sometimes necessary steps toward the traditional model of a market economy.

The Chinese leadership adopted a gradual approach to transition because of its aversion to the serious risks associated with a fast transition. The Chinese Communist Party (CCP) had made many significant mistakes during its first thirty years of rule—the grand experiments in social engineering including aggressive collectivization of agriculture, the Great Leap-Forward, and the catastrophic Cultural Revolution. With this legacy, a rapid transition to a full-blown market economy was seen by the CCP as quite a risky endeavor that is best avoided. At the same time,

---

[a] An abridged version of the paper has been published in *Foreign Affairs Online* by the title 'The End of Beijing Consensus' on 2 February 2010. http://www.foreignaffairs.com/articles/65947/the-end-of-the-beijing-consensus. I thank Daniel Bromley, Edward Friedman, Ashok Gurung, Yukon Huang, Sanjay Ruparelia, and Jianying Zha for their helpful comments and suggestions.

[1] The National Bureau of Statistics (NBS) website: www.stats.gov.cn.

[2] Ibid.

many of China's somewhat unconventional organizational forms can be understood as reactions to the unconventional political and economic circumstances encountered along its transitional path. For example, government ownership in the township and village enterprises (TVEs), which was hailed by some as a challenge to the conventional private ownership, was a consequence of the government's ambiguous—even conflicting—attitudes toward private firms in the 1980s. After private firms were made legal in the 1990s, TVEs vanished quickly. Although there are debates, the consensus inside China is that China is not creating a new model of economic organization and growth. As evidence of this, the idea of a 'Beijing Consensus' has not received widespread approval within China.

Indeed, if we lay out a list of the reforms China has undertaken, and then compare that list with the recommendations of the Washington Consensus, we might be surprised by the similarities in those two lists. According to John Williamson's original formulation (Williamson 1990), the Washington Consensus has the following ten policy recommendations:

1. financial discipline to avoid the inflation tax;
2. public expenditure redirected from redistribution to productive areas, such as primary education, health care, and infrastructure;
3. tax reform so as to broaden the tax base and cut marginal tax rates;
4. financial liberalization, involving an ultimate objective of market-determined interest rates;
5. a unified exchange rate at a level sufficiently competitive to induce a rapid growth in nontraditional exports;
6. quantitative trade restrictions to be rapidly replaced by tariffs;
7. abolition of barriers impeding the entry of foreign direct investment (FDI);
8. privatization of state enterprises;
9. abolition of regulations that impede the entry of new firms or restrict competition; and
10. provision of secure property rights. Over the past thirty years, China has closely followed most of these recommendations.

In terms of fiscal discipline, the Chinese government has been very cautious in maintaining a roughly balanced budget; its debt has never surpassed its tax revenue. The rate of inflation has been kept in single digits in most years. On the expenditure side, pure redistributive programs have been kept to a minimum; central government transfers have been primarily limited to infrastructure spending. Before 2003, the share of 'social spending' in government budgets had been declining. It has slowly picked up in recent years, but its level is still low.

In terms of taxation, the overall tax burden, measured by the ratio of taxes to GDP, declined dramatically from 31 per cent in 1978 to 12 per cent in 1993, largely because of fiscal decentralization in the 1980s.[3] The 1993 fiscal reform has greatly strengthened governments' taxation capacities, and the amount of government revenues has increased to approximately 25 per cent of GDP. However, this rate of growth has begun to concern both the government and the general population. The rate of corporate income tax was reduced from 33 per cent to 25 per cent, and the permissible deductions for personal income taxes have been raised several times. Even the value-added tax has begun to provide a deduction for capital investment.

On the international front, China has taken a road that decisively leads to the liberalization of trade and FDI although it has successfully followed its own pace of opening-up. The Special Economic Zones have served as windows for China to reach the outside world. Export-led growth model was adopted as a national development strategy in the mid-1980s. Joining the WTO in 2001

[3] Ibid.

marked China's full integration into the world economy. Since then, China's trade dependence ratio, that is, the ratio of imports and exports in GDP has been maintained at a level higher than 60 per cent, one of the highest among the large economies.

Domestically, the two major themes of the Chinese reform have been privatization and deregulation. After fifteen years of privatization that started in the mid-1990s, most of China's state-owned enterprises (SOEs) have been released to private hands, or transformed into publicly listed companies. Only a handful—though powerful—SOEs are still owned by the government. The removal of price controls happened even before privatization. By the end of the 1990s government reforms had removed many barriers to the entry and exit of individual firms into specific markets.

Although protection of property rights is still weak in many arenas (especially intellectual property rights), China has made noticeable progress in the last thirty years. Several amendments to the Constitution, and the passage of the *Property Law*, have established a reasonable—though still incomplete—legal framework for property rights protection. The situation is far from perfect, but the direction has been decisively set for better and stronger protection in the future.

It is noteworthy that the Washington Consensus, as Williamson correctly emphasizes, is different from the so-called 'neoliberal doctrine' that adds to the list capital account liberalization, a floating exchange rate, and above all, the relentless working of the un-bridled market, which China has clearly rejected. On the other hand, China has also adopted other policies frequently prescribed by neoclassical economics as essential for economic growth—among which high saving and investment rates, and an emphasis on primary education, are the most significant.

The only prescription that China has not followed closely is liberalization of interest rates. Despite vast deregulation, the state still maintains tight controls on what it calls 'the strategic sectors' like petroleum, telecom, and banking. Controlling interest rates is a tactic the government believes to be essential for its control of the financial sector. However, this approach, even if it was warranted in the past, now seems problematic. We will come back to this point later. For now it is sufficient to conclude that China's economic success has been a triumph of neoclassical economics to which the Washington Consensus is a core set of auxiliary policy recommendations.

THE DISINTERESTED GOVERNMENT

Yet we have to ask a further question when we think about China's economic success more carefully—why has the Chinese government adopted the principles of neoclassical economics, particularly when the CCP still claims that Marxism is its ideological anchor?

The answer to this question, I suggest, is that the Chinese government has been a disinterested government. Here I am using the word 'disinterested' in one of its three meanings in aesthetics,[4] which is 'detached' or 'unbiased' when one makes judgments on objective existences. Thus, by a disinterested government I mean a government that takes a neutral stand when conflicts of interests among different social and political groups arise. In other words, it is a government that does not consistently represent—and is not captured by—any social or political groups in the society. This does not mean that such a government is devoid of self interests; quite to the contrary. It can not only have its own interests, but also be predatory toward society at large. The key is that its predation is 'identity-blind' in the sense it does not care about the social and political statuses of its particular prey. As a consequence, it is more likely to adopt growth-enhancing policies than is a government that consistently represents the interests of certain social or political groups.

[4] The other two meanings, according to Rind (2002), are 'uninterested' and 'without self interests' when a person examines an objective existence.

To understand this assessment, we first realize that biased governments are obliged to adopt policies that consistently benefit their own favored groups, and thus create a mismatch between productivity and government allocation of resources because other groups, not similarly favored, might well be more productive. In contrast, a disinterested government is autonomous in the sense that it is free of social and political constraints and thus is more likely to allocate public resources according to sector/group productivity. In that sense, a disinterested government promotes economic growth. It is willing to make this happen for two reasons. First, higher economic growth brings tangible gains (rewards) to its members. Second, higher economic growth brings satisfaction to the people, who in turn may be more willing to acknowledge its legitimacy.

A corollary of the above reasoning is that the policies adopted by a disinterested government are often selective and have the potential to enlarge income gaps in the society. Unless the gaps lead to serious threats to its rule, however, a disinterested government will have little incentive to correct them.

The Chinese government has acted as if it has been disinterested over the last thirty years. This started with the establishment of the 'growth consensus' at the end of the 1970s. This consensus came out of the CCP's realization that continuing the Stalinist socialism would not only retard China's rise in the world, but also endanger its own legitimacy—which was already faltering in the mid-1970s. The need was to discourage growing discontent, and put economic growth at the center of all governmental and societal endeavors.

Looking back, it is clear that the Chinese government intentionally adopted selective policies to promote reform and economic growth. China's integration into the world economy is a case at point. At the end of the 1970s the United States was eager to bring China into its camp as a buffer against the Soviet hegemony. China quickly grasped the opportunity. Yet that early adoption of an 'open-door' policy was not without domestic resistance. The special economic zones enjoyed an abundance of preferential treatments that other parts of the country envied. The export-led growth model required that China embrace an unbalanced development path that encouraged rapid growth on the east coast, and relative neglect of the interior; today, nearly 90 per cent of China's exports come from the nine coastal provinces. China's accession to the WTO in 2001 was also a selective move. Before accession it was widely believed that China would have to undergo painful structural adjustments in agriculture, automobile manufacturing, banking, telecom, and retailing if it were to join the WTO. Amidst the debate, the central government actually speeded up negotiations with the WTO members, especially the United States. Despite many detrimental effects, accession to the WTO has greatly accelerated China's growth of exports. Between 2002 and 2007, Chinese exports grew by an annual rate of 28.9 per cent, comparing with the average rate of 14.5 per cent in the prior decade.[5]

Privatization of the SOEs was another case. In the 1990s, during the most dramatic transformations, the CCP had to face new challenges emerging from an increasingly diversified population. Between 1995 and 2004—the peak of privatization—nearly 50 million SOE workers lost their jobs. This put the CCP in a conundrum: by supporting privatization it risked losing support from its main power base—the working class; on the other hand, its larger goal of transition to a market economy would be halted if it abandoned privatization. The CCP finessed this difficult passage by quietly pushing continued privatization while simultaneously doing all it could to re-employ laid-off workers. This strategy has worked. By the mid-2000s when SOE privatization drew to a close, most unemployed workers had found new jobs, or had come onto government welfare programs.

[5] The figures quoted in this paragraph are all from the NBS website: www.stats.gov.cn

Perhaps the most controversial illustration of the government's selective policies is the urban–rural divide. With urban per capita income standing at 3.5 times of rural per-capita income, China has the largest urban–rural income differential in the world. There are many explanations for this large gap, some of which are related to the institutional barriers inherited from the planning period. However, from an efficiency point of view, this large gap would not be bothersome to the government because cities enjoy much higher productivity and wages than can be found in the countryside.

The government has also been willing to correct mismatches between government policies and group productivity. The dual-track price system instituted between 1985 and 1994 is a case at point. Under this system, SOEs were given the opportunity to sell their products and buy inputs in the emerging market after they fulfilled their planned quotas. While this system opened up a wide door for economic incentives to play a role in SOE decision making, increasing gaps between market prices and quota prices created enormous scope for rent seeking. SOE managers and government officials who controlled the quotas of key inputs could easily get rich by selling their quotas to other enterprises and individuals. The brighter side of the dual-track system, however, was that it also created—unintentionally—new elements that benefited only from the market. The TVEs and private firms were particularly helped in this regard. They did not have access to planned resources such as bank credits and key inputs, but instead had to rely on the market to survive. Despite these perils, they had become important players in the Chinese economy by the early 1990s. For example, TVEs contributed 40 per cent to China's industrial growth and 40 per cent of its exports (Lin and Yao 2001). These new circumstances forced the government to give up the dual-track system so they were treated equitably with the SOEs. This happened even when the beneficiaries of the system were mostly powerful members of the CCP.

Government policy toward migrant workers is another example. Until very recently, free mobility of labor was hampered by various barriers including the household registration system (*hukou*), which is still in place today. In the 1990s migrant workers were often treated as second-rate citizens deprived of basic rights to free mobility, workplace safety, health care, and even equitable salaries. However, by the end of the 1990s it had become clear that they were indispensable in the national economy as China became the 'world's factory.' It seems that urban dwellers had gained undue benefits with the government's suppression of migrant workers' rights, and the share of national income going to migrant workers fell below their relative contribution to the national economy. This unequal treatment ignited wide-spread grassroots rights movements and petitions by intellectuals. The CCP was alarmed by the potential of social unrest. Soon the discriminatory policies toward migrant workers began to wither away after the more equity-conscious Hu Jintao-Wen Jiabao government took office in 2003.

The question remains as to why the Chinese government remained 'disinterested' during the reform era? The CCP's search for legitimacy is one of the major reasons. Despite its absolute power, the CCP has never been free to ignore the general wishes of the people. The April Fourth Movement in 1976, the June Fourth Movement in 1989, and numerous protests in later stages, show that people are quite willing to stage organized resistance. In addition, fiscal decentralization of the 1980s had considerably weakened the central government's authority over local governments, thereby making it more prudent in carrying out regional policies. International monitoring has also played an important role. As it has emerged as one of the largest international players, China now must care about its legitimacy on the world stage. Since it is not democratically elected, the CCP does not have the legitimacy derived from the set of procedures pre-proved by the people. As a result, it has to seek for performance-based legitimacy, that is, legitimacy coming from the delivery of continuous improvements toward people's welfare.

However, many other authoritarian regimes also tried to obtain legitimacy from economic growth, yet they often did not enjoy power for long. It has a lot to do with the absence of extreme social inequality in China that the CCP remained disinterested in the reform era.

In societies with extreme social inequality, like many of those where other authoritarian regimes existed, forming an alliance with the strongest social groups provides the best chance for the government to survive because those groups can provide sufficient resources for it to suppress any challenge from the disfavored groups. However, the biased policies ultimately lead to stagnation of economic growth and the erosion of the regime's legitimacy. In contrast, it is dangerous for the government in an equal society to side with any particular groups because other groups can form an alliance to block the government—and perhaps even to unseat it.

China was made a more equal society through a series of revolutions in the twentieth century. The 1911 Xinhai Revolution led by the nationalists ended the Manchu rule of imperial China and established a republic. The communist revolution of 1949 further leveled out the Chinese society. Through a comprehensive yet brutal land reform, the landed class was effectively eliminated and land distribution became equalized. Large businesses originally tied to the nationalist government were nationalized. By the early 1950s, the Mainland and Taiwan, despite their diametrically opposite ideological outlooks, were surprisingly similar in terms of social structure and government policies. Like the communists in the Mainland, the nationalists in Taiwan also carried out thorough—though peaceful—land reform. Both governments established SOEs and extracted surpluses from agriculture in the hope of speeding up the industrialization process. Many commentators believe that both economies benefited from land reform in their early stages of development. The divergence occurred in 1956 when the Mainland began to eliminate family farming in the countryside and private businesses in the city. Between 1956 and 1978 the Mainland took a long detour and the reform has largely been a process of moving the country back on the track set for it in the early 1950s.

THE FUTURE?

The selective and efficiency-biased policies have, predictably, led to large income inequality in China. The overall Gini coefficient has reached 0.47 and the gap between the richest and the poorest is increasing even faster. Worse than that, governments at various levels constantly infringe on people's political and economic rights in order to create short-term growth. Arbitrary land acquisitions are but one example. Political and economic inequality has led to wide-spread protests in the country. In a sense, China is indeed a 'fragile superpower' as Susan Shirk calls it. Yet it seems that there are no clear signs of an imminent collapse. How has the CCP managed to minimize the downsides of its selective policies?

First, the government has delivered continuous economic growth, and rising living standards, to the population. One of the curious things about China is that the government has constantly received an approval rate of 70 per cent or above, no matter who does the survey.[6] The reason behind this is that the majority of the Chinese population is quickly moving into the rank of the middle class which actually benefits from the current regime. In China, the middle class, at least for now, is not a force for change, but rather a force for stability.

Second, the government has carried out specific programs that quickly and effectively address early signs of discontentment in the population. This includes an urban subsistence maintenance program that covers 20 million low-income people, reemployment centers that provide

---

[6] For a recent independent survey, see ISSS (2009).

unemployment benefits to laid-off workers and train them for reemployment, several programs (for example, Go West) that aim at lowering regional disparities, and the recent New Countryside Movement to improve infrastructure, health care, and education in the rural areas.

Third, the government has gradually begun to give more respect to people's expressed interests in response to large-scale protests. The policy change for migrant workers is but one example. Other examples include the passage of The Property Law, increased levels of compensation for those who lose land and buildings to urban and industrial expansion, and limited transparency of government budgets.

Lastly, the selective policies themselves have certain self-correcting effects. Being disinterested, the government does not consistently favor specific groups and so in the long run favors are likely to be distributed roughly equally, at least in areas where institutional impediments are relatively weak. For example, the Gini coefficients within the city and within the countryside alone are not high, both at the range of 0.35 to 0.37—approximating the levels found in South Korea and Japan (Cheng 2007).

However, those measures are only 'pain relievers'—being too weak to break institutional barriers and market imperfections that might stimulate new and threatening social groups. While the private business community is realizing the importance of cultivating the government for larger profits, it is the government itself, its cronies, and government-controlled SOEs that are quickly forming strong and exclusive interest groups. This is the result of the CCP's two political strategies to improve its chances of continuous control of the society. One is its transformation to become an all-people's party, and the other is its intention to follow the Singaporean model to merge itself with the government. The first strategy is aimed at broadening its power base, while the second is aimed at controlling the country in the 'shell' of the government. In the last several years, government involvement in the economy has increased; the current four trillion RMB stimulus plan, mostly carried out by the government, reinforces this trend. However, China is too big for the CCP to follow the Singaporean model even if it were a model worth pursuing. The CCP's strategies will only create strong and exclusive interest groups; there is no assurance that the government can remain disinterested and growth will continue.

In the last several years, government involvement in the economy has increased —most notably with the current four-trillion-yuan (USD 586 billion) stimulus plan. Government investment helped China reach a GDP growth rate of nearly nine percent in 2009, which many applaud; but in the long run, it could suffocate the Chinese economy by reducing efficiency and crowding out more vibrant private investment.

The economy currently depends heavily on external demand, creating friction among major trading partners. Savings account for 52 per cent of GDP, and consumption has dropped to a historic low. Whereas governments in most advanced democracies spend less than eight per cent of government revenue on capital investment, this figure is close to 50 per cent in China. Residential income as a share of national income is declining, making the average citizen feel poorer while the economy expands. As the Chinese people demand more than economic gains as their income increases, it will become increasingly difficult for the CCP to contain or discourage social discontent by administering the medicine of economic growth alone.[7]

More importantly, the government in its current form is cumbersome in dealing with multiple goals that are increasingly demanded by the society. The concerted efforts to promote GDP growth will still result in infringements on people's economic and political rights, which in turn will arouse periodic resistance. Despite its absolute power and recent track record of delivering economic

---

[7] The figures quoted in this paragraph are from the NBS website: www.stats.gov.cn.

growth, the CCP has still periodically faced resistance from citizens. The Tiananmen incident of 5 April 1976, the first spontaneous democratic movement in PRC history, the 4 June movement of 1989, and numerous subsequent protests proved that the Chinese people are quite willing to stage organized resistance when their needs are not met by the state. International monitoring of China's domestic affairs has also played an important role; now that it has emerged as a major global power, China is suddenly concerned about its legitimacy on the international stage.

All this suggests that some form of explicit political transition will be necessary to counterbalance the formation of strong and exclusive interest groups, to allow the government to deal with multiple goals, and even to enhance the CCP's own rule. While the prospect of a multi-party and competitive democracy may not be so clear at the current stage, pressures from the larger society are forcing the CCP to open up the political process. There is a silent yet steadily growing civil society movement that presses the government to show greater respect for people's rights. The internet is serving as a platform not just for information sharing among concerned citizens, but also for them to coordinate public protests against perceived government wrongdoings. The most powerful resistance, however, is likely to come from marginalized people and the 'rights movements' representing them. They are the group that suffers the most from arbitrary government infringements and benefits the least from the status quo.

The CCP must soon realize that there is no other alternative to fuller democratization if it wishes to maintain both high economic growth and enhanced social stability. The emergence of strong and privileged groups will block equal distribution of the benefits of economic growth in the society, which will then render futile the CCP's strategy of trading economic growth for people's consent to its absolute rule. The CCP needs to act now to enable 'ordinary people' to challenge privileged groups on an open and institutionalized platform. Indeed, this will also ease the CCP's own task of controlling the bureaucracy because the democratic institutions will carry it out. Although interest group politics is widely spread and often damaging in democratic societies, an open and inclusive political process has been proven to be the most effective way to reach a balance between different groups. Indeed, this is precisely the mandate of a disinterested government—to balance the demands of different social groups. A democratic government can still be disinterested if the right institutions are in place to keep the most powerful groups at bay.

REFERENCES

Cheng, Yonghong (2007) 'The Gini Coefficient and Its Rural-Urban Decomposition Since the Reform,' *Chinese Social Sciences* (in Chinese), No. 4, pp. 24–36.
ISSS (2009) *The China Report*, Institute of Social Science Survey, Peking University Press, Beijing.
Lin, Justin and Yang Yao (2001) 'Chinese Rural Industrialization in the Context of the East Asian Miracle,' in Joseph Stiglitz and Shahid Yusuf (eds), *Rethinking the East Asian Miracle*, the World Bank and Oxford University Press, New York.
Ramo, Joshua (2004) 'The Beijing Consensus: Notes on the New Physics of Chinese Power', Foreign Policy Centre, http: www.fpc.org.uk.
Rind, Melise (2002) 'The Concept of Disinterestedness in Eighteenth-Century British Aesthetics,' *Journal of the History of Philosophy*, Vol. 40, No. 1, pp. 65–76.
Shirk, Susan, L. (2007) *China: Fragile Superpower: How China's Internal Politics Could Derail Its Peaceful Rise*, Oxford University Press, New York.
The Growth Commission (2008) *The Growth Report: Strategies for Sustained Growth and Inclusive Development*, The World Bank, Washington, D.C.
Williamson, John (1990) 'What Washington Means by Policy Reform?', in John Williamson (ed.) *Latin American Adjustment: How Much Has Happened?* Institute for International Economics, Washington.

Subject Index

1943 Yalta global political settlement 16
2001 Census of India 59
2006 World Economy Forum 25
    2006–7 Global Competitive Power Report 25
Accountability 58, 77, 79
Adventurism 16
Africa 14
Agra 89
Agriculture 10, 15, 18, 30, 33, 37, 46, 53, 85, 93, 133, 144, 149, 153-154, 156-157, 160, 165–169, 171, 175–177, 183, 186, 188
American Chambers of Commerce 49
Amsterdam 137
Andhra Pradesh 132, 155, 160
Andhra Pradesh Infrastructure Investment Corporation 132
    Polavaram project 155
Annual Compound Growth Rate (ACGR) 152
Anti-Monopoly Law 49
Arthashastra, the 1
Asia 14, 16, 20-21, 54-55
Association of Southeast Asian Nations (ASEAN) 55
    Surveillance Process 55
Authoritarianism 58

Bangalore 16, 129, 131
Bankruptcy 21
Beijing 2, 6, 14, 16, 46, 56, 65–67, 71, 75–76, 79, 87–88, 106–109, 115, 126–132, 134, 149–150, 152, 172, 180, 182, 184
    5th Plenary Session of CPC 46
Bilateral trade agreement (BTA) 53-54
Brain drain 35
Brazil 53, 56, 122
Bretton Woods institutions 16
Buddhism 1
Burma 177
Business process outsourcing (BPO) 25, 38, 159, 167

Canada 54, 56, 177

Capital 10-11, 13, 16–20, 27, 33, 39, 44, 49, 52, 64, 68, 91, 106, 108-109
    allocation 44
    availability 13
    cultural 10
    domestic 13
    foreign 11, 49
    human 10-11, 17, 19, 27
    venture 33
Capitalism 11, 13-14, 78
    command 11, 13
Chengdu 67, 107, 134, 172
Chennai 131, 160
Chhattisgarh 155
Chifeng 172
China and India 1–3, 5–6, 9–12, 14–17, 19–23, 30, 35, 37, 38, 42-43, 54, 58-59, 79, 85, 90, 107, 118, 120, 121–124, 129, 132, 137, 151, 153, 157, 167
    1962 War 2
    agriculture 10, 15, 18, 30, 33, 37, 46, 53, 85, 93, 133, 144, 149, 153-154, 156-157, 160, 165–169, 171, 175–177, 183, 186, 188
    bilateral economic and political relationship 42
    bilateral relations 9
    bilateral trade 20, 42, 48, 53-54
    border disputes 1, 12
    cellular phones 13
    cities 18, 31, 44–44, 52, 58–61, 64–68, 71, 74–75, 77, 79, 85–93, 105–107, 109, 115
    coal and oil 18, 19, 45
    comparative growth 22
    competition 15, 22, 38, 43, 48-49, 54, 78, 86-87
    demographic transition 17
    development,
        models of 167
        transition 19
    distinctiveness 137
    divergence 10–11, 13, 17, 70
    economic- and trade-based engagement 10–11

economic growth 2-3, 6, 11, 13, 15, 18, 24-25, 28, 30, 35, 37, 74-75, 78, 85, 125, 161-162, 165, 167, 183, 185-186, 188-190
economic stature 27
economic strategy 10
economic strength 152
economic transformation 5, 118, 132
education transition 17
elite diaspora 16
energy transition 18
environmental transition 19
expenditure 17, 20, 27, 35-36, 39, 93
'failed' Asian neighbor 12
GDP 19-21, 28, 33, 35-37, 39, 42-46, 48, 51-52, 71, 79, 86-87
geopolitical resurgence 17
globalization and development 15
growth differential 11
households save 120
industrial development 31, 45
infrastructure 11-13, 18, 27-28, 30, 33, 35, 38, 42-45, 60, 62-63, 69-70, 88-89, 95, 101, 115
innovation 11, 17-18, 25-31, 33-35, 37-39
  systems 26-28, 38-39
interstate engagement 9
misinterpretation 174
mutual understanding and knowledge 11
National Innovation Systems (NIS) 2, 24-30, 37-39
  advancements 26
  comparative studies 27
  concept 26
  definition 26
  descriptive model 27
  organization 26
  set-up 27
negotiations 9, 20, 53
partition 10, 22
perceptions 12
population 3-4, 12, 15, 17-18, 33, 45, 50-51, 58, 59, 62-66, 68, 70-72, 74-76, 79, 90-92, 95, 108, 111, 119, 121, 122-124, 143, 149, 152-153, 155-156, 165, 168, 184, 188, 188
post-1980 divergence 10
poverty alleviation 153
R&D expenditure 27, 36, 39
relationship 1, 14
small and medium enterprises (SMEs) 31-32
social transition 143
socio-cultural and political systems 17

special economic zones (SEZs) 119, 146, 157-166
  comparison 162
  cost and benefit analysis 164
  foreign and domestic investment 158
  structure of 158
trade 9-11, 13-14, 16, 18, 20, 22, 42-44, 46-48, 50, 51-57, 85, 92, 108, 111
urban growth 121
urban transition 17
women 6, 57, 130, 133, 150, 169-173
China and USA 46
China, People's Republic
  11th Five-Year Plan 30
  agriculture 151
  Beijing propaganda 14
  China Social Science Institution 30
    Knowledge Innovation Program (KIP) 30
  Chinese Academy of Sciences (CAS) 30
  Chinese Communist Party (CCP) 9-10, 78, 125, 151, 154, 174-175, 178, 183, 185-190
    5th Plenary Session, Beijing 46
    Mao-led consolidation of the revolution 9
  Chinese State Council 150
    informal settlers 2-3, 61, 79
  cities in 3-5, 91, 105-106, 123, 125, 134-135, 180
  computer software 46
  Constitution 92, 185
  Cultural Revolution 10, 13-14, 78, 144, 170-171, 178, 183
  currency 44, 46-48
  defeated the Japanese 9
  developmental paradigm 85
  domestic market 14
  economic growth 11, 13, 23
  economic success 183, 185
  economy 2-3, 37, 43, 52-53, 145, 161, 168, 183, 187, 189
  education 35
  farmers' suicides in 151
  FDI 22
  fundamental challenges 14
  GDP 37, 143
  Great Leap Forward 10
  Great Power 10, 16
  guided democracy 14
  household registration 58, 65-66
  infrastructure 129
  integration of Tibet 9

Subject Index

intellectual property rights 185
International Marine Container 50
Joint Venture Law 147
labor organizations in 172
Land Administration Law 92
Land Resources Administration Law 93
local and ethnic disaffection 13
migrant children in 65
migration policies 63
military system 10
National Economic and Social Development 31
National People's Congress 49, 114, 127, 146, 161
national security 10
New Left 6, 174-175, 177–180
one-child policy 14, 17
Open Door Policy 146
People's Liberation Army 16
performance-based system 79
Planning Commission 126
political hiccups in 13
Property Power Law, the Urban and Rural Planning Law 92
Property Right Law, section 4 93
reformers 14
reform processe 6
rural 5, 11, 130, 153
rural–urban divide in 154
rural–urban segregation 64
savings rate in 44
self-sufficiency 10
SEZs 157, 162-163
Small and medium enterprises (SMEs) 31
Standing Committee of National People's Congress 49
State Environmental Protection Administration (SEPA) 114, 123
state-owned enterprises (SOEs) 185
Strategic Action Plan for Science and Technology (S&T) Innovation (SAPI) 30
Suggestions on Carrying on Efforts of Compulsory Education of Migrant Children in Urban Areas 66
Three Gorges Dam 155
urban development 5
urbanization 91-92, 118, 123
Wal-Mart and 56-57
water, bodies and urban design in 107
WTO and 44, 47, 49, 53-54
Chindia 12, 15, 16-17
 urban 16
Chinese silk 1
Chongqing 66, 134, 137
Chung, Tan 136
Citizenry 58, 60
Citizens' Research Collective 164
Civil war 9, 22
Climate change 15, 18-19, 21
Colonialism 10
Competitiveness 18, 27, 37
Conflict 9-10, 12, 19, 65, 86, 88-89, 93
 interstate 10
Corruption 11-12
Costa Rica 56
Culture 9, 14, 18, 21, 44, 71, 85, 86-87, 90
 and private enterprise 44
 urban 18, 86

Darfur 47
Deficit
 budget 13, 51
 trade and macroeconomic 13
Democracy 10–14, 58, 78, 86-87, 89, 119, 125, 144, 154, 178-179, 190
 guided 14
 liberal 12, 14
 Parliamentary 10
 plural 10, 13
 Western 14
Deprivation 11-12, 15, 65
Development indicator 11, 13
Discrimination 18, 75
Disparities 13, 62, 107
Dominican Republic–Central America–United States Free Trade Agreement (CAFTA-DR) 54
Drinking water 11, 62, 69, 90, 108

Economic boom 13, 17
Economy 1–6, 10–17, 19, 22–23, 28-29, 31, 34, 37, 39, 42–54, 64, 71, 76, 86–90, 106, 108, 111-112, 115, 119-120, 126, 129, 133–135, 143–147, 151–154, 157, 160-161, 165, 167–169, 171, 174–175, 177, 180, 183, 185–187, 189
 capitalist 14
 capital-starved 11
 Chinese 3, 37, 52, 53, 161, 168, 183, 187, 189
 developing 44
 energy 19
 global 10, 13-14, 19, 22, 51–54, 145, 151
 Indian 11, 22-23, 37, 89, 160, 167

knowledge 17, 31, 37, 39
market 5-6, 47–49, 86, 88, 119, 129, 143-144, 153, 167, 171, 174, 177, 180, 183, 186
market oriented 24, 88
mixed 10
optic fiber 167
planned 86, 88, 177
political 1, 2, 157
private-sector 34
western 14
western-style 12
world 10, 11, 31, 43, 51
Education 10–13, 15, 17, 27, 34–35, 38, 45, 58, 61–63, 65–79, 95–96, 111, 114
basic 35, 45, 65–68
universalization of 17
elementary 11, 17, 61–63, 69–70, 79
foreign 34
free and compulsory 61
higher 12, 34-35, 38, 65–66
investment in 13, 78
primary 12, 34, 62, 70
provision of 58, 77–79
quality 15, 76
secondary 17
student–teacher ratio 62, 69
technical 35, 111
El Salvador 56
Emerson, Ralph Waldo 157
Encouragement of Foreign Investment 147
EU-15 26
Europe 16-17, 34, 42, 50-51, 55, 143, 176–179, 182
European Economic Community (EEC) 50
European Union (EU) 19–20, 26, 48–50, 52-53
Export 10–11, 13–16, 18–19, 22, 32, 39, 42–44, 46–48, 51–53, 57, 64, 111
Chinese 14, 48
manufacturing 16
market 11, 19, 51

Financial Express, The 2-3
Foreign direct investment (FDI) 11, 16, 22, 30, 33-34, 39, 44, 55, 143–149, 151, 157, 160, 162–164, 169, 184
inflow 146-147
Foreign institutional investor (FII) 11, 16
Foreign Trade Agreements (FTAs) 53–55
Fossil fuels 14, 18
conventional 18
Fujian 66, 68, 146, 161, 176

Gandhi, Mahatma 9–10, 89, 118, 182
non-violent struggle 9–10
Gandhi, Rajiv 131
Gender 62, 171
consciousness 171
differences 171
General Agreement on Tariffs and Trade (GATT) 53
Geopolitics 10
Germany 26, 27, 53, 56
Ghanta 5-6, 143
Global economy 10, 13–14, 19, 22, 51–54
Globalization 1–2, 5–6, 10, 15–17, 19, 43, 54, 86, 143, 174–177, 179–181
Global Trade Agreement 54
Governance 1, 3-4, 14–15, 18, 38, 58–59, 61, 77–78, 87–88, 123, 163, 183
global 14
inadequate 18
Indian 18
urban 18
Gross domestic product (GDP) 19–21, 28, 33, 35–37, 39, 42–46, 48, 51-52, 71, 79, 86-87, 122, 143, 150–152, 167–169, 178, 183–185, 189
Guangdong 68, 146, 152, 161
Guangxi 66
Guangzhou 65, 85
Guardian 175
Guatemale 56
Guilin 85
Guitierrez, Carlos 56
Gujarat 124, 160
Industrial Pollution Corridor 124
Gurgaon 129, 160, 164

Hangzhou 3–5, 85, 91–99, 101-102, 105–115, 128, 130–137, 169–170
basic policies 94
Che Cun Jian Ju policy 3–4, 92, 94–96, 98, 101-102, 105, 130-131, 133, 135
Grand Canal 5, 106–109, 113
Hangzhou Economic and Technological Development Zone 133
State Environmental Protection Administration (SEPA) 114
urbanization process 91–92, 99, 105
West Lake 106–115
Harbin 85
Health care services 15
investment in 13
Hebei 66

Hindu, The 151
Hitler 179
   state socialism 179
Honduras 56
Hong Kong 13, 21, 34, 45, 115, 137, 143, 147, 162–164
Hubei 66-67
Human development 12
Hyderabad 130-131

Import 48, 51, 54
India
   asymmetries 10
   British colonial regime 9
   Central Bureau of Investigation 119
   Central Vigilance Commission 119
   Chinese perceptions of 12
   cities of 60-61, 119, 124, 131, 136, 149
   coalition politics 13
   Communist Party of India (Marxist) 132
   Congress party 9
   Constitution 11, 58, 93
   currency 171
   disabilities 10
   Draft National Slum Policy 59
   economic growth 11, 13
   economic performance 10
   economic policy document 1
   economic reforms 11, 13, 63-64
   economy 11, 22, 23, 37, 89, 160, 167
   education 34-35
   Environmental Improvement of Urban Slums (EIUS) Programme 60
   EXIM Policy 160-161
   Export-Oriented Units (EOU) Scheme 160
   GDP growth rate 122
   higher education 34-35
   informal settlements 58
   Licence–Permit Raj 11
   Local Area Development Schemes 60
   market-based systems 10
   National Census of Small Scale Industries 32
   National Emergency 11
   National Environmental Assessment Authority (NEAA) 155
   National Rural Employment Guarantee Scheme 122
   National Slum Policy 59
   non-violent struggle in 10
   procedure-based system 79
   Rajiv Awas Yojana (RAY) 131
   reform processe 6
   Satyam Computer Services 129
   savings and investment 11, 13, 20, 53
   SEZ Act 158-159, 166
   Slum Networking Program (SNP) 60
   Slum Upgradation Program 60
   Small and medium enterprises (SMEs) 31
   social revolution 11
   Supreme Court 127, 132
   technological capability 10
   Tenth Five-Year Plan 31
   urban growth 18
   urban landscape in 129
India and Pakistan 10
   partition 10
   three wars 11
      1971 war 11
India China Fellowship 1
India China Institute at The New School, New York 1
India Infrastructure Report 2004 33
Indian Institute of Technology (IIT) 34
Indian Ocean 9
Indore 60-61
Industrialization 10, 30, 46, 107, 111
Inequality 13, 15, 45
Information technology (IT) 10-11, 20, 32-33, 35, 37, 42
   use of 32
Innovation 11, 17-18, 25–31, 33–35, 37–39
   human resources 34
   infrastructure 33
   institutional 38
   operation subsystem 35
   scientific 30
   S&T 30
   system 27, 30, 33, 37, 39
   technological 31
Intellectual Property Rights (IPRs) 20, 33, 53, 185
International Monetary Fund (IMF) 145
International remittances 11
Investment 10-11, 13-14, 20, 22-23, 33–36, 38–39, 42, 44–48, 50–54, 63, 78, 88-89, 91, 108, 111, 115
   external 13
   inadequate 89
Irrigation 107, 110, 144, 152-153, 155

Japan 13-14, 16, 20, 26, 34, 44, 48, 51, 53, 56, 108, 114-115, 143, 147, 164, 175–177, 189
Jawaharlal Nehru National Urban Renewal Mission (JNNURM) 61, 131

Subject Index

Jiangsu 66-67, 123, 152

Kandla 85
Kochi 86

Labor 18, 24–26, 37, 44-45, 49, 54, 57, 76, 79, 92, 146–149, 163–169, 171–172, 175, 177, 187
Latin America 14, 122
Lausanne International Management School, Switzerland 25
2006 World Competitive Power Yellow Book 25
Legitimacy 3, 15, 17, 58-59, 77-78, 79, 186–188, 190
   performance-based 17, 58, 77-78
   procedure-based 58, 77
Liaodong 146, 161
Liaoning 66-67, 123, 161, 172
Liberalism 175, 178, 179, 182
Liberalization 13, 53–55
Liberation 9, 90

Madras Institute of Development Studies (MIDS) 151
Mahabharata, the 1
Maharashtra 59
Mao 6, 9-10, 18, 109, 113, 149-150, 167-168, 170, 175–180
   hukou edict of 1956 18
Maoism 13
Maritime contact 9
Market 5-6, 10–20, 24, 26–27, 37–39, 42–56, 68-69, 77–78, 86, 88, 94, 99, 101, 106, 115, 119–120, 129, 133, 143–147, 150, 153, 157, 162, 166–167, 171, 174-175, 177, 180, 183–187, 189
   Chindian 20
   domestic 11, 14-15, 19-20, 54
   economy 5-6, 47–49, 86, 88, 119, 129, 143–144, 153, 167, 171, 174, 177, 180, 183, 186
   export 11, 19, 51
   financial services 47
   forces 14, 54, 77, 86
   international 11
   localities 16
   national 11, 13, 20
   opportunity 12, 15
   pan-Asian 11
   socialist 24
   system 86, 129
   world 44
Mass mobilization 119
Media 11, 14, 20, 21, 22, 46-47
Mergers and acquisitions (M&A) 50

Mexico 54, 56
Modernization 10, 13, 17, 19, 32
   hyper 13
   industrial 10
Monopoly 16, 49-50, 88
Multinational corporations (MNCs) 38, 44, 48
Mumbai 2-3, 16, 58–60, 62–63, 68–69, 76–77, 85, 89, 118, 124, 127, 129, 135, 160, 163, 165
   Education Committee 70
   informal settlements 58
   Mumbai Municipal Corporation Act 1888 62
   municipal education system in 62
   Santacruz Export Processing Zone (EPZ) 160
   Transit Camp School Education Committee 70

NASDAQ 52
NASSCOM 167
National innovative capacity (NIC) 27-28
National resources 29, 39
National Science & Technology Entrepreneurship Development Board 32
Nehru, Pandit Jawaharlal 10, 61
Neo-liberalism 175, 178, 179, 182
Nepal 9
New Delhi 13, 16, 61, 62–63, 89, 118, 127, 129–132, 134-135, 143
   Delhi Master Plan 127
   lal dora areas 132
New York 1-2, 128, 180
New York Times, The 180
Nicaragua 56
Nikkei 52
Non-governmental organizations (NGOs) 61, 62, 70, 155
Non-resident Indians (NRIs) 143, 164
North America 17, 112, 178
North American Free Trade Agreement (NAFTA) 54
North Korea 47, 177-178

Opportunity 11-12, 15–18, 20, 35, 54, 56, 64, 71-72, 76–77, 89, 95
   business 12
   social 18
Organization for Economic Cooperation and Development (OECD) 10, 13, 20, 26-27
Orissa 155

Pakistan 10-11, 13, 24
Patel 10
Peoples Bank of China (PBOC) 47

Subject Index

Ping, Deng Xiao 42
Political maturity 1
Population 3-4, 12, 15, 17, 18, 33, 45, 50-51, 58-59, 62–66, 68, 70–72, 74–76, 79, 90–92, 95, 108, 111, 119, 121–124, 143, 149, 152-153, 155-156, 165, 168, 184, 186, 188
    rural 50, 64, 68, 76
    urban 59, 63, 91, 95, 122-123, 165
Poverty 4, 11-12, 14-15, 45, 50, 58, 62-63, 143-144, 152-153, 165, 168, 172
    alleviation 153
    line 153
    rural and urban 12
    urban 12
Power 10, 12, 14–16, 19, 21, 25, 31, 33, 39, 42, 44–46, 50, 53, 61, 78, 79, 89, 93, 96, 107
    coal-based 19
    economic and political 16
    global balance of 15-16
    infrastructure 12
    military 15
    structures of 16
    technological 25
Property Law 87, 185, 189
Public expenditure 17
Public health care 12
Public service 12
Pudong 146, 161-162
Puerto Rico 56
Purchasing power parity (PPP) 127, 145

Qiantang river 5, 96, 106–109, 113–115, 169

Recession 13, 47, 51-52
Rehabilitation 127, 155–157, 165
Religion 9, 21, 109
Renewable energy 19, 46
Resource optimization 29
Reurbanization 137
Rui'an 58-59, 68, 70–72, 74–77, 79
    Educational Subsidy Certificates 71-72
    migrant communities 58
    Sunshine Project 71, 74
Russia 14, 51

Security 10, 14–16, 18, 21, 30, 49-50, 64, 85, 90, 92
    challenges of 15
    employment 90
    global 16, 21
Services sector 10
Shaanxi 66-67

Shandong 66-67, 146, 161, 176
Shanghai 14, 16, 34, 52, 65–66, 85, 107, 109, 115, 130, 134, 146, 152, 161-162, 170, 172, 180
Shantou 146, 161
Shenyang 67, 85
Shenzhen 56, 65, 66, 68, 131, 132, 146, 161–163, 165
Sichuan 66-67, 134, 172, 174
Singapore 137
Slum 59–63, 68, 77, 89, 118, 129–131, 135
Small Industries Development Bank of India (SIDBI) 32
Socialism 78, 144, 174, 176, 179, 186
South America 178
South Korea 162, 164, 175, 176, 180, 189
Special Economic Zones (SEZs) 119, 127, 144, 146–147, 157–166, 168, 171-172
Superpower 14
Surat 85
Switzerland 25

Tagore, Rabindranath 136
Taiwan 13, 21, 147, 162–164, 177, 180, 188
Tamil Nadu 59
Technology transfer 27, 30
Tiananmen Square 10, 13
Tianjin 85, 107, 152
Tibet 1, 9
    integration into China 9
Tibetan plateau 1, 9
TIME magazine 150
Tokyo 135, 141
Tourism 16, 21, 106, 112
Township and Village Enterprises (TVEs) 130, 168-169, 184, 187
Trade 9–11, 13-14, 16, 18, 20, 24, 42–44, 46–48, 50–57, 85, 92, 108, 111, 114, 145, 151, 153, 159, 166, 175
    agreement 48, 53–55
    deficit 44, 46–47, 51-52, 56
    foreign 24, 43, 111
    policy 55
    surplus 44
Trade-off 10, 124-125
Trade pact agreement (TPA) 47
Transportation 11-12, 19, 85, 111, 115
    air 11
    rail 11

United Kingdom (UK) 56
United Nations Conference on Trade and Development 145

United Nations (UN) 16-17, 122, 153
   projections 17, 122
United States of America (USA) 1, 3, 13, 15–20, 28, 34, 42–48, 50–57, 90, 132, 143, 149-150, 155, 164, 167, 169, 176–178, 180
   economy 44, 46, 48, 51–52
   trade deficit 51, 56
Urbanism 1
Urbanization 1–6, 18, 59, 62, 76, 85–88, 90–92, 99, 105, 107, 115, 118, 121–127, 129, 131-132, 137, 149, 168
   Chinese 118, 123
   democracy and 127
   nature of 123
   process of 91
   rapid 3, 18, 86, 91, 105
   slums and 129
US–Korea FTA 54
USPTO 28

Wal-Mart 55–57
   China and 56-57
Walton, Sam 56
West Bengal 132, 160
   Singur agitation 133
West Lake 5, 106–115, 136-137

Wittgenstein 181
   Philosophical Investigations 181
Women 6, 57, 130, 133, 150, 169–173
   Chinese 170-171
      organization 171
   physical and psychological health of 172
World Bank 33, 48, 54, 121, 155-156, 183
World Bank Growth Report 183
World Investment Report 145
World Trade Organization (WTO) 44, 47, 49, 53-54, 153, 175–176, 184, 186
   Doha Development Round (DDR) 53
World War II 9, 12, 13, 17, 53, 59

Xiamen 68, 146, 161
Xiaoping, Deng 78, 144, 151, 168
Xintang 4, 96–102, 131, 132, 134
Xiuhong, Ma, Chinese minister of the Ministry of Commerce 46

Yangtze river 107–109, 111, 146, 156, 161-163

Zedong, Mao 6
Zengwei, Jian 56
Zhejiang 66, 68, 70, 91, 111
Zhuhai 146, 161

Editors and Contributors

AMITA BHIDE, *Tata Institute of Social Sciences*
Amita Bhide works to ensure that the urban poor are not marginalized by the process of urbanization that is currently shaping India's global economy. As a member of the District Urban Development Agency, she has played an instrumental role in pushing the local government of Greater Mumbai to redress the question of poverty in the city. She is also associated with the Committee for Right to Housing in Mumbai. Amita Bhide is involved in developing a rehabilitation plan for people displaced by recent slum demolitions. She is currently working on concentration in urban development as part of the newly configured Master's curriculum in social work at her institute, which is soon expected to evolve into a Center for Urban Development. She has a formidable record of accomplishments in the field of urban poverty and development communication.

HIREN DOSHI, *Infosys Technologies Limited*
Hiren Doshi has traveled and worked around the globe during his career with Infosys. As an Indian who has lived in China, he is uniquely poised to observe the triumphs and challenges each country faces as it undergoes economic and social change. Sparked by his experience at Infosys, he is particularly interested in examining the role of information technology in catalyzing the development of both countries. Specifically, he aims to analyze the potential for increased sharing of resources and knowledge between India and China—a united front in the journey toward globalization. His international experience offers keen insight into dilemmas facing India and China today.

CHAKRAPANI GHANTA, *Dr B.R. Ambedkar Open University*
Chakrapani Ghanta is a human rights activist and scholar studying globalization. He maintains that globalization adversely affects the Dalit communities of India—economically, socially and culturally oppressed groups branded untouchable and considered impure. He has organized several workshops for Dalit NGOs on human rights and globalization, including the World Social Forum Desk on Dalit rights. He has been part of the international conferences and seminars, including a conference organized by the Human Rights Commission of the United Nations. Moreover, Chakrapani Ghanta has been instrumental in introducing progressive and innovative courses at the University on human rights, women's studies, and mass media. Widely published as an academic and journalist, he has participated in serious social debates in Telegu print media and research journals and developed content for TV and radio documentaries.

YUKUAN GUO, *Tsinghua University*
Yukuan Guo organized the first investigative journalism training program in China and established a cross-district collaborative network for journalists. He was the chief journalist at Nanfengchuang Magazine and did hard-hitting segments on medical fraud, environmental issues, urbanization and equality in education for CCTV's high profile program News Probing. He has reported

on urban land seizures in the country after interviewing more than 100 victims, lawyers and government officials. He has interviewed Islamic leaders and also studied the volatile relationship between the Han (the majority population) and various minority groups. Guo is a fervent and influential advocate of free thinking, critical thought and truth-seeking in the Chinese media. He has published widely in the Chinese press and on the Internet. He was a journalist at Southern Metropolis Weekly, and is currently a Post-doctorate in Tsinghua University.

ASHOK GURANG, *India China Institute*
Ashok Gurang is the founding Director of India China Institute and a Faculty member at the Graduate Program in International Affairs at The New School. Ashok's research and teaching interests include project design and development management, capacity building, inequality, environment, and inclusive democracy. Ashok has over twenty-five years of international development experience in several countries, with a particular focus in South and South East Asia. Prior to joining The New School, Ashok was the program officer for the International Fellowships Program, the largest global leadership initiative of the Ford Foundation, and an Adjunct Professor at Columbia University. He holds a MA in Economic and Political Development from the School of International and Public Affairs at Columbia University, and a BA in International Service and Development from World College West in Petaluma, California.

BRIAN MCGRATH, *Parsons The New School for Design*
Brian McGrath is a founding faculty member of the Masters of Architecture Program at Parsons, The New School for Design, where he teaches urban theory and architectural representation. His research is focused on linking high resolution remote sensing technology with various local urban actors and agents on ground. His India China Institute research project 'Sensing Shanghai' will look at the urban fringe between Shanghai and Hangzhou China from airborne imagery and from ground level surveys of agricultural villages and landscapes near newly constructed ring roads which are recently absorbed by urbanization.

PARTHA MUKHOPADHYAY, *Centre for Policy Research*
An economist by profession, Partha Mukhopadhyay is currently a Senior Research Fellow at the Centre for Policy Research, New Delhi. In his previous assignment with the Infrastructure Development Finance Company (IDFC), as Vice President of the Policy Advisory Group, Partha was actively involved in fostering public-private partnerships between policymakers and stakeholders to enable the implementation of efficient infrastructure services to various sectors in India. In this capacity he has worked closely with the Government of Karnataka and was an active member of the staff of the Prime Minister's Taskforce on Infrastructure. Partha is keenly interested in conducting research to compare the ways in which India and China deliver their social and economic infrastructure services, and aim to focus on the participation of public and private sectors and examine locational disparities. He has not only published consistently and extensively, but taught at various institutions in India including IIM Ahmedabad and XLRI Jamshedpur. He has also taught at NYU as a University Fellow.

AROMAR REVI, *Indian Institute for Human Settlements*
Aromar Revi is currently Director, Indian Institute for Human Settlements. He is also the Founding Director of TARU, a South Asian research and consulting firm that undertakes groundbreaking work in public policy. He has served as Senior Advisor to government ministries and the Planning Commission of India. He has two decades of experience in economic reform, public policy,

development planning and technology. He has consulted with World Bank, UNDP, UNEP, DFID, SIDA and AusAID. His contributions and commitment to sustainability as well as economic, environmental and social change have been recognized by Ashoka and the Balaton Group.

ZONGYONG WEN, *Beijing Municipal Urban Planning Commission*
Zongyong Wen, with fifteen years of experience in urban planning with the Beijing Government is a leader in the field of historic preservation. As the Deputy Chief Planner and Head of the Detailed Planning Section, he has managed many urban planning efforts at the Beijing Municipal Urban Planning Commission, and has led major surveys that produced important preservation and renovation plans for Beijing's old city areas. He focuses on the issues of urbanization in the age of globalization and has consistently participated in programs and studies centering on urban planning and space development. He is currently the Head of Beijing Topography and Design Research Institute.

XIAOBO WU, *National Institute for Innovation Management, Zhejiang University*
Xiaobo Wu teaches and researches on strategic management and technological innovation at Zhejiang University. He has participated in more than twenty national research projects and three international projects on global manufacturing, sustainable development, regional policy and information technology. Wu has published widely on the topics of management and technology co-authoring several books on this subject. He is currently the Deputy Dean of the School of Management, Zhejiang University.

ZUOJUN YANG, *Hangzhou Urban Planning Bureau*
Zuojun Yang has been responsible for the recent development of the historic Hangzhou into a city poised for participation in the global arena. An architect and urban planner by training, he aided in the contemporary urban planning of Beijing before working in Hangzhou. He is deeply interested in the future of urban China and how it dovetails with similar development efforts in the cities of India and the United States. He is currently the Director General of the Hangzhou Urban Planning Bureau.

YANG YAO, *China Center for Economic Research, Peking University*
Yang Yao has been following issues of land acquisition, ownership transformation and migration in China for the past decade. He has taught Economics, at various institutions in China, Japan, and the US. He has served as a consultant to the World Bank and participated in numerous contemporary debates about China's economic reforms. Yao is currently the Director of the China Center for Economic Research, the Deputy Dean of the National School of Development, Peking University, and the editor of China Economic Quarterly. He has published widely in international and domestic journals as well as several sole authored and coauthored books on institutional economics and economic development in China including Ownership Transformation in China, Economic Reform as A Process of Institutional Innovation. He is an associate editor of Agricultural Economics and a respected authority on rural development. He is also a prolific writer for the popular press in China.

JIANYING ZHA, *India China Institute*
Jianying Zha is the China representative of the India China Institute and works closely with ICI's partner organization Horizon Research Consultancy Group. A writer, columnist and media commentator, she is the author of five books, including China Pop and the award-winning The

Nineteen Eighties (Bashi Niandai Fangtanlu). Her writing has appeared in The New Yorker, The New York Times, Dushu, Wanxiang, and other magazines and newspapers. A recipient of a Guggenheim Fellowship, she is finishing a new book on China.